Suicide

Volume 1
Understanding

Volume 2
Prevention

Suicide

A Global Issue

Volume 1
Understanding

David Lester and James R. Rogers, Editors

PRAEGER

AN IMPRINT OF ABC-CLIO, LLC
Santa Barbara, California • Denver, Colorado • Oxford, England

Library of Congress Cataloging-in-Publication Data

Suicide : a global issue / David Lester and James R. Rogers, editors.
    p. ; cm.
  Includes bibliographical references and index.
  ISBN 978-1-4408-0080-1 (hardback : alk. paper) — ISBN 978-1-4408-0081-8 (e-ISBN)
  I. Lester, David, 1942– editor of compilation.   II. Rogers, James R., editor of compilation.
  [DNLM: 1. Suicide—psychology.   2. Suicide—prevention & control. WM 165]
  RC569
  362.28—dc23   2013018980

ISBN: 978-1-4408-0080-1
EISBN: 978-1-4408-0081-8

18 17 16 15 14   1 2 3 4 5

This book is also available on the World Wide Web as an eBook.
Visit www.abc-clio.com for details.

Praeger
An Imprint of ABC-CLIO, LLC

ABC-CLIO, LLC
130 Cremona Drive, P.O. Box 1911
Santa Barbara, California 93116-1911

This book is printed on acid-free paper ∞
Manufactured in the United States of America

These books are dedicated to Jim Rogers, a wonderful scholar yet an even more wonderful person.

Jim dedicated so much of his life and his energy to understanding and preventing suicide, it is fitting that co-editing this set was his final literary creation before passing away and returning to the universe as these manuscripts were completed in early 2013.

We hope the readers of these volumes will see the importance of this work, and continue the research mission that so moved Jim.

Contents

Volume 1
Understanding

1

Defining Suicide and Suicidal Behavior

Morton M. Silverman

What's in a name? That which we call a rose
By any other name would still smell as sweet
—(Juliet in "Romeo and Juliet,"
by William Shakespeare, 1600)

A rose is a rose is a rose is a rose
—("Sacred Emily," by Gertrude Stein, 1913)

As the two quotations above suggest, throughout many centuries we have been able to communicate similar concepts through the use of commonly understood language and images. However, after more than a century of serious attention to the public health problems of suicide and suicidal behaviors, one of the "thorny issues" that still remains is the inability of clinicians and researchers to speak to each other with a common language that conveys the same concepts and images.

Although there have been significant advances in the field of suicidology, many challenges remain. We now know a great deal about the epidemiology of suicide and suicidal behaviors. For example, we know a great deal about the risk factors for suicide: age, gender, race, geographical location, employment status, marital status, family history, personal history (including a prior suicide attempt), psychiatric disorder (including alcohol and other drug use and abuse), and so forth. We are beginning to develop a body of knowledge about the biological underpinnings of suicidal behavior through research on the neurobiology and genetics of risk for suicidal behaviors. However, we still know little about protective factors and what places an individual at acute risk for self-injury. We have few validated treatments for suicidal individuals, and no agreed-upon screening questions or instruments. As our knowledge base about the etiology and transmission of suicidal behaviors expands, we need to bridge the gap between this knowledge and the development of effective clinical and population-based practices, protocols, procedures, and policies.

In order to bridge the knowledge-to-practice gap, we need to translate what we have learned from epidemiological surveillance and research studies into practical clinical applications. Similarly what is learned in clinical settings needs to be communicated to researchers and public health policy makers. One major stumbling block is that the suicide literature remains replete with confusing, and sometimes derogatory and pejorative, terms, definitions, and classifications that make it difficult, if not impossible, to compare and contrast research, epidemiological, or clinical findings (Silverman, 2006). Efforts at generalization and extrapolation are also hampered (Linehan, 2000). Toward the goal of sharing information and observations to help identify and treat truly suicidal individuals, and to develop interventions to prevent the onset, exacerbation, and recurrence of these thoughts and behaviors, all the components of the suicidal process must be uniformly identified, labeled, and classified (O'Carroll, 1989).

Clinically, the adoption of a standardized nomenclature for suicide is an essential foundational step toward increasing the accuracy of risk assessment, clinical management, and both short-term and long-term intervention (Rudd, 2000). The eventual mapping of commonly accepted terms onto a spectrum of risk will provide information that is essential to intervention and case management of at-risk individuals. From a research perspective, comparing studies and analyzing suicide statistics across cohorts is virtually impossible without a common language (Malone, Szanto, Corbitt, & Mann, 1995). In terms of surveillance, the accurate reporting of suicide attempts and suicide deaths is extremely difficult without clear and universal understanding of how each of these terms is defined. Improved fidelity in terms of facility reporting standards for suicidal behaviors will provide policy makers with increasingly accurate information regarding the rate of self-directed violence (SDV) behaviors.

One of the major difficulties in communicating about the phenomena of SDV with patients and both within and across disciplines is that we do not speak the same scientific language. An issue that has been noted by members of the Veterans Health Administration's (VHA) Blue Ribbon Work Group on Suicide Prevention in the Veteran's Population (VHA, 2009), the Institute of Medicine of the National Academies of Science (Goldsmith, Pellmar, Kleinman, & Bunney, 2002), the World Health Organization (WHO) (Krug, Dahlberg, Mercy, Zwi, & Lozano, 2002), as well as suicide experts (Mann et al., 2005) is the absence of uniform definitions of terms related to SDV. The lack of a common nomenclature has inhibited epidemiological efforts, as well as evidence-based assessment and treatment of individuals who are at high risk for suicide.

Although there are a large number of scales and measures that purport to quantitatively and qualitatively measure the presence of suicidal ideation, intent, and behavior (Brown, 2001), most measures assume that the respondent already possesses a definition and understanding of the terms for suicidal ideation, intent, and attempt. Rarely do these measurement tools provide the respondent with clear definitions for the suicide-related terms that they are measuring (Kessler, Berglund, Borges, Nock, & Wang, 2005).

We also do not share the same conceptualizations of what constitutes self-harm, self-injury, SDV, and the suicidal process. The terminology we use is often based on our training (theoretical, political, social, psychological, biological, and religious perspectives) and the professional needs to identify and count these behaviors in the first place (e.g., clinical, epidemiological, public health, research, etc.). One clearly identified problem is the difficulty that different professionals have in communicating with each other. For example, conceptual, methodological, and clinical problems result from widely varying definitions and classification schemes for such terms as suicide attempt (Nock & Kessler, 2006).

For example, epidemiologists are interested in counting discrete outcomes (deaths). Primary care physicians need to know the 1–2 suicide screening questions to ask that will elicit an answer that broadly places the patient in the category of needing immediate intervention or a referral to a mental health professional for a more extensive assessment. The emergency room physician needs to know the criteria to determine whether the behavior being assessed is intentional. The clinical researcher needs to accurately differentiate the populations being studied who are engaged in self-destructive behaviors, and to be able to compare populations across research sites. Given the multidimensional aspects of suicidal thoughts and behaviors, the researcher needs to use uniform criteria to clearly place the study samples into discrete categories. The mental health clinician needs to know the specifics of the current ideation, intent, plans, and actions, as well as the history of prior self-destructive behaviors (e.g., who, where, when, why, how much, how often) in order to determine the best treatment approach. The mental health clinician also needs to determine the contribution of a mental disorder or an altered state of consciousness to the expression of self-destructive behaviors. The public health policy maker needs to know which preventive interventions have been shown to work for which at-risk populations.

It is a known fact that there is inaccuracy in the reporting of suicidal deaths by coroners and medical examiners (Jobes & Berman, 1985). Estimates of underreporting have ranged from 10 to 50 percent, and Jobes, Berman, and Josselson (1987) have identified over 20 possible sources of variability in the official reporting of suicide data. They suggest that perhaps the single most important source of variability and error in suicide statistics arises from the virtual absence of any standardized classification criteria that coroners and medical examiners might more uniformly use to evaluate cases of equivocal suicide. Until we establish a standardized nomenclature, we will continue to have differences between and among official reporting sources (e.g., police, coroner, medical examiner death certificates), research studies, clinical population reports (e.g., hospital discharge summaries, emergency department reports, first-responder reports), and epidemiological surveys (self-report).

If we cannot even agree upon what are the essential features that define a suicide, then how are we to determine what is an attempt to die by suicide? There is considerable debate about the differential attributes of those who die by suicide and those who attempt suicide. The resolution of this controversy is hampered because studies have used different descriptive methods and dissimilar definitions for suicide attempts (Linehan, 1986; Maris, 1992). When the suicide attempts are medically serious (e.g., needing extensive, specialized medical care), the characteristics of these two populations overlap considerably (Hawton, 1997). However, because most epidemiological studies are based on self-report of prior suicidal behaviors (without defining these terms for the population being surveyed), the profile of those engaging in nonmedically serious suicide attempts remains inconsistent and unreliable.

CLARIFYING TERMINOLOGY

Before discussing some of the current issues related to the development and implementation of nomenclature and classification systems, it is pertinent to provide some definitions for these constructs. The following terms and definitions illustrate the degree of overlap or "fuzziness" when discussing classification systems.

Nomenclature: a set or system of names or terms, as those used in a particular science or art; a system of words used to technically name things in a particular discipline.

Classification: the act of distributing things into classes or categories of the same type; the act or method of distributing into a class or category according to characteristics.

Taxonomy: the practice and science of classification as well as the laws or principles underlying such a classification; the science dealing with the description, identification, naming, and classification of organisms.

Almost anything (e.g., behaviors, concepts, events) may be classified according to some taxonomic scheme. Hence, a nomenclature is simply establishing the words (and definitions) chosen for use in the development of a classification, using taxonomic principles.

CHALLENGES TO DEVELOPING AND IMPLEMENTING A STANDARDIZED NOMENCLATURE AND CLASSIFICATION SYSTEM

The ongoing confusion concerning nomenclature has perpetuated the use of multiple terms to refer to the same behavior, frequently with pejorative connotations (e.g., threat, gesture) and derogatory descriptors (e.g., "manipulative," "hostile," "nonserious") (Bille-Brahe, Kerkhof, De Leo, & Schmidtke, 2004; O'Carroll et al., 1996; Silverman, 2006), or the same term is used to refer to many different, albeit related, behaviors. Such variability in terminology has consequences that extend beyond imprecise communication, limiting comparison of epidemiological prevalence rates and hampering clinical and preventive efforts (Silverman, Berman, Sanddal, O'Carroll, & Joiner, 2007a). Precise assessment of suicidal events is necessary both to better inform research-derived risk-benefit analyses and to foster improved clinical management and identification (Posner, Oquendo, Gould, Stanley, & Davies, 2007).

There are currently a number of nomenclatures and/or classification systems that are being tested in the United States (Brenner et al., 2011; Crosby, Ortega, & Melanson, 2011; Posner et al., 2007; Silverman, Berman, Sanddal, O'Carroll, & Joiner, 2007b), as well as internationally (De Leo, Burgis, Bertolote, Kerkhof, & Bille-Brahe, 2006). I have recommended that there be an international conference to resolve these differences such that there is a universal adoption of a uniform set of terms and definitions. I argue elsewhere that not only must we use the same terminology and definitions, but also these terms must be easily understood, easily applied, and internally consistent (Silverman, 2006). The terms must relate to each other in a way that has utility, meaning, and relevance to the real world of at-risk individuals.

A nomenclature or classification system for suicide and related phenomenon should be characterized by its generalizability within and across settings and disciplines (DeLeo et al., 2006), its ability to facilitate and improve communication amongst those who employ it (O'Carroll et al., 1996), and ultimately the degree to which it enhances the quality of clinical care for individuals who are at risk for self-injurious behavior (Rudd, 2000). Whereas a nomenclature is a set of commonly understood and logically defined terms, a classification system is a more exhaustive, systematic arrangement of terms into superordinate categories and subtypes (O'Carroll et al., 1996) that are related to a particular subject of interest.

Regarding suicide, several prior efforts have been made to develop and implement standard nomenclatures and classification systems (Beck et al., 1973; O'Carroll et al., 1996; Posner et al., 2007; Silverman et al., 2007b), and yet, to date, none have been widely adopted. Instead, clinicians and researchers have encountered various obstacles to implementing such classifications. The perception of clinical infeasibility is sometimes encountered because systems developed in the research laboratory are overly complex or laborious, or include terms that are novel or confusing to clinicians. Consequentially, prior systems have not been widely adopted in practice, and thus, terms pertaining to suicide and self-harm phenomena remain poorly operationalized, ambiguous, and inconsistently applied within and across clinical settings.

This reliability conundrum brings to light two related issues that are of utmost concern to both suicide researchers and clinicians working with individuals who are potentially at risk for suicide: (a) threat to the external validity of past and future empirical studies of suicide; and (b) the potential for detrimental impacts with regard to clinical decision-making (Rudd, 2000; Silverman, 2006). With regard to research, operationally defining terms *a priori* is inherent to understanding data. If variables of interest are not clearly defined, interpreting and generalizing findings can be highly problematic. As for the clinical implications, poorly differentiated and/or ambiguous terms utilized to denote suicide risk can lead to miscommunication among clinicians and consumers, and ultimately to treatment recommendations that lack efficiency and/or are contraindicated.

In summary, measures of suicide and nonfatal suicidal behavior continue to be hindered by the lack of (1) a standard nomenclature; (2) clear operational definitions; and (3) standardized lethality measures. It has been recognized for over 20 years that reliable statistics on the numbers, types, and methods of nonfatal, intentional self-inflicted injuries, in conjunction with national and regional suicide mortality data, are required for the development, targeting, and evaluation of national and regional suicide prevention strategies.

TERMINOLOGY IN SUICIDE CLASSIFICATION SYSTEMS

Although one can argue about the degree of specificity for describing suicidal behaviors, there is a set of commonly used terms that generally describes the universe of suicidal thoughts and behaviors. These suicide-related generic terms are suicidal ideation (with or without a plan); suicidal intent; motivation; preparatory acts (toward imminent self-harm); self-harm or self-directed violent behaviors (with or without injury); undetermined suicide-related or self-directed violent behaviors (with or without injury); suicide attempt (with or without injury); and suicide.

The definitions of terms such as "suicide attempt," "nonsuicidal self-injury," or "self-harm" are predicated on the definition of "suicide." After all, a true suicide attempt is an action whose purpose is to die by suicide. However, as noted elsewhere, there are at least 15 definitions of "suicide" in our scientific literature, 9 definitions of "suicide attempt," and well over 35 synonyms for a nonfatal self-injurious behavior with the intent to die (Silverman, 2006).

A brief listing of the current difficulties in communicating between and among professionals as well as their patients includes (1) limitations of hindsight bias and informant bias regarding the reporting of suicidal thoughts, intent, and behaviors (Duberstein & Conwell, 1997); (2) difficulty in comparing and contrasting epidemiological surveys or clinical research studies; (3) inconsistency of scale development and validation when most measures assume that the respondent already possesses a definition and understanding of the suicidal behaviors being measured; and (4) lack of specificity and consistency of definition for such terms as suicide attempt, self-injurious behavior, and self-harm. Furthermore, each clinical specialty, research group, or surveillance team has developed its own reporting forms and systems to gather similar information.

A brief list of the challenges to resolving these conundrums include the following:

1. Agreeing on which terms to be used and defining them as mutually exclusive. There remains confusion about when to apply and what exactly constitutes terms such as suicidality, deliberate or intentional self-harm (DSH), suicide-related behavior, and nonsuicidal self-injury (NSSI).

2. Developing a nomenclature that is free of bias—philosophical, theoretical, biological, sociological, political, religious, cultural, and so forth. A nomenclature must be sensitive to different needs, depending upon the professional making the assessment and the audience receiving the information. Often, different data-gathering procedures require different standards of evidence, different levels of certainty for such evidence, and place different emphases on different aspects of the evidence.

3. Remaining internally consistent. Inasmuch as there are over a dozen definitions of "suicide" in the literature, clearly defining the concept and its defining criteria has remained elusive, and, as a result, has implications for defining those terms which are related to the act of death by suicide, such as "suicide ideation," "suicide intent," and "suicide attempt." The nomenclature must be internally consistent and all the terms must be based on, and relate to, the clear definition of what is a "suicide."

4. Remaining consistent with the terminologies and approaches used by scientific fields that study other forms of violence (e.g., homicides and sexual assault) and unintentional injuries (e.g., motor vehicle crashes). However, there must be a clear "cross-over table" to demonstrate equivalencies between and among terms currently used in existing nomenclatures, so that clinical, research, and epidemiological studies can be compared.

5. Deciding which terms are pejorative or have a negative bias and should be eliminated from the lexicon. For example, suicide gesture, suicide threat, completed suicide, failed attempt, and so forth.

6. Resolving the distinctions between what we label as a suicide attempt and DSH, or NSSI.

We look to other scientific fields of inquiry to help us understand how aspects of cognition, brain development (acquisition of reasoning, cognitive skills, executive functioning), social behavior, and risk-taking behaviors impact the development of suicidal thinking, and the unfolding of suicidal actions. For example, when does the development of suicidal ideation become clinically significant, and under what conditions? What triggers suicidal thoughts and behaviors? What are the elements that go into an individual's risk appraisal? At what age and under what conditions does an individual develop and/or access executive functioning, such as accurately perceiving or understanding the consequences of certain risk-taking behaviors?

We must get beyond our almost total reliance on self-report for understanding and recording such important components of the suicidal process as suicidal thoughts, intent, motivation, and planning, or accurately remembering and reporting prior life events, assigning significance to certain life events, appraisal of current stressors, history of prior self-destructive behaviors, and the like.

SOME EXAMPLES OF DEFINITIONAL OBFUSCATION

In this section I briefly highlight some of the terms and definitions that are confusing and misleading.

Intent to Die

Determining the presence or absence of intent to die is a key factor in differentiating nonsuicidal from suicidal self-harm behaviors (Beck, Beck, & Kovacs, 1975; Hjelmeland & Knizek, 1999; Silverman, 2006; Silverman et al., 2007a). Determination of the intent to die is a critical consideration, and has been used to differentiate between terms in prior nomenclature and classification systems (DeLeo et al., 2006; Silverman et al., 2007a). Some would argue that a suicide attempt is a subcategory under self-injurious behaviors, while others see a clear distinction between self-harm behaviors and suicidal behaviors based on the presence or absence of intent. When asked by clinicians at the time of their self-injury many patients will deny that they had an intent to die, despite the evidence to the contrary (e.g., high lethality of the act, prior history of near-lethal suicide attempts, collaborative information received from family, friends, or support network). Linehan (2000) has suggested that the presence or absence of the intent to die during self-harm is a critical factor that can differentiate the two behaviors. Although determining the intent to die at the time of the self-directed violent behavior is the critical variable that distinguishes suicide from nonsuicidal thoughts and behaviors, difficulties in categorization can arise when the assessment of the intent to die is denied by the patient, yet there is some ambivalence present regarding the intent to die.

Clinically inferring "intent" on behalf of a patient is a subjective, albeit clinically informed act, which may involve a set of decisions and clinical experiences that may not be transferable to other settings or situations. As Rosenberg et al. (1988) have stated, "with respect to intent, absence of evidence is not evidence of absence" (p. 1446). Some have argued that it is better to avoid the inclusion of intent as a necessary component in the definitions for suicidal thoughts and behaviors. However, alternative conceptualizations and definitions of thoughts and behaviors have their own sets of problems when applied to clinical and research settings. Continued refinement and operationalizing of this concept is warranted, particularly given its salience to clinical practice.

Suicidality

There is no definition of "suicidality" other than that it is the state of being suicidal. But what does that mean? Does that mean having suicidal ideations, intent, motivations, and plans? Does it mean that you have had a suicide attempt, been exposed to others who have been suicidal, or rehearsed a suicidal act? Is it the equivalent of being in a "suicidal state of mind"? For the most part it has been used to categorize individuals who have expressed a combination or permutation of cognitions (ideations, intent, motivation, and planning), as well as behaviors (rehearsals and attempts). It has also been used to categorize mentally ill patients who are so depressed that they feel suicidal (emotions). Hence, it becomes nearly impossible to compare populations who are deemed to be expressing suicidality. Because these phenomena are vastly different in occurrence, associated factors, consequences, and interventions, the U.S. Centers for Disease Control and Prevention (CDC) has recently determined that, for purposes of describing self-directed violent behaviors, suicidality is an unacceptable term (Crosby et al., 2011).

Suicide Attempt

The determination of whether a suicide attempt had occurred has remained "in the eye of the beholder," that is to say, the individual self-reporting whether or not their self-directed violent behavior was initiated by an intent to die. Until recently, there was no standardized definition of "suicide attempt" by which a clinician or researcher could provide an individual with a definition of what is being investigated, or determine independently whether an SDV behavior was a suicide attempt.

Why is it so important to know whether an SDV behavior was suicidal in nature? Two lines of evidence suggest that suicidal behaviors are repetitive. Many of those who die by suicide have made a previous suicide attempt; and many of those who make a nonfatal suicide attempt will make subsequent attempts (Beautrais, 2004; Conner, Langley, Tomaszewski, & Conwell, 2003). In a study of all patients admitted to a hospital for any degree of attempted suicide, Gibb, Beautrais, and Fergusson (2005) found that, within 10 years, 28.1 percent of those who had been admitted for an index suicide attempt were readmitted for a further nonfatal suicide attempt, and 4.6 percent died by suicide. Hence, a prior suicide attempt is statistically the best predictor of future suicide attempts and death by suicide and a history of repeated attempts further increases the risk of death by suicide.

A nonfatal suicide attempt is the strongest known clinical predictor of eventual suicide (Harris & Barraclough, 1997). Suicide risk among self-harm patients is hundreds of times higher than in the general population (Owens, Horrocks, & House, 2002). It is often estimated that about 10–15 percent of attempters eventually die by suicide. The risk is highest during the first months and years after the attempt, but a history of a suicide attempt by self-poisoning appears to be an indicator of high risk for completed suicide throughout the entire adult lifetime.

Souminen et al. (2004) studied the outcome of suicide attempts, with the use of suicide mortality as the outcome criterion, for a follow-up period of 37 years (1963–2000). The study group consisted of 100 consecutive patients who had attempted suicide by self-poisoning in Helsinki in 1963 (by far the most common method used), and who were subsequently admitted to the hospital for treatment. After 37 years, 13 percent (13 of 98) had died by suicide: 6 of 71 women (8%) and 7 of 27 men (26%). The method of suicide was drug overdose in 62 percent of the cases (8 of 13; 5 men and 3 women), hanging in 31 percent (4 of 13; 2 men and 2 women), and jumping in 8 percent (1 of 13; 1 woman). Two-thirds of the suicides (62%, 8 of 13) occurred at least 15 years after the first suicide attempt. They found that, after index suicide attempts by self-poisoning in 1963, completed suicides continued to accumulate for almost four decades. Inclusion of undetermined and undetermined plus accidental deaths as possible suicides raised the proportion of suicides up to 16 percent and 19 percent of the group, respectively, but had little influence on the temporal pattern of their accumulation.

When digesting these statistics it becomes evident that concerted efforts need to be made to identify those at most risk of engaging in an index suicide attempt, as well as providing services to those who have engaged in an index suicide attempt, irrespective of its level of lethality (Beautrais, Joyce, & Mulder, 1999; Luoma, Martin, & Pearson, 2002). It then becomes imperative that clinicians, researchers, and epidemiologists have a clear and consistent definition of what is a "suicide attempt." A standardized definition does not exist on the international level, and only recently has a uniform definition been agreed upon by the CDC and other federal agencies.

Deliberate Self-Harm and Nonsuicidal Self-Injury

The development of the concept of DSH arose out of Kreitman's original creation of the term "parasuicide" to label all suicide-related self-injury that did not result in death by suicide (Kreitman, 1977). As a result, the term gained much favor in Europe broadly, but not so in the United States. The WHO used the term to describe a number of large-scale epidemiological studies that were undertaken in multiple sites (Schmidtke et al., 1996; Schmidtke, Bille-Brahe, De Leo, Kerkhof, & Wasserman, 2001).

Over time, the term "deliberate self-harm" replaced "parasuicide," but this term has a potentially pejorative connotation, because it suggests that the self-harming behavior is deliberate and under the full control of the individual. Hence, the current term being used in Europe to describe self-injury that does not lead to death is intentional self-harm (with or without suicidal intent). In the United States, the term "nonsuicidal self-injury" (NSSI) is gathering momentum to describe similar behaviors. A further complication is that the term "suicide gesture" has not left the lexicon in the United States. In fact, it was used in the National Comorbidity Study (NCS) to describe "self-injury in which there is no intent to die, but instead an intent to give the appearance of a suicide attempt in order to communicate with others" (Nock & Kessler, 2006, p. 616).

The original definition of DSH included all self-injurious behaviors whether the individual had any intent to die or not, confusing the key factor (intent) that differentiates suicidal from nonsuicidal SDV. DSH has been identified as a behavior that carries considerable risk of subsequent self-harm, including death by suicide. It is a deliberately initiated act of self-harm with a nonfatal outcome, including both self-poisoning and bodily self-injury.

An early study by Hawton and Fagg (1988) found that at least 1 percent of patients referred to general hospitals in the United Kingdom for DSH died by suicide within a year of an episode of DSH, and 3–5 percent within 5–10 years. Another study found that 1–2 percent of patients died by suicide in the year following being seen in a hospital emergency department or admitted for treatment (Owens et al., 2002), with an estimated 7–10 percent of individuals eventually dying by suicide (Nordentoft et al., 1993).

The DSH literature as well as the suicide attempt literature rarely distinguishes the populations by method (self-poisoning, cutting, etc.), location of the injury (wrists, arms, legs, head, etc.), physical location at the time of self-injury, time of day, day of week, and so forth. Without such a classification system it is more difficult to differentiate between the two self-directed violent behaviors.

Some studies suggest that self-harm differs from suicidal behaviors in clinically important ways. Reasons for suicide attempts are more likely to involve making others better off (reducing burdensomeness), while reasons for self-harm included "anger expression" and "distraction" (Brown, Henriques, Sosdjan, & Beck, 2004; Chapman, Gratz, & Brown, 2006). Individuals who engage in self-harm will report that the behavior relieves unendurable anxiety or tension, while in other studies individuals report that DSH temporarily reduces anger, anxiety, sadness, depression, and shame (Chapman & Dixon-Gordon, 2007). Other observers suggest that individuals engage in DSH as a form of self-punishment, which relieves anger directed inward, self-blame and self-loathing for perceived social transgressions (Krasser, Rossmann, & Zapotoczky, 2003). Chapman and Dixon-Gordon (2007) found that relief was the most common consequence of self-harm, whereas anger was the most common consequence of a suicide attempt. They suggest that self-harm serves an emotion regulatory function. However, a significant proportion of individuals reported that their predominant emotional consequence following self-harm was negative, most notably sadness.

Preparatory and Undetermined Behaviors

Clinicians and researchers alike have long recognized that suicide or self-harm related events are often preceded by a series of events. Precursory actions can range from nonlethal behaviors, such as an individual pursuing information about suicide on the Internet, to more lethal actions, such as purchasing a gun, loading it, and even holding it to one's head. Furthermore, determining the presence of intent to die is not always an either/or determination because sometimes the individual is unable to tell us (e.g., due to cognitive impairments while under the influence of drugs), the individual is just not sure (due to their own ambivalence), or the evidence is not compelling. Hence, as discussed below, the VA and CDC has incorporated the concepts of preparatory and undetermined into their classification systems. Although adding these terms expands a SDV classification system, it also allows for a richer and more representative system.

Table 1.1.   CDC's Self-Directed Violence Uniform Definitions

Self-directed violence (analogous to self-injurious behavior)

Behavior that is self-directed and deliberately results in injury or the potential for injury to oneself.

This does not include behaviors such as parachuting, gambling, substance abuse, tobacco use, or other risk taking activities, such as excessive speeding in motor vehicles. These are complex behaviors some of which are risk factors for SDV but are defined as behaviors that, while likely to be life-threatening, are not recognized by the individual as behavior intended to destroy or injure the self. These behaviors may have a high probability of injury or death as an outcome but the injury or death is usually considered unintentional.

Self-directed violence is categorized into the following:
Nonsuicidal (as defined below)
Suicidal (as defined below).

Nonsuicidal self-directed violence

Behavior that is self-directed and deliberately results in injury or the potential for injury to oneself.

There is no evidence, whether implicit or explicit, of suicidal intent.

Suicidal self-directed violence

Behavior that is self-directed and deliberately results in injury or the potential for injury to oneself.

There is evidence, whether implicit or explicit, of suicidal intent.

Undetermined self-directed violence

Behavior that is self-directed and deliberately results in injury or the potential for injury to oneself.

Suicidal intent is unclear based on the available evidence.

Suicide attempt

A nonfatal self-directed potentially injurious behavior with any intent to die as a result of the behavior. A suicide attempt may or may not result in injury.

Interrupted self-directed violence—by self or by other

By other—A person takes steps to injure self but is stopped by another person prior to fatal injury. The interruption can occur at any point during the act such as after the initial thought or after onset of behavior.
By self (in other documents may be termed "aborted" suicidal behavior)—A person takes steps to injure self but is stopped by self prior to fatal injury.

Other suicidal behavior including preparatory acts

Acts or preparation toward making a suicide attempt, but before potential for harm has begun. This can include anything beyond a verbalization or thought,

(Continued)

Table 1.1. (*Continued*)

such as assembling a method (e.g., buying a gun, collecting pills) or preparing for one's death by suicide (e.g., writing a suicide note, giving things away).

Suicide

Death caused by self-directed injurious behavior with any intent to die as a result of the behavior.

Suicide Threats, Suicide Gestures, and Manipulative Acts

Over time, the terms "suicidal threats," "suicidal gestures," and "manipulative acts" have developed pejorative connotations (see Tables 1.1 and 1.2). They are usually used to describe an episode of low lethality SDV. Each of these three terms connotes a negative value judgment of the person's intent. Threats can be dismissed as "not serious," and "gestures" can be seen as "poorly enacted attempts" or "having missed the mark." In some cases these terms are assigned to characterize a form of SDV at a time when an individual is experiencing great psychological distress and uncertainty about the intent to die. When is a gesture not a suicidal attempt? First of all we must agree that both gestures and threats are forms

Table 1.2. Unacceptable Terms

The panel that advised the CDC's NCIPC on the development of the Self-Directed Violence Uniform Definitions felt the following terms are unacceptable for describing self-directed violence:

Completed suicide—This terminology implies achieving a desired outcome, whereas those involved in the mission of "reducing disease, premature death, and discomfort and disability" would view this event as undesirable. Alternate term: suicide.

Failed attempt—This terminology gives a negative impression of the person's action, implying an unsuccessful effort aimed at achieving death. Alternate terms: suicide attempt or suicidal self-directed violence.

Nonfatal suicide—This terminology portrays a contradiction. "Suicide" indicates a death while "nonfatal" indicates that no death occurred. Alternate term: suicide attempt.

Parasuicide—Formally used to refer to a person's self-directed violence whether or not the individual had an intent to die. However, the World Health

(*Continued*)

Table 1.2. (*Continued*)

Organization is now favoring the term suicide attempt. Alternate terms: nonsuicidal self-directed violence or suicidal self-directed violence.

Successful suicide—This term also implies achieving a desired outcome whereas those involved in the mission of "reducing disease, premature death, and discomfort and disability" would view this event as undesirable. Alternate term: suicide.

Suicidality—This terminology is often used to refer simultaneously to suicidal thoughts and suicidal behavior. These phenomena are vastly different in occurrence, associated factors, consequences, and interventions, so should be addressed separately. Alternate terms: suicidal thoughts and suicidal behavior.

Suicide gesture, manipulative act, and suicide threat—Each of these terms gives a value judgment with a pejorative or negative impression of the person's intent. They are usually used to describe an episode of nonfatal, self-directed violence. A more objective description of the event is preferable such as nonsuicidal self-directed violence or suicidal self-directed violence.

of behavior. If the behavior did not involve the intent to die then it is a non-suicidal SDV and should not be labeled with the adjective "suicide" (as in suicide gesture or suicide threat). If the nonlethal behavior was initiated by the intent to die, then it is better classified as a suicide attempt, with or without injury. If the individual is ambivalent about the intent of the "threat" or "gesture," then it is best classified as "preparatory" or "unde-termined." Removing "threats," "gestures," and "manipulative acts" from our vocabulary not only adds rigor to our classification system, but also communicates sensitivity and compassion to those who may be undergo-ing great pain and distress.

A BRIEF OVERVIEW OF NOMENCLATURE CLASSIFICATION SYSTEMS

The intent of this overview is not to present an exhaustive review of all prior attempts to develop nomenclatures and classification systems for the study of suicide and suicide-related thoughts and behaviors, but to simply highlight some notable examples and milestones.

Beck et al.'s Classification of Suicidal Behaviors

The first modern attempt to systematically develop a "classification and nomenclature scheme" in the United States was put forth by Beck and colleagues in 1973. This system validated the key terms of "suicidal ideas," "suicide attempts," and "completed suicide" to describe the entire range of suicidal phenomena. Each of these three terms is further subclassified by (a) certainty of the rater (0–100%); (b) lethality (zero, low, medium, or high); (c) intent to die (zero, low, medium, or high); (d) mitigating circumstances (zero, low, medium, or high); and (e) method (by listing actual method used). Beck and colleagues proposed that a key variable in the three types of suicidal behavior was the intent to die, especially when the behavior was nonlethal in nature. However, they acknowledged that intention is difficult to measure, as evidenced by allowing for four categories (zero, low, medium, high). Intent "includes consideration of subject's statements, the likelihood of rescue, past history, and other evidence, and requires inference and judgment on part of the rater" (p. 9).

In their classification schema, a suicidal idea "includes all overt suicidal behavior and communications except for overt acts classifiable under suicide attempt or completed suicide. It includes suicide threats, suicide preoccupation, expressions of wish to die, and indirect indicators of suicide planning, etc." (p. 11). Hence, this is a very broad conceptualization of "suicide ideas." Beginning with this initial work, Beck et al. developed many psychometric scales, including the Beck Suicide Intent Scale, the Beck Hopelessness Scale, and the Beck Suicide Ideation Scale (Beck, Herman, & Schuyler, 1974a; Beck, Weissman, Lester, & Trexler, 1974b).

Operational Classification for Determination of Suicide (OCDS)

In the mid-1980s, the CDC convened a working group representing coroners, medical examiners statisticians, and public health agencies to develop operational criteria to assist in the determination of suicide. These criteria are based on a definition of suicide as "death arising from an act inflicted upon oneself with the intent to kill oneself" (Rosenberg et al., 1988). This definition highlights two clear components: that the lethal outcome is self-inflicted (the agent) and that it is intentionally inflicted (awareness of outcome).

The purpose of the criteria was to improve the validity and reliability of suicide statistics by (1) promoting consistent and uniform classifications; (2) making the criteria for decision-making in death certification explicit; (3) increasing the amount of information used in decision-making; (4) aiding certifiers in exercising their professional judgment; and (5) establishing common standards of practice for the determination of suicide.

Rosenberg et al. (1988) argued that all suicides, by definition, must be self-inflicted and that the deceased intended to die. Hence, emphasis is placed on establishing the evidence of intent to die. They introduced the concept of explicit (verbal or nonverbal) and implicit (or indirect) evidence of intent, and provided 11 examples of implicit or indirect evidence of intent to die. They acknowledged that some of these examples of indirect evidence included many commonly identified risk factors (e.g., previous suicide attempt). Yet they also acknowledged that a risk factor is not necessarily a causal factor.

For them, "intent" requires that the decedent knew or had in mind that a specific act would probably result in death. They acknowledged that intent may be difficult to determine. Nonetheless they agreed that the establishment of intent may require judgment and that "absolute certainty is not the goal in certifying deaths" (p. 1451). Instead, the basis for the determination should correspond to the legal notion of "preponderance of the evidence." Otherwise stated it is an opinion based on "reasonable probability" (p. 1451).

Despite its name, this is not a classification system because they only defined the term suicide and it was not operationalized. What they accomplished, through a consensus of experts, was to establish the evidence needed to define a suicidal death to assist the decision-maker in answering two fundamental questions: (1) whether or not the injury was self-inflicted; and (2) whether or not the decedent intended to kill himself or herself. This tool has both relatively high content and face validity.

O'Carroll et al.'s "Beyond the Tower of Babel" Nomenclature

In 1996, O'Carroll et al. published their "Beyond the Tower of Babel" nomenclature which distinguished suicidal behaviors by three characteristic features: intent to die, evidence of self-inflicted injury, and outcome (injury, no injury, or death). They attempted to build on the Beck et al. (1973) classification system and provide definitions for commonly used terms in suicide research. Although a number of investigators and professional organizations adopted the nomenclature (American Psychiatric Association, 2003; Daigle & Cote, 2006; Rudd & Joiner, 1998), the nomenclature was not widely used in the research and clinical communities, partially due to its introduction of unfamiliar terms and definitions, such as instrumental suicide-related behavior.

WHO/EURO Terminology

In the 1980s, the WHO embarked on the EURO/WHO Parasuicide Multi-Centre Study, which required the development and application of a nomenclature to differentiate various suicidal behaviors (with a specific emphasis on the identification of parasuicidal behaviors) (Schmidtke et al., 1996). The use of the term "parasuicide" was based on Kreitman's definition of parasuicide as a nonfatal act in which an individual deliberately causes self-injury or ingests a substance in excess of any prescribed or generally recognized therapeutic dosage. As is evident, Kreitman's term avoids any reference to intent or motivation (Kreitman, 1977).

Subsequently, after the study ended, members of the multicenter study (De Leo et al., 2006) revised the initial WHO nomenclature based on some of their observations from the study. They established the key components that determine fatal and nonfatal suicidal behaviors: self-initiated; with or without intent to die; and outcome. One criticism is that although they collapsed "parasuicide," "deliberate self-harm," and "attempted suicide" under the one term of "non-fatal suicidal behavior," this term can be applied with or without the presence of intent to die, and therefore captures a broad set of behaviors. It is also potentially confusing because of the use of the phrase "suicidal behavior" to include behaviors without the intent to die.

Columbia University Suicidality Classification

Suicidologists at Columbia University were approached by the U.S. Food and Drug Administration (FDA) to assist them in reviewing all the adverse event reporting associated with antidepressant drug trials involving children and adolescents. The FDA was concerned about whether some of the adverse events being reported were appropriately being labeled as "suicidality." Under contract to the FDA, the Columbia team developed a "Classification Scheme"—a nomenclature of terms and definitions. They introduced the terms "aborted" and "interrupted" suicide attempts. These researchers reviewed all of the adverse events reports to determine how many actually were related to suicidal behaviors. The "Classification Scheme" was subsequently used for the review of adverse event reporting for drug trials with adults (Posner et al., 2007). The hope was that this classification scheme would lead to better systematic assessment of suicidality and identify high-risk groups for research protocols.

Subsequent to conducting the FDA analysis, the Columbia group developed the "Columbia Suicidality Severity Rating Scale" (C-SSRS). Specifically it measures the degree of suicidal ideation and the level of lethality. Suicidal ideation is measured on a 1–5 point scale (from "wish to die," "active suicidal ideation," "method," "intent," to "plan"). Hence, the assessment of intent, motivation, and plans are part of the measurement of suicidal ideation. Suicidal behavior is measured on five levels: (1) actual attempt; (2) interrupted attempt; (3) aborted attempt; (4) preparatory act or behavior; and (5) nonsuicidal self-injury. Lethality is measured on a 0–4 scale. The instrument measures the frequency, duration, controllability, determinants to an active attempt, and the reasons (motivation) for ideation. In many ways they advanced the establishment of criteria for assessing and assigning suicidal risk (Posner et al., 2011).

Silverman et al.'s Revised Nomenclature

In 2006, with the support from the Department of Veterans Affairs' Mental Illness, Research, Education, and Clinical Center (MIRECC) located in Denver, Colorado, and critical input from the medical and psychiatric staff at the Denver VA Medical Center, as well as from representatives from the Department of Defense, Silverman et al. (2007a, 2007b) published a revised nomenclature based on the O'Carroll et al. "Beyond the Tower of Babel" nomenclature. This revision also benefited from numerous recommendations and contributions from the international suicidology community that were received after the publication of the O'Carroll nomenclature.

One improvement was to include a category of "undetermined," which includes "undetermined suicide attempt," "undetermined suicide-related death," and "self-inflicted death with undetermined intent." The goal was to simplify the nomenclature and definitions in a manner that would increase communication between and among clinicians, researchers, administrators, policy makers, and the public. The hope was that a standardized nomenclature would lead to a standardized set of questions for determining the presence or absence of suicidal cognitions, motivations, emotions, and behaviors. As with the initial O'Carroll effort, the authors struggled with the concepts of intent, motivation, risk, threat, gesture, and nonsuicidal self-harm, all the while distilling the existing nomenclature to its most basic conceptual categories.

Denver VA's MIRECC Self-Harm and Suicide Classification System

Using the Silverman et al. (2007b) nomenclature as a template, in 2008 researchers at the Denver VA MIRECC developed a nomenclature and classification system that had clinical utility and could be used across the U.S. Department of Defense and the Veterans Administration Hospital system. The system was developed to "map" onto the CDC's

Self-Directed Violence Surveillance System, which was undergoing development at that time (Silverman, 2011), and subsequently released in 2011 (Crosby et al., 2011).

The VISN 19 Suicide and Self-Harm Classification System was devised with respect to the following four assumptions:

1. The establishment of a valid and reliable system of classifying suicide-related and self-harm phenomenon is the foundation of all suicide research and clinical practice.
2. All suicide-related and self-harm phenomenon can be classified according to thoughts, communications, and behaviors, and ultimate term identification is predicated on the ability to make basic typological distinctions about the phenomenon of interest.
3. The continuum of self-injurious behaviors includes precursory actions that have critical clinical implications for ascertaining suicide risk.
4. Discerning the intent of the patient is a critical factor that differentiates suicidal from nonsuicidal phenomenon and that is most salient with respect to informing clinical decision-making.

While refining the VA's Self-Harm and Suicide Classification System, the MIRECC researchers were instructed to coordinate efforts with other federal agencies. The CDC was already working on a Self-Directed Violence Surveillance System. Recognizing the need to improve the quality of SDV data, in 2003 the CDC's National Center for Injury Prevention and Control (NCIPC) initiated a process to address some of the conceptual difficulties inherent in the task. As a result, the MIRECC researchers worked closely with the team at the CDC to mutually develop the Self-Directed Violence Classification System (SDVCS) (see Table 1.1). From the beginning, the CDC's interest in developing uniform terms and definitions for SDV was for purposes of surveillance. In the collaborative process, the MIRECC researchers also developed a clinical tool to assist clinicians in the application of the classification system to clinical settings (Brenner et al., 2011).

CDC's Self-Directed Violence Classification System (SDVCS)

The Self-Directed Violence Classification System (SDVCS) has standardized the definition of terms related to most frequently discussed forms of suicidal thoughts and behaviors. The SDVCS terms relate to each other in a way that has utility, meaning, and relevance to the clinical world of at-risk individuals. The central aims of the SDVCS are to improve communication, improve consistency of reporting across settings and disciplines, enhance understanding of self-directed violent behaviors among clinicians (DeLeo et al., 2006), and facilitate improved quality of care. Furthermore, the SDVCS has applicability across theoretical perspectives, is considered free of cultural biases, judgments, beliefs, or values (culturally normative), and contains mutually exclusive terms (Crosby et al., 2011).

The SDVCS will allow all healthcare systems to develop an accurate suicide mortality database in order to do meaningful research, clinically intervene with individuals identified as being at risk, and develop and implement prevention efforts. For example, to address suicide as a public health problem would require the sustained and systematic collection, analysis, and dissemination of accurate information on the incidence, prevalence, and characteristics of fatal and nonfatal suicidal behavior. Surveillance, using uniform definitions and data elements, allows for realistic priority setting, facilitates the design of prevention programs, and the ability to evaluate such programs. Official suicide rates have been used to chart trends in suicide, monitor the impact of change in legislation, treatment policies, and social change, and to compare suicides across regions, both within and across countries. In addition, suicide rates afford a method by which to assess population-based risk and protective factors for geographical areas (counties, states, and countries).

This system was officially adopted throughout the VA in April 2010, and since then the MIRECC research group has been centrally involved in nationwide VA efforts to implement the SDVCS. Thus far efforts have included trainings for Suicide Prevention Coordinators and other mental health professionals at national meetings, web-based live meetings, and via the dissemination of materials associated with the nomenclature. Subsequently, the Department of Defense has also adopted the system for its use.

The effort undertaken by the Department of Veterans Affairs to adopt the CDC's SDVCS for clinical use throughout the VA health-care system is a major effort to standardize how veterans at risk for suicide are evaluated, assessed, treated, and managed. Training is underway throughout the VA healthcare system for all clinical personnel. This effort has major implications for the national adoption of a uniform set of definitions to be used in research and clinical settings. These materials are available free-of-charge at: http://www.mirecc.va.gov/MIRECC/visn19/ordersdvcs/or derclipboard.asp.

CHALLENGES TO OVERCOME WITH IMPLEMENTING A UNIFORM NOMENCLATURE AND CLASSIFICATION SYSTEM

Despite a clear need for a uniform nomenclature and classification system in the field of suicidology, there are a number of obstacles to implementing such a system. These include the following:

1. Any standardized nomenclature runs the risk of ignoring or not capturing the nuances of human thinking, intent, motivation, and behavior.
2. Even if we are able to differentiate a range of self-destructive thoughts and behaviors into broad categories, such as suicide-related ideations and behaviors, and subcategories, such as suicide ideation, suicide attempt, and suicide, not all suicide-related phenomena are identical across many domains (e.g., time, duration, frequency, context, degree of lethality, degree of planning, etc.). Although it is a goal to have as few categories and subcategories as needed to accurately label an event, there will always be exceptions to the rule. This does not negate the need for adoption of a uniform nomenclature.
3. Within each subcategory (subclassification) we need to provide more levels of detail and depth to fully describe the presentation in as many domains as possible. To differentiate further within each subcategory, we need to recognize and establish criteria for finer differentiations that are believed to be critical to understanding and classifying suicidal behaviors: levels of lethality, time frames, degree of intent, types of methods used, degree of planning, likelihood of rescue, degree of impulsivity, and presence and status of psychiatric or medical illness. Scales or ranking systems can be developed to measure these elements and provide clinicians and researchers with a richly nuanced approach to classifying the full range of suicidal thoughts, communications, and behaviors.
4. Arriving at the appropriate suicide-related term is almost totally dependent on the individual's self-report for such important components of the suicidal process as suicidal thoughts, intent, motivation, planning, accurately remembering prior life events, assigning significance to life events, appraisal of current stressors, history of prior self-destructive behaviors, and so forth.
5. The role that "clinical inference" plays in determining suicide risk has not been well studied, yet remains an important skill when assessing at-risk individuals.

6. Despite several noteworthy attempts to address the absence of uniformity, the implementation of prior classifications systems has encountered a number of challenges. To date, there have been no known empirical investigations to understand the reasons for the ineffectiveness of implementation efforts. Anecdotally, however, reasons why past suicide nomenclatures have been applied sporadically include clinician unfamiliarity with elements of the proposed terminology, the complexity of the systems, and/or terminology focusing on surveillance efforts instead of on clinical decision-making.

7. Systematic field studies or pilot tests are needed to gauge the usefulness of SDV surveillance, to identify optimal methods of data collection, and to specify resource requirements for implementation. This testing will help to identify unforeseen problems with the data elements and adaptations needed for various settings, and to ensure that categories are mutually exclusive.

CONCLUSIONS

A shared language to describe suicide and suicidal behaviors should be considered the foundation for all suicide prevention efforts and clinical best practice interventions. Adoption of a uniform language aimed at streamlining communications between patients, clinicians, administrators, and researchers is needed. Such a nomenclature is the foundation to the development of a classification system, which should serve as the bridge from research and theory to clinical application. A classification system can be used as a tool to investigate and better understand suicidal phenomena across many domains, such as timing, duration, frequency, intensity, level of intent, method used, degree of lethality, and degree of planning. In addition, different treatments may be indicated for different, albeit related, behaviors, highlighting the need for clarity in assigning patients to different categories of suicide-related behaviors.

The central aim of any suicide nomenclature should be to develop a foundation upon which we can disseminate a system that improves communication, has practical utility across settings and disciplines, enhances understanding among those who employ it, and ultimately facilitates improved quality of care. Will a consistent nomenclature actually result in better identification, intervention, monitoring, and prevention? To date, we do not know for sure. The selection of one or two classification systems for field-testing is an essential next step. Data can be collected to determine whether the classification system has clinical utility and acceptability, and will allow for exploration of the relationship between the use of SDV terms and mental health-care utilization and outcomes.

The adoption of a uniform language aimed at streamlining communications between participants, clinicians, mental health professionals, administrators, and researchers is warranted. Erroneous typological distinctions and overgeneralizations are all too frequent. Clinicians and researchers alike continue to struggle to discern one thought, communication, or behavior pertaining to suicide from another, and sometimes even employ terms that can be pejorative (e.g., suicidal gesture). Incomplete understanding regarding terms utilized to denote suicidal risk can lead to flawed communications among clinicians, and ultimately to treatment recommendations that, at best, lack efficiency, and, at worst, are contraindicated for a particular individual. Research implications are as salient. In light of the lack of consistency in defining operationally distinct manifestations of suicide-related thoughts and behaviors, the adoption of a shared language to discuss suicide and associated phenomena should be considered inherent in, and the foundation of, all suicide prevention efforts and clinical best practice interventions.

All the components of the suicidal process then must be identified, labeled, and classified if we are ever to hope for the day when we all can share information and observations to help identify and treat truly suicidal individuals, and ideally develop interventions to prevent the onset, maintenance, duration, intensity, frequency, and recurrence of these thoughts and behaviors. Classifying individuals on the basis of the intent of their self-injury is a useful scientific and clinical endeavor (Nock & Kessler, 2006). Carefully defining key constructs, such as suicide attempts, will reduce variation in responding and will enhance interpretation and communication of study results (Linehan, 1997; Meehan, Lamb, Saltzman, & O'Carroll, 1992).

Although progress is being made on a number of different fronts, there still remains a need for a convening of an international workgroup to resolve differences between and among the existing nomenclatures, definitions, and classification systems. Unless and until the field of suicidology (comprising epidemiologists, sociologists, psychologists, physicians, neurobiologists, researchers, clinicians, first-responders, survivors, community leaders, etc.) speaks the same language and approaches the classification of suicidal behaviors in a clear, concise, and consistent manner, I believe that communications between and among all those who work for the goal of suicide prevention will remain clouded.

REFERENCES

American Psychiatric Association. (2003). Practice guidelines for the assessment and treatment of patients with suicidal behaviors. *American Journal of Psychiatry, 160 (Supplement),* 1–60.

Beautrais, A. (2004). Further suicidal behavior amongst medically serious suicide attempters. *Suicide & Life-Threatening Behavior, 34,* 1–11.

Beautrais, A., Joyce, P., & Mulder, R. (1999). Personality traits and cognitive styles as risk factors for serious attempts among young people. *Suicide & Life-Threatening Behavior, 29,* 37–47.

Beck, A. T., Beck, R., & Kovacs, M. (1975). Classification of suicidal behaviors: 1. Quantifying intent and medical lethality. *American Journal of Psychiatry, 132,* 285–287.

Beck, A. T., Davis, J. H., Frederick, C. J., Perlin, S., Pokorny, A. D., Schulman, R. E., . . . Wittlin, B. J. (1973). Classification and nomenclature. In H.L.P. Resnik & B.C. Hathorne (Eds.), *Suicide prevention in the seventies,* pp. 7–12. Washington, DC: U.S. Government Printing Office.

Beck, A. T., Herman, I., & Schuyler, D. (1974a). Development of suicidal intent scales. In A. T. Beck, H.L.P. Resnick & D. Lettieri (Eds.), *The prediction of suicide,* pp. 45–56. Bowie, MD: Charles Press.

Beck, A. T., Weissman, A., Lester, D., & Trexler, L. (1974b). The measurement of pessimism: The hopelessness scale. *Journal of Consulting & Clinical Psychology, 42,* 861–865.

Bille-Brahe, U., Kerkhof, A., De Leo, D., & Schmidtke, A. (2004). Definitions and termination used in the World Health Organization/EURO Multicentre Study. In A. Schmidtke, U. Bille-Brahe, D. De Leo & A. Kerkhof (Eds.), *Suicidal behaviour in Europe,* pp. 11–14. Göttingen, Germany: Hogrefe and Huber.

Brenner, L. A., Breshears, R. E., Betthauser, L. M., Bellon, K. K., Holman, E., Harwood, J.E.F., . . . Nagamoto, H. T. (2011). Implementation of a suicide nomenclature within two VA healthcare settings. *Journal Clinical Psychology in Medical Settings, 18,* 116–128.

Brown, G. K. (2001). *A review of suicide assessment measures for intervention research with adults and older adults.* Rockville, MD: U.S. Department of Health and Human Services.

Brown, G. K., Henriques, G. R., Sosdjan, D., & Beck, A. T. (2004). Suicide intent and accurate expectations of lethality: Predictors of medical lethality of suicide attempts. *Journal of Consulting & Clinical Psychology, 72,* 1170–1174.

Chapman, A. L., & Dixon-Gordon, K. L. (2007). Emotional antecedents and consequences of deliberate self-harm and suicide attempts. *Suicide & Life-Threatening Behavior, 37,* 543–552.

Chapman, A. L., Gratz, K. L., & Brown, M. (2006). Solving the puzzle of deliberate self-injury: The experiential avoidance model. *Behaviour Research & Therapy, 44,* 371–394.

Conner, K. R., Langley, J., Tomaszewski, M. S., & Conwell, Y. (2003). Injury hospitalization and risks for subsequent self-injury and suicide: A national study in New Zealand. *American Journal of Public Health, 93,* 1128–1131.

Crosby, A. E., Ortega, L., & Melanson, C. (2011). *Self-directed violence surveillance: Uniform definitions and recommended data elements, Version 1.0.* Atlanta, GA: Centers for Disease Control and Prevention, National Center for Injury Prevention and Control.

Daigle, M. S., & Cote, G. (2006). Nonfatal suicide-related behavior among inmates: Testing for gender and type differences. *Suicide & Life-Threatening Behavior, 36,* 670–681.

De Leo, D., Burgis, S., Bertolote, J. M., Kerkhof, A. J.F.M., & Bille-Brahe, U. (2006). Definitions of suicidal behavior: Lessons learned from the WHO/EURO Multicentre Study. *Crisis, 27,* 4–15.

Duberstein, P. R., & Conwell, Y. (1997). Personality disorders and completed suicides: A methodological and conceptual review. *Clinical Psychology: Science & Practice, 4,* 359–376.

Gibb, S. J., Beautrais, A. L., & Fergusson, D. M. (2005). Mortality and further suicidal behaviour after an index suicide attempt: A 10-year study. *Australian & New Zealand Journal of Psychiatry, 39,* 95–100.

Goldsmith, S. K., Pellmar, T. C., Kleinman, A. M., & Bunney, W. E. (2002). *Reducing suicide: A national imperative.* Washington, DC: The National Academies of Science.

Harris, E. C., & Barraclough, B. (1997). Suicide as an outcome for mental disorders: A meta-analysis. *British Journal of Psychiatry, 170,* 205–228.

Hawton, K. (1997). Attempted suicide. In D. M. Clarke & C. G. Fairburn (Eds). *Science and practice of cognitive behavior therapy,* pp. 285–312. Oxford, UK: Oxford University Press.

Hawton, K., & Fagg, J. (1988). Suicide, and other causes of death, following attempted suicide. *British Journal of Psychiatry, 152,* 359–366.

Hjelmeland, H., & Knizek, B. L. (1999). Conceptual confusion about intentions and motives of nonfatal suicidal behavior: A discussion of terms employed in the literature of suicidology. *Archives of Suicide Research, 5,* 275–281.

Jobes, D. A., & Berman, A. L. (1985). The numbers game: A critique of mortality stats. Paper presented at the 18th annual meeting of the American Association of Suicidology, Toronto.

Jobes, D. A., Berman, A. L., & Josselson, A. R. (1987). Improving the validity and reliability of medical-legal certifications of suicide. *Suicide & Life-Threatening Behavior, 17,* 310–325.

Kessler, R. C., Berglund, P., Borges, G., Nock, M., & Wang, P. S. (2005). Trends in suicide ideation, plans, gestures, and attempts in the United States, 1990–1992 to 2001–2003. *Journal of the American Medical Association, 293,* 2487–2495.

Krasser, G., Rossmann, P., & Zapotoczky, H. G. (2003). Suicide and auto-aggression, depression, hopelessness, self-communication: A prospective study. *Archives of Suicide Research, 7,* 237–246.

Kreitman, N. (1977). *Parasuicide.* London, UK: Wiley.

Krug, E. G., Dahlberg, L. L., Mercy, J. A., Zwi, A. B., & Lozano, R. (2002). *World report on violence and health.* Geneva, Switzerland: World Health Organization.

Linehan, M. M. (1986). Suicidal people: One population or two? *Annals of the New York Academy of Sciences, 487,* 16–33.

Linehan, M. M. (1997). Behavioral treatments of suicidal behavior: Definitional obfuscation and treatment outcomes. *Annals of the New York Academy of Sciences, 836,* 302–328.

Linehan, M. M. (2000). Behavioral treatment of suicidal behavior: Definitional obfuscation and treatment outcomes. In R. W. Maris, S. S. Canetto, J. L. McIntosh & M. M. Silverman (Eds.), *Review of suicidology 2000,* pp. 84–111. New York: Guilford.

Luoma, J. B., Martin, C. E., & Pearson, J. L. (2002). Contact with mental health and primary care providers before suicide: Review of the evidence. *American Journal of Psychiatry, 159,* 909–916.

Malone, K. M., Szanto, K., Corbitt, E., & Mann, J. J. (1995). Clinical assessment versus research methods in the assessment of suicidal behavior. *American Journal of Psychiatry, 152,* 1601–1607.

Mann, J. J., Apter, A., Bertolote, J., et al. (2005). Suicide prevention: A systematic review. *Journal of the American Medical Association, 294,* 2064–2074.

Maris, R. W. (1992). The relationship of nonfatal suicide attempts to completed suicides. In R. W. Maris, A. L. Berman, J. T. Maltsberger & R. I. Yufit (Eds.), *Assessment and prediction of suicide,* pp. 362–380. New York: Guilford.

Meehan, P. J., Lamb, J. A., Saltzman, L. E, & O'Carroll, P. W. (1992). Attempted suicide among young adults: Progress toward a meaningful estimate of prevalence. *American Journal of Psychiatry, 149,* 41–44.

Nock, M. K., & Kessler, R. C. (2006). Prevalence of and risk factors for suicide attempts versus suicide gestures: Analysis of the national comorbidity survey. *Journal of Abnormal Psychology, 115,* 616–623.

Nordentoft, M., Breum, L., Munck, L., Nordestgaard, A., Hunding, A., & Bjaedager, P. (1993). High mortality by natural and unnatural causes: A 10-year follow-up study of patients admitted to a poisoning treatment centre after suicide attempts. *British Medical Journal, 306,* 1637–1641.

O'Carroll, P. W. (1989). A consideration of the validity and reliability of suicide mortality data. *Suicide & Life-Threatening Behavior, 19,* 1–16.

O'Carroll, P. W., Berman, A. L., Maris, R. W., Moscicki, E. K., Tanney, B. L., & Silverman, M. M. (1996). Beyond the Tower of Babel: A nomenclature for suicidology. *Suicide & Life-Threatening Behavior, 26,* 237–252.

Owens, D., Horrocks, J., & House, A. (2002). Fatal and non-fatal repetition of self-harm: Systematic review. *British Journal of Psychiatry, 181,* 193–199.

Posner, K., Oquendo, M. A., Gould, M., Stanley, B., & Davies, M. (2007). Columbia Classification Algorithm of Suicide Assessment (C-CASA): Classification of suicidal events in the FDA's pediatric suicidal risk analysis of antidepressants. *American Journal of Psychiatry, 164,* 1035–1043.

Posner, K., Brown, G. K, Stanley B, Brent D. A., Yershova K. V., Oquendo M. A., . . . Mann J. J. (2011). The Columbia-suicide severity rating scale: Initial validity and internal consistency findings from three multisite studies with adolescents and adults. *American Journal of Psychiatry, 168,* 1266–1277.

Rosenberg, M. L., Davidson, L. E., Smith, J. C., Berman, A. L., Buzbee, H., Gantner, G., . . . Jobes, D. (1988). Operational criteria for the determination of suicide. *Journal of Forensic Science, 33,* 1445–1456.

Rudd, M. D. (2000). Integrating science into the practice of clinical suicidology: A review of the psychotherapy literature and a research agenda for the future. In R. W. Maris, S. S. Canetto, J. L. McIntosh & M. M. Silverman (Eds.), *Review of suicidology, 2000,* pp. 49–83. New York: Guilford.

Rudd, M. D., & Joiner, T. E. Jr. (1998). The assessment, management and treatment of suicidality: Towards clinically informed and balanced standards of care. *Clinical Psychology: Science & Practice, 5,* 135–150.

Schmidtke, A., Bille-Brahe, U., De Leo, D., Kerkhof, A., Bjerke, T., Crepet, P., et al. (1996). Attempted suicide in Europe: Rates, trends and sociodemographic characteristics of suicide attempters during the period 1989–1992. Results of the WHO/Euro Multicentre Study on Parasuicide. *Acta Psychiatrica Scandinavia, 93,* 327–338.

Schmidtke, A., Bille-Brahe, U., De Leo, D., Kerkhof, A., & Wasserman, D. (Eds.) (2001). *Suicidal behavior in Europe: Results from the WHO/Euro multicentre study on suicidal behavior.* Göttingen, Germany: Hogrefe & Huber.

Silverman, M. M. (2006). The language of suicidology. *Suicide & Life-Threatening Behavior, 36,* 519–532.

Silverman, M. M. (2011). Challenges to classifying suicidal ideations, communications, and behaviors. In R. O'Connor, S. Platt & J. Gordon (Eds.), *International handbook of suicide prevention: Research, policy and practice,* pp. 9–25. Chichester, UK: Wiley Blackwell.

Silverman, M. M., Berman, A. L., Sanddal, N. D., O'Carroll, P. W., & Joiner, T. E. (2007a). Rebuilding the Tower of Babel: A revised nomenclature for the study of suicide and suicidal behaviors. Part I: Background, rationale, and methodology. *Suicide & Life-Threatening Behavior, 37,* 248–263.

Silverman, M. M., Berman, A. L., Sanddal, N. D., O'Carroll, P. W., & Joiner, T. E. (2007b). Rebuilding the Tower of Babel: A revised nomenclature for the study

of suicide and suicidal behaviors. Part II: Suicide-related ideations, communications and behaviors. *Suicide & Life-Threatening Behavior, 37,* 264–277.

Suominen, K., Isometra, E., Suokas, J., Haukka, J., Achte, K., & Lonnqvist, J.
(2004). Completed suicide after a suicide attempt: A 37-year follow-up study.
American Journal of Psychiatry, 161, 563–564.

Veterans Health Administration (VHA) (2009). Report of the Blue Ribbon Work
Group on Suicide Prevention in the Veteran Population. http://www.mental
health.va.gov/MENTALHEALTH/suicide_prevention/Blue_Ribbon_Report-
FINAL_June-30-08.pdf, Accessed July 2011.

2
The Phenomenology of Suicide

Bernard S. Jesiolowski and James R. Rogers

*We must at all times remember, that the decision
to take your own life is as vast and complex and
mysterious as life itself.* (italics in original)
—(Paraphrased from Alvarez (1971)
by Webb (1971) [2012])

We are born, we live, and we die. In a sense, everything is born, lives, and dies, from a virus to the universe itself. However, we are rare among living creatures in that we are phenomenologically conscious of our existence and our experiences. Phenomenology is generally defined as the study of consciousness as it is experienced from the first-person point of view. From this point of view, as we mature and develop, we become increasingly conscious of our inevitable death. In addition, and perhaps more importantly, we may also grow to apprehend that we are unique beings. We experience choice and intentionality, and we can begin to understand our place in the universe. We are also self-aware beings and conscious of the presence, thoughts, and feelings of others. We care about other people, and our relationships with them help define who we are throughout our lives. However despite, or perhaps as a consequence of, the fact that we are complex, aware, conscious, and from many perspectives unique in evolutionary adaptation, we can and sometimes do make what appears to be the conscious phenomenological choice to end our own lives, that is, some among us choose to die by suicide.

Can we better understand and prevent suicide by considering the phenomenology of suicidal people? Although it is the case that more traditional research and scientific approaches to understanding and preventing suicide have advanced our understanding of suicidal behaviors and influenced our prevention and intervention approaches, the evidence supporting the efficacy of those efforts in terms of reducing suicide is generally lacking (Rogers & Lester, 2010). According to Rogers and Soyka (2004):

> Taken together, the aggregate data available with regard to suicide attempts and completed suicide, coupled with the dearth of empirical support for the effectiveness of clinical work with suicidal individuals, are both disheartening and compelling. Disheartening in that, despite the activities of public health officials, researchers, and clinicians focusing on the issue of suicide, there is little in the way of concrete evidence in support of our efforts. (p. 9)

Consequently many clinicians and researchers alike agree that suicidal behavior cannot be fully understood through quantitative methodologies alone, that there are qualitative or phenomenological experiences of suicidal people that must be understood. The purpose of this chapter is to provide an introduction to phenomenology and a phenomenological perspective on suicidal behavior and offer an example of one person's journey toward suicide as he experienced it.

INTRODUCTION TO PHENOMENOLOGY

Historically phenomenology is anchored in a philosophical tradition promulgated in the first half of the 20th century by Edmund Husserl (1989), Martin Heidegger (1962), Maurice Merleau-Ponty (1996), Jean-Paul Sartre (1956), and others. Since human beings themselves are the instruments through which the universe is apprehended and, therefore, from which philosophy is generated, phenomenology is viewed from this tradition as being the foundation of all philosophy. We as human beings are bound by the limits and nature of our sensory organs and experiences as we individually experience our humanness through our brains, neurochemistry, and ecology and through the evolution that has astoundingly produced it all. We all think, feel, and behave as human beings, and our phenomenological experience of all that we apprehend, create, or develop is a product of these variables and constraints. Hence, phenomenological philosophy would be considered by many to be the primary perspective from which any other philosophy emerges, and is, therefore, superior even to ethics, epistemology, and even metaphysics.

Phenomenology became central to the tradition of continental European philosophy during the 20th century, and in many ways it dovetails rather neatly with the more analytical philosophy of mind which evolved in the Anglo-American tradition in that same century. Indeed, phenomenology continues to be explored and celebrated around the world through events such as the World Conferences on Phenomenology as a means to unify reason with life, objective truth with first-person experience, and strict knowledge with ethics (Toadvine, 2011). Along these lines, the First Global Conference Making Sense of Suicide which was held in November of 2010 in Prague (the Czech Republic) had a session on phenomenological approaches to suicide. Schlimme (2011) presented a paper there entitled "Self Determination and the Suicidal Experience: A Phenomenological Approach." Her findings indicated that there is a measure of subjective freedom in the decision to die by suicide or to continue to live, although a suicidal person may have difficulty phenomenologically bringing the decision completely into focus.

Although a lengthy discourse regarding phenomenology may be fascinating to some, for the more practical purposes of this chapter, the less philosophical and more contemporary and integrative definition of phenomenology presented below will prove sufficient to our needs. In a somewhat circular way, various sources cite that phenomenology is literally the study of phenomena—the appearances of things, or rather things as they appear in our experience, as well essentially the ways in which we experience things. Therefore, by way of logical extension, phenomenology includes the meanings that people assign to their experiences since we human beings tend to be pattern-forming and order-seeking entities. Phenomenology investigates conscious experience from the subjective or first-person point of view, sifted through these uniquely human templates. For example, a beautiful sunset would certainly be differently sensed and have different meanings when sifted through the templates of a praying mantas, a bat, a whale, or a human being.

PHENOMENOLOGY AND SUICIDAL BEHAVIOR

Pompili (2010) succinctly offered the following integrative presentation of his contemporary conceptualization of phenomenology.

In recent philosophy of mind, the term "phenomenology" is often restricted to the characterization of sensory qualities of seeing, hearing, etc.: what it is like to have sensations of various kinds. However, our experience is normally much richer in content than mere sensation. Accordingly, in the phenomenological tradition, phenomenology is given a much wider range, addressing the meaning things have in our experience, notably, the significance of objects, events, tools, the flow of time, the self, and others, as these things arise and are experienced in our "life-world." (p. 240)

Pompili (2010) continued:

Phenomenology studies conscious experience as experienced from the subjective or first person point of view. The experiencing subject can be considered to be the person or self. Subjective experiences are those that are, in principle, not directly observable by any external observer. (p. 240)

Pompili further contends that, "Although the early pioneers of suicidology, like Edwin S. Shneidman and Erwin Stengel, asked 'What is it like to be suicidal?', the trend in recent decades has been for the phenomenology of suicidality to almost disappear from the research agenda of the discipline" (p. 1). In the chapter on the "Phenomenology of Suicide," from Shneidman's book *On the Nature of Suicide* (1973), Farber states:

A few words about the place of this conscious will and the willing to die: such a person, I have to assume, is undergoing the questioning of his entire existence. His [sic] whole life has been put into question: who is he [sic], where is he [sic], what has he [sic] been about all of these years, what acts of betrayal has he [sic] committed, either actively or by omission, and so on. (p. 108)

Without knowledge and empathic understanding of the world in which an individual may arrive at the questioning of his entire existence, how can we successfully help this person? Doing our very best to comprehend the phenomenological world of that person is surely a good start in this process.

Congruent with this line of reasoning, researchers, in attempts to know that which is "not directly observable by an external observer," have examined suicide notes and other personal narratives to better understand the suicidal person through understanding those behavioral expressions. For example, Leenaars (1988) concluded from his study of suicide notes that suicide often appears as a solution to an individual's present interpersonal situation as well as a reflection of the individual's history. He also contended that, although an act of suicide is intentional and conscious, it may also involve substantial unconscious processes, thereby creating a model of suicide in which both conscious and unconscious processes are present (Leenaars, 1994). Indeed, as Sigmund Freud, Carl Jung, or Fritz Perls might say, the incongruent expressions we observe may in fact give us some clues to the unconscious processes which act as drivers in some suicidal actions. Perls was known to assert that when verbal and body language are incongruent, the body is more likely to convey the truth. Hence, his double-entendre direction to go out of your mind and into your body. Orbach, Mikulincer, Gilboa-Schechtman, and Sirota (2003) similarly suggest that the life narrative of a suicidal person may offer insight into her or his subjective world and can be formulated in terms of a sequence of losses, their nature, and their essence. They believed, therefore, that it is possible for a therapist and client through empathic understanding to review the past together in order to learn how the person's life and perspective for the future have perhaps become phenomenologically untenable and unendurable to that person.

Empathic understanding allows therapists and clients to work together to comprehend how it is that suicide seemed the only available alternative and, perhaps, to move on therapeutically from that shared understanding. Jesiolowski (1988), using a process he called *Life Syntegration* with clients who had severe mental illnesses such as schizophrenia and bipolar disorder, supports the concept that a review of the past in a narrative form can be helpful to some individuals. In this case, the narrative was in the context of a Gestalt-oriented group life-review methodology incorporating elements of neurolinguistic programming theory. In this predominantly qualitative study, he found that such a process enhanced the participant's sense of personal meaning and supported positive recollections of their accomplishments in life. For some participants, significant life-path changes occurred during and after their six-month involvement in the group.

Other researchers have also quantitatively and qualitatively studied notes, poems, diaries, letters, and songs, as well as other personal narratives and documents, which are artifacts of people who have died by, contemplated, or attempted suicide. Although much of this line of research has been plagued by methodological problems, as well as difficulty in obtaining sufficient data for study, it appears that, if such difficulties could be resolved, this research may eventually prove useful in providing insight into the suicidal mind (Rogers & Lester, 2010) and by extension into their phenomenological world. Attempts to know and understand that which is subjective and "not directly observable by an external observer" through an examination of artifacts is promising. To use a holography metaphor (i.e., the development of a three-dimensional perspective based on two-dimensional data), we need to shine a more cohesive and holistic methodological light through all of the data to see the "whole" of the person through the "parts" and to make sense of them as well as their conscious and unconscious expressions.

THE CONSCIOUS PHENOMENOLOGICAL EXPERIENCE OF BEING SUICIDAL

To many of us, suicidal intentionality or action does not make sense from our respective phenomenological worlds, and we cannot imagine wanting to truly end our own lives. Yet research informs us that a relatively high percentage of people consider suicide at some time during their existence. In fact the American Association of Suicidology website (www.suicidol ogy.org) informs us that, "By some estimates, as many as one in six people will become seriously suicidal at some point in their lives." In the day-to-day living of our lives, ostensibly most people appear to enjoy being alive and seem to work assiduously and proactively to extend their years on this planet through various self-care and nurturing activities. Most people, indeed most organisms, work against the process of entropy, which is the second law of thermodynamics. Entropy dictates that everything, including higher energy states and order (which take energy from the environment to sustain their states), ultimately degrades to lower energy states and chaos. In everyday language, this means that entropy increases as matter and energy in the universe inexorably degrade to an ultimate state of inert uniformity; into the lowest energy state possible. The ultimate fate of the universe is chaos. Entropy therefore increases as we move toward death and personal chaos.

Living is work and requires human beings to work against the inevitable pull of entropy. Living things are, for the most part, genetically programmed to remain alive for a period of time and to work to sustain this life through interactions with their environments. Therefore, human beings exist and thrive by using the energy stored in surrounding ecologies and resources to sustain their complex systems and to decrease the probability of their death. Even counseling and family support for a person considering suicide represents this process metaphorically, with the counselor and family members using self-energy when giving energy and helping to instill a more cohesive order into the suicidal person who seems to be in desperate need of this help and whose subjective life seems to be filled with disorder and chaos.

Indeed, such supportive experiences may often leave the counselor and family members who are attempting to help the suicidal person feeling "emotionally and physically drained." The suicidal person, when depleted of cohesive and ordered energy, literally seems to need energy from others in order to hold entropy at bay. From this perspective, entropy is the ally of suicide since suicide increases entropy.

Yet, in defiance of entropy, we all intuitively realize that, as organisms, we are designed to sustain life. Subsequently, it is little wonder that, from the perspective of a friend, a family member, or a behavioral health practitioner, the mere consideration of an individual engaging in suicidal intention or behavior is frequently viewed as irrational, senseless, and (although we dislike using this word) "crazy." However, from the phenomenological frame of reference of the suicidal person being seduced into the dark and powerful vortex of suicide contemplation, perceived burdensomeness, isolation, despair, and hopelessness, such an action may appear to be a viable and perhaps even a logical and rational choice.

One suicidal client, in retrospect, gave us a powerful glimpse into her phenomenological world of suicidal contemplation through the following statement:

> Those around me were very distraught and frustrated with my mental state. My life style had become life threatening and I was imposing emotional pain on loved ones with my disruptive, self-destructive behavior. My failed attempts to "pull myself together," coupled with my awareness of the continual distress I was causing, led me to view suicide as a logical option . . . it eventually became the only option I could conceive of to prevent myself from inflicting pain on those I loved. (Rogers & Soyka, 2000, p. 90)

This decision to end one's life, in essence, represented to the suicidal person the best and most logical approach to solving what seemed to be an insurmountable problem of living, given the pain, the feeling that others will be better off without them, the available resources and the phenomenologically perceived unsustainable and inextricably complex situations at that point in their lives. Entropy pulls them. In addition, suicide increasingly becomes a most seductive option to such an individual in that this single action of self-destruction will end the lingering deep pain, the hopelessness, and the complex turmoil so intensely and unremittingly experienced. Extending our entropy metaphor, with far too much emotional, cognitive, behavioral, and spiritual information to reorganize, integrate, and reframe to make things phenomenologically consistent than seems humanly impossible for that person to undertake and inhabit, with far more entropy to fight than there are internal or external resources available to accomplish this battle, it feels easier to simply let it all go and succumb to entropy. There may be a sense of impending peace, as described by some suicide attempters, when they finally decide to end their lives. Due to the unbearable psychological pain phenomenologically experienced prior to this decision, there seems to be a sense of relief in letting entropy follow its course.

As an aside, although we have not seen this expressed or reflected in the literature, we conjecture that the psychologically powerful negative reinforcement (i.e., the removal of pain) experienced by the decision to take one's own life and let entropy do its effortless work, may actually operate behaviorally to reinforce the decision itself to die by suicide, from a behavior reinforcement theory perspective. If this is the case, then intermittent decisions to die by suicide, followed by the reinforcement of experiencing relief (even after the suicidal crisis has passed), may greatly increase the probability of future decisions related to suicide. Intermittent reinforcement theory would predict that the probability of any behavior increases according to reinforcement schedules and is most powerful when an intermittent reinforcement schedule is employed. Therefore, through a humanized, nonrigid, nonmechanistic, phenomenologically based assessment and intervention process, through the client feeling support, human caring, and learning about the reinforcement process, she or he may actually agree to reveal the frequency of such phenomenological decisions and, through informed mindfulness and support, be able to actively reduce the effects of the internal intermittent negative reinforcement resulting from the sensation of removal of unbearable psychological pain.

Shneidman (1993), who was the creator of the field of study that he named *suicidology,* first named this unbearable pain *psychache.* He defined psychache as an intolerable, very deeply experienced, severe psychological pain. Although the concept of psychache is clinically and empathically acknowledged by behavioral health practitioners as a consuming, hopeless, and all-encompassing psychological pain, it appears to be evident on a face validity basis to those not actually experiencing such pain that suicide is "a permanent solution to a temporary problem." Solutions other than suicide in such situations are always perceived as possible from the phenomenological perspective of the observer. Yet, in most cases, these solutions feel inescapably unknowable or impossible to access to a person so immersed in the despair and hopelessness of the suicidal maelstrom.

Steinbock (2007) investigated the phenomenological experience of hope and the "rivals of hope" which he suggested create hopelessness. He found these rivals of hope to include disappointment, desperation, panic, hopelessness, and despair. He examined the varieties of experiences that seem to counter hope, and he found that despair is the greatest phenomenological challenge to hope. This hopeless pain and untenable subjective situation is further complicated in that the highly distressed and unbalanced subjective internal state of the suicidal person seems often to be equally unknowable or impossible to access by those of us who want to prevent the suicide and help the person regain balance.

Thomas Joiner (2010) has a great deal to convey about the phenomenological mind of a suicidal person. Joiner acknowledges that, because people who have never been suicidal cannot possibly imagine taking their own lives, they frequently view those who contemplate, attempt, or die by suicide as "crazy," psychotic, demented, or delusional. He concludes from his research in the field that this is typically not the case and that:

> Anecdotes abound in which a person was seen or spoken with at one point in time; seemed coherent, calm, in tune with reality, and sober; and then was dead by suicide minutes or hours later. . . . The high school president who gave a lucid and rousing talk to students, faculty and others on the future of the school, both for the short- and long-term, is a good example. This kind of performance from him was typical; no one noticed anything unusual or erratic about his appearance or behavior. On the contrary, he was composed and articulate, just as he usually was, and then approximately 4 hours late, he jumped to his death from the upper floors of a downtown hotel. . . . There are numerous documented cases in which people have been in communication with family or authorities in the seconds and minutes leading up to their deaths by suicide. In the vast majority of these cases, those about to die were not incoherent or psychotic. (pp. 87–88)

Again, this is not to say that those who die by suicide may not have a mental health disorder, as research indicates that a very high percentage of those who die by suicide indeed have a diagnosable mental health disorder or "are experiencing sub-clinical variables of mental disorder" (Joiner, 2010, p. 89). However, these people are not usually out of touch with reality and, furthermore, may believe that their choice to end their lives is rational from their subjective frame of reference. The following statements by Joiner eloquently describe another aspect of the suicidal individual based on his research, experience, and his own phenomenological frame of reference:

> Those who die by suicide have two simultaneous mental processes unfolding. One is mundane (and yet in a way incredible) and is happening in virtually everyone (including those whose deaths by suicide are impending): "Should I change jobs? What will I do this weekend? Should I get a new car? Should I ask so and so on a date, or to marry me?" The other is far from mundane, and is difficult for most people to even conceive of: "Why don't I just die? It would be a relief. There's an aspect to death that is comforting, even beautiful, people would be better off, why don't I just get it over with?" Though it is difficult and uncomfortable to conceive of this process, that does not change the fact that it is a true process that characterizes the minds of suicidal people. (p. 69)

Joiner's view of the individual's primary motivation for suicide (in conjunction with an experience of thwarted belongingness and desensitization to pain) is "the mental calculation that the individual's death will be worth more than his or her life to others" (p. 45), which he also refers to as perceived burdensomeness.

As a further reflection of this, Hersh (2010), a person who survived several suicide attempts, recounts much of what she experienced in her life through her phenomenological experiences. Hersh recounts the following statement she said to herself before a suicide attempt: "You are not needed, the voice in my head taunted. They're better off without you" (p. 151). The content of this first-person inner voice supports Joiner's position that a primary motivation for suicide is often perceived burdensomeness.

From a different perspective, Roy Baumeister (1990) gives us his version of the intolerable first-person tunnel vision that he is convinced is experienced by a genuinely suicidal person. Suicide, in his model, is analyzed in terms of motivations to escape from aversive, painful self-awareness and ultimately escape from the self. A number of sources agree that escape from the relentless, excruciating pain (psychache), and the conscious conviction that all is hopeless and that there will be no relief from this internal hell, invariably leads to a desire to escape from the source of this pain which ultimately is the self. According to Baumeister, there are six primary steps in this escape theory, culminating in a probable suicide when all criteria are met. These are as follows:

Step 1: Falling short of standards.

Step 2: Making self-loathing attributions to self.

Step 3: High self-awareness in comparing oneself ceaselessly and unforgivingly to a preferred self.

Step 4: Powerful negative affect such that negative suicidal emotions are experienced as an acute inescapable state rather than a prolonged one.

Step 5: Cognitive deconstruction in which the outside world becomes a much simpler affair in our heads, but usually not in a good way. This is actually a defensive mechanism helping the person to withdraw cognitively from thinking about past failures and the anxiety of an intolerable, hopeless future.

Step 6: Disinhibition which is required to overcome the intrinsic fear of causing oneself pain through death, not to mention the anticipated suffering of loved ones left behind to grieve. In this model, the suicidal person has, through time, constructed a phenomenological world for herself or himself so self-denigrating and self-loathing that it is utterly unbearable to inhabit. In this world, moment-to-moment existence is so painful (and it feels as though changing it is an impossibility) that the only choice is to escape the self through death by suicide.

These models contribute to the observer's understanding of a suicidal person, help to explain how such a person can consider this act to be logical, rational, and necessary when so many others cannot, and point toward interventions that may be ameliorative based upon the theoretical constructs and tenants of the respective models. Hence, through these models of suicidal phenomenological consciousness, the subjective first-person experience of being suicidal, that experience which seems unobservable, vast, and mysterious to all but the suicidal person, can be at least experienced cognitively by those of us who are not suicidal yet and who quest to understand.

Furthermore, because we are all human and share many of the same human templates, our amazing biocomputers (i.e., brains) can simulate the rest of the experience for us if we mindfully care to experience this state. By understanding the thinking, the logic, and the human pain of the suicidal person, we can extrapolate to the rest of her or his phenomenological world and work to fully comprehend another's phenomenological perspective, or at least simulate it for ourselves.

What follows now in an attempt to provide one example of a phenomenological experience of suicidality is an interview with a person who was previously suicidal. In it, you will see much of what has been discussed throughout this chapter. Here is an opportunity to consider what you may have come to understand about the phenomenology of suicide by applying it to the case of an actual human being who has been suicidal. Try to be fully aware and mindfully acknowledge this experience as you read the words of John and understand his world as he almost terminated his own life. Try to connect with his phenomenological experience.

A PHENOMENOLOGICAL INTERVIEW

Whenever Richard Cory went down town,
We people on the pavement looked at him:
He was a gentleman from sole to crown,
Clean favored, and imperially slim.
And he was always quietly arrayed,
And he was always human when he talked;
But still he fluttered pulses when he said,
"Good-morning," and he glittered when he walked.
And he was rich—yes, richer than a king—
And admirably schooled in every grace:
In fine, we thought that he was everything
To make us wish that we were in his place.
So on we worked, and waited for the light,
And went without the meat, and cursed the bread;
And Richard Cory, one calm summer night,
Went home and put a bullet through his head.

To set the stage, the first author of this chapter is going to tell you a brief story about one of my best friends in this life whom I will call John in this interview. John is an intelligent, gentle, compassionate, kind, funny, artistic, and talented man who loves astronomy, understanding the universe, music, his wife, his children, his friends, and people in general—a man who would stop in an instant if he saw you in trouble and do whatever he could to help. This story demonstrates how difficult it often is to see the internal struggle that people may experience as they grapple with questions of life and death. The struggle can continue unobserved by us despite our willingness and desire to help. Despite knowing John for over 40 years, it was only recently that I became aware of how closely he had approached the threshold of suicide.

By way of context, John had deeply struggled with his son's heroin addiction for years leading up to his consideration of suicide. His son's reoccurring pattern of using heroin, seeking help, beginning a program, and then relapsing had the family in a state of perpetual chaos and turmoil since they all lived under the same roof. Despite dealing with his fears, frustrations, and disappointments regarding his son on a daily basis, John was always pleasant when we spoke. He seemed as though he was managing as well as could be expected, and I could not discern that phenomenologically John was feeling hopeless, helpless, and agitated, but there were no objective signs that John was considering suicide. No one knew what was really going on inside John. Everyone missed any signs and signals that might have been revealed as John arrived at the conclusion that he needed to end his life to stop the pain. What follows is John's phenomenological account of his descent into the suicidal maelstrom, including the moment he decided to end his life and the moment when he changed his mind.

When John discovered that we were writing this chapter, he asked me if he might be able to help others understand the world of the suicidal person by telling his story. He said that his hope was that, by so doing, those who read this account and are interested in helping people who may be suicidal will have "a little more insight into how it feels to be suicidal, to feel that there is no other way out, and to not leak a word of intending to do it to anyone, even your best friends or wife." The following account, therefore, is about an event which occurred a year ago, and he had never talked about it before. We had been talking about phenomenology for an hour before I started the tape recorder, and I know we had a shared understanding of the phenomenological perspective.

Bernie: Could we begin with you telling me what was going on with you around that time, the pressure you have mentioned to me before in previous conversations, that was building up? What was going on inside, what it felt like to you, what it felt like to be you then?

John: Well, first I was very disappointed and then I got very angry. I had this anger thing with him [his son]. Yeah. Really disappointed that he kept relapsing over and over no matter what we tried. Really angry, really pissed, that he was stressing the family more and more every time he did. I was deeply disappointed and pissed.

Bernie: That was beginning of the process which led you to consider suicide?

John: I think so. I think so. (Long pause) But it was building up for a year or so I think. (Long pause) Before that, you know I threw him out of the house then, just before I lost it.

Bernie: Yeah, I remember that, John. When I called you at the hospital, you mentioned that to me. So you threw him out.

John: Yeah, just for one night. But Sally [John's wife] . . . Sally couldn't do that. It hurt her. It really hurt her. I was ready to, I don't know why, I was ready to just throw him out. I had more than I could take.

Bernie: So when you "threw" him out, he had been out of recovery, dropped out a couple of times, and when you threw him out, Sally was really upset over that. That kicked it up a notch, is that right?

John: Right.

Bernie: Did you kind of feel like Sally was mad at you, disappointed in you?

John: No, I didn't feel that she was mad at me, but she couldn't do that to her son. She begged and begged me to let him back in, and actually I eventually went along with that the next day. I didn't want to do that either, kick him out I mean. I didn't want to do that as much as Sally didn't want me to do that, you know, but I did kick him out though. I said "You're outta here. It's been too many times." I was crying. "You know it's been years now. We tried to help you, but you're going to have to go because Mom and I can't live like this." It seemed like it didn't matter to him how we felt. You know what I mean? So I tried to get rid of the problem. "Just get out of the house!" But that wouldn't have gotten rid of the problem.

Bernie: Well, you sound as though you had just reached the point where you had tried to help him every way you could and tried what some people call tough love.

John: Yeah. Then it just turned into total despair, hopelessness, helplessness and being guilty, like I couldn't do enough to help.

Bernie: Like nothing made or would make any difference?

John: No nothing at all. I'm thinking that I'm going to have the rest of my life like this. You know what I mean? I walked around this house for four hours on that day. Thinking, agitated, hopeless. I kept staring out the window in the living room, just wondering what I was going to do.

Bernie: Around the house. You mean pacing?

John: Oh yeah, pacing for four hours in a circle through the house. From the living room to the dining room, to the kitchen, to the hall, to the living room! Sally was at work. I was by myself.

Bernie: So could you feel pressure building up inside, or something like that?

John: Yeah, yeah. I had to do something, like I had to do something, but I didn't know what I had to do. I kept saying to myself, "What can I do? What the hell can I do? I can't live like this. Sally can't live like this. No one can," over and over. Then this thought came to me that maybe it would be a good time to end this. I can't make phone calls feeling like that. I said to myself, "You can't do anything else." I don't know. I was by myself.

Bernie: It felt like that completely?

John: Yeah, completely. It was like I had blinders on. It's just that single thought takes over your whole being and I don't know. I just decided to go and buy a gun.

Bernie: So when all this stuff was building up, did anybody in your family, any of your friends know you were to that point? Did we miss something?

John: No.

Bernie: You didn't tell anybody?

John: No, no, no. Until that day.

Bernie: Until that day?

John: Until that minute. I remember exactly what happened. I was looking out the window and said, "I'm going to town and getting a gun."

Bernie: And then?

John: I went down to town. Yeah, and the whole time, I was not completely myself, but I knew what I was going to do. It was just such a disconnect with myself. But I was really good at it. No one knew what I really felt and was thinking. I just went down there and said I needed something for protection, you know. Just to buy a gun. You know I'm allowed to buy a gun just like that where I live.

Bernie: Yeah.

John: Yeah, I'm allowed to buy a gun. It was, you know, this is this much money. "Oh yeah, sure, sure," the shop owner said. And the whole time, it feels like there's two of me. Yeah, the one in the front that's doing the talking and sounding cheerful and acting like it's an everyday thing, and the real me that's just pondering what I'm going to do next at home, you know.

Bernie: Did you already have a plan in mind? Did you already know in advance what exactly you were going to do?

John: Yeah. I thought that out when I was walking around in the thing there. Pacing. I had it all worked out. (Long pause)

Bernie: After you bought the gun, throughout the whole time you're driving home with it, what were you thinking and feeling? What was going on in your head?

John: I'm not sure. I really don't remember that part very well right now. It's like watching somebody do it, and I don't really remember driving home.

Bernie: Okay.

John: Obviously, I must have been thinking what I was going to do, but I don't remember that now.

Bernie: um.

John: And I came home, loaded it up and went outside and fired two shots.

Bernie: Oh, you did? To test it out?

John: Yeah, just fired into the ground, just to get a feel for. (Long pause) You know, I'm not good at speaking.

Bernie: You're doing fine. This is really helping me to understand what you experienced. Are you feeling like you want to continue?

John: Yeah. I really want to tell this story. I never told it before, and it kind of feels good to tell a good friend. (Pause)

John: So, I came home, loaded it up and went outside and fired two shots. You know, just to get a feel for it, you know, the trigger and how the gun felt to fire it.

Bernie: Yes. So you loaded it up in the house?

John: Yeah, in the kitchen.

Bernie: Where's Sally?

John: Still at work.

John: Yeah, and my son was upstairs and, you know, was not doing good at all. He was out of recovery then, and I had just thrown him out of the house the day before. And, you know, he heard the shots and came down, and he saw me with the gun.

Bernie: Where did you shoot the gun? Out front, out back?

John: Back of here. I think it was like, you know, it was pretty new to me. You know, I've never had a gun in my life. Just to feel it, feel the power of it, and how this is going to be to use it. It was all new to me. By the way, when I went down to the store and came home, I loaded it up. I went right out, you know. So it wasn't like coming home and waiting for hours. I went right to it, and then I kind of pondered it before I fired the shots. I went out the garage door, fired a couple of shots into the ground. My son heard that and came down and said, "What are you doing?" I didn't answer him. I just walked straight back into the woods back there. Then he saw me going back there, and he called Sally. I didn't know this at the time. It was a snowy day, a windy, snowy day. I didn't feel the wind, the cold, or anything. I sat down in the snow by this big tree, leaned against it, and just fiddled around with the gun a little bit. Then I said, "Well, I went this far. This still sounds like a good idea to me." So I held it up to my temple, and I squeezed the trigger a little. And then, uh, I couldn't do it right then. I couldn't do it, so I shot at the tree. I don't know why. I'm just firing this gun off.

And I think now that people who actually do die by suicide; they must really have horrible, horrible, horrible problems and no help to get through it. I know mine was bad too, but nowhere near what other people have, I guess. But at the time, I think to myself that I'm going to spend the rest of my life like this, and I can't do that can't do that. It's a selfish thing. That's all you think about is yourself, you know. The whole time I was out there, I wasn't thinking about anybody but me, when am I going to do it.

I couldn't do it there, so I got up and walked about two-hundred yards to the end of the property on a trail that goes way down in the woods. I went down there, and I said, "This is the spot. Yeah, this is the spot, right here." So I think I shot a tree again. By this time my wife had come home. They had called the police, but I didn't know about it. And I held the gun up to my temple again, and I thought about my grand-daughter. She came to my mind, my granddaughter. And that's what actually kept me from doing it. I don't think I really wanted to do it. But I almost did. I was just a second away from it twice! It turned out that I didn't have the nerve to do it because I thought of my granddaughter. Just her face, and I don't know why it was her and not anybody else in my family. But it was her. "I want to, but I just can't." The detective was already down there behind a tree, and he was yelling at me. I think he is saying, "Don't do it. Don't do it," or something like that, and I can't. Plus he's hiding, and I'm carrying a gun and behind a tree. He doesn't know if I'm going to . . . (Very long pause)

Bernie: If you were going to shoot him?

John: Yeah, right. He didn't know who I was or if I would shoot him. So it was very strange. Talk about a disconnect right there! That was just like, "Wow. I can't actually believe I did that, went through that whole thing." So I gave up and laid the gun on the ground. He saw me put it on the ground.

Bernie: Then what did you do?

John: I walked away, walked away from it so that he would know that I'm not going to do anything else. Not hurt him in any way. He came down real fast once I got so far away, about 20 feet away. Boy, he came flying down and grabbed me and knocked me to the ground. He held me down there, and two other policemen came after him and dragged me up out of the woods. And off to the hospital I went.

Bernie: Can we go back into your story a little bit so I can understand a few more things?

John: Absolutely.

Bernie: You said earlier that it felt like you had blinders on.

John: Well, I wasn't thinking about anybody else. You know, the only thing I was thinking about was me and how I was going to end this problem. Well, I know how I'm going to end this problem. You know. I just didn't think it was going to go away. I couldn't live like that.

Bernie: You didn't see solutions anywhere?

John: No, not talking to anybody, not making any phone calls. Could not think of anything other than to kill myself. No, that was the only thing that I could think of. It was the only thing that made any sense to me at all. Kind of logical in a different kind a way. They'd be better off if I was gone anyway. So I just knew I had to do it, and no one can stop me.

Bernie: Do you think that anybody, if they would've come through the door while you were thinking about all this, while you were pacing, do you think anybody could've diverted you? Do you have any sense about that?

John: That's possible. That's a possibility, yeah. That might've averted it, but I'm not sure how long I would've felt like that. Like not doing it. I wouldn't have done it right then. (Long pause) Might've just delayed it. I'm not sure. The only thing I'm pretty sure about is I really wanted to do it, but I didn't know that I didn't really want to do it in the end.

Bernie: Yeah.

John: But I thought I did. I was very, very close. I squeezed the trigger. Yeah it moved. It moved a little bit.

Bernie: Did that scare you?

John: Yeah. I was quite frightened. But like I said, in the end I couldn't do it.

Bernie: But at the time, before you had thoughts of your granddaughter, it felt sort of rational to kill yourself, like a real solution?

John: Yeah, yeah. I was thinking this could be a solution to this. That's how stupid that was in looking back on it. You know, but that's about it. I wanted to do it really deep, deep, deep down, but I went through that action, and I think it was maybe a call for help because it takes a lot of guts to do that. It takes an awful lot of guts and, I don't know what the word would be, despair. I just don't know. It takes an awful lot of guts and despair and thinking that you're making things worse by being around, alive. The people that actually do it, I don't know, that's what it takes I think. That's what it took for me—guts and despair.

Bernie: You were so down and so despairing, it sounds like you can imagine how down and despairing someone would have to be to actually complete suicide.

John: Yeah, actually do it. Yeah, right.

Bernie: You mentioned you felt hopeless.

John: Hopeless and helpless.

Bernie: Both. With all the pain you were experiencing, it just seemed like a good solution as you have said.

John: Yeah. I just kept thinking I won't have the problem anymore, you know. I've lived this long, you know. At least I made it into my sixties. That's what I was telling myself, you know. I've lived that long, so let's do it and get it over with. It would be so nice not to have the problem. I'd do anything.

Bernie: It had to feel so deep to take you to that point, the feeling of despair.

John: Oh yeah, it's total despair. Whatever despair means, that was it! Yeah, there's no other choice when you feel that way. No other choice. You seem so far gone that no one or nothing can help.

Bernie: And it's like you said, you can't live with this pain anymore.

John: No, no. It's definitely that I wasn't going to, I couldn't live with it. No, absolutely not, and that was the way out! That was the way out and, like what we talked about before, the disassociation and being behind myself when I was buying the gun. It was like there were two of me. That's what was really weird, you know. One guy was like okay, and I'm talking to the guy down there. Meanwhile, the person in back of me is just thinking about what I'm going to do when I get home. (Pause) Wait. I think that's what I was thinking about while I was driving home. Where am I going to do it? Yeah, that's what I was thinking. Where I was going to do it. Not when, because I was going to do it right away.

Bernie: So you ruled out doing it in the house?

John: Yeah, I ruled out doing it in the house. It just didn't seem right to me. I don't know. I just thought that was a good place right there, up the hill. Nobody could see me.

Bernie: When you think back to the John of that time, what do you think?

John: I think about how selfish I was.

Bernie: That's the first thing that comes to your mind?

John: Yeah, just selfish. That all I was thinking about was me. I'm not thinking about my family or anyone but me. It's a totally selfish thing that I did, even though I thought it was best for everyone at the time. But, like I said, it's like having blinders on. You can only see that one thing. That was the worst day of my life. I couldn't even think about any other possible solutions that were there. No, I wanted to get rid of the problem right away—today. I had had enough. I couldn't live like that anymore. All I would do was walk around this house. Everyday, up and down the steps, around the thing, downstairs, just stewing.

Bernie: For days you did this?

John: For days and days. I did absolutely nothing but think about it all and pace. Just walking around the house, upstairs, downstairs, thinking, "What am I going to do?" Not what are we going to do to help my son, but what am I going to do to help me. And that's why I think it's a selfish thing to do when you commit suicide. You're only thinking about yourself. Not thinking about what you're doing to your family. It was such a help for me to put it down, the gun. Actually it felt good to put it down. So like I said I don't think I really wanted to do it in the end, but I did while it was happening all that while. (Pause) It was more of a call for help.

Bernie: And I'm so glad. I keep thinking how close you came.

John: Yeah, it could've slipped. You just don't know. So I'm really glad I didn't do it.

Bernie: So what do you think when people reach that despairing state, how will anyone who loves them ever know about it? How would they know that? How would they be able to help before it got to that point?

John: I don't know the answer to that.

Bernie: Thank you so much for sharing your story here. I feel really privileged to hear it.

—(John, personal communication,
December 10, 2011)

Comment

Upon reflection, this interview with John revealed not only his internal, slowly rising tide of hopelessness and of the unfulfilled needs in his life, but also the tsunami of emotional pain that finally reached intolerable, devastating intensity as his son's unrelenting addiction stressed his family and seemed to leave John "no way out" of the pain. This was John's phenomenological existence, and he shared it with no one, not even his trusted best friends or loving wife. Phenomenological experience, as we have discussed, by its very nature can sometimes remain unobserved and unobservable. With John, his internal experience did not manifest easily recognizable outward signs and symptoms when he was with others. If it had, these signs could have served as clues to those who loved him that he had reached the end of his ability to tolerate his inexorable pain. This level of unrelenting powerful psychological pain frequently leads to what is termed and experienced as psychological tunnel vision, that is, the inability of an individual to see solutions to a problem even when they may be evident to others. Perhaps further exacerbating this internal psychological tunnel vision experience is the actual physiological experience an individual may have with psychache. Extreme and intolerable fear, anxiety, distress, worry, and agitation can result in the body being flooded with adrenaline and oxygen, which may lead to the actual physical sensation of tunnel vision accompanied by a feeling of unreality and disassociation. Indeed, tunnel vision and disassociation are revealed throughout John's interview, as a result of his own increasing psychache. They can, for example, be ascertained from his words as he described his inability to see any way to solve his problem except to escape it through suicide (i.e., tunnel vision) and when he purchased his gun and he described feeling as though there were two of him, one smiling as he procured the weapon and another observing this process and knowing how he planned to use it to end his existence (i.e., disassociation).

It may interest the reader to know that John's son has been in recovery since this incident and is working at a full-time job. John eventually received the helpful and healing counseling he needed and is living a happy and fulfilling life.

CONCLUSION

We must at all times remember, that the decision to take your own life is as vast and complex and mysterious as life itself. (italics in original)

We began this chapter with the above paraphrase from Alverez. We believe it is fitting to end this chapter with the same paraphrase, along with the addition of a small reflection.

It is our hope, as well as John's, that this brief introduction to the phenomenology of being suicidal will be enlightening and perhaps encourage us to look more deeply into each other's phenomenological worlds, beyond the surface words we say, or facial expressions that may be incongruent with our inner selves. Perhaps, in so doing, we can help to reduce the psychache in others before they find themselves on the threshold of suicide.

REFERENCES

Alvarez, A. (1971). *The savage god: A study in suicide.* New York: Random House.

Baumeister, R. F. (1990). Suicide as escape from self. *Psychological Review, 97,* 90–113.

Heidegger, M., (1962). *Being and time.* Trans. by John Macquarrie & Edward Robinson from the German original of 1927. New York: Harper & Row.

Hersh, J. K. (2010). *Struck by living: From depression to hope.* Dallas, TX: Brown Books.

Husserl, E. (1989). *Ideas pertaining to a pure phenomenology and to a phenomenological philosophy.* Trans. by Richard Rojcewicz & André Schuwer from the German original unpublished manuscript of 1912, revised 1915, 1928, known as *Ideas* II. Boston, MA: Kluwer Academic Publishers.

Jesiolowski, B. S. (1988). *The use of gestalt therapy in the process of life review: A conceptual and, theoretical synthesis.* PhD dissertation, Kent State University.

Joiner, T. E., Jr. (2010). *Myths about suicide.* Cambridge, MA: Harvard University Press.

Leenaars, A. A. (1988). *Suicide notes.* New York: Human Sciences Press.

Leenaars, A. A. (1994). Crisis intervention with highly lethal suicidal people. In A. A. Leenaars, J. Maltsberger, & R. Neimeyer (Eds.), *Treatment of suicidal people,* pp. 45–59. London, UK: Taylor & Francis.

Merleau-Ponty, M. (1996). *Phenomenology of perception.* Trans. by Colin Smith from the French original of 1945. New York: Routledge.

Orbach, I., Mikulincer, M., Gilboa-Schechtman, E., & Sirota, P. (2003). Mental pain and its relationship to suicidality and life meaning. *Suicide & Life-Threatening Behavior, 33,* 231–241.

Pompili, M. (2010). Exploring the phenomenology of suicide. *Suicide & Life-Threatening Behavior, 40,* 234–244.

Robinson, Edwin Arlington. (1897). "Richard Corey." In Cary Nelson (Ed.), *Anthology of Modern American Poetry* (p. 26). New York: Oxford University Press, Inc.

Rogers, J. R., & Lester, D. (2010). *Understanding suicide: Why we don't and how we might.* Cambridge MA: Hogrefe.

Rogers, J. R., & Soyka, K. M. (2000). Toward a phenomenological understanding of suicide. In M. Weishaar (Ed.), *Suicide 99: Proceedings of the 32nd annual conference of the American association of suicidology,* pp. 89–91. Washington, DC: American Association of Suicidology.

Rogers J. R., & Soyka K. M. (2004). "One size fits all": An existential-constructivist perspective on the crisis intervention approach with suicidal individuals. *Journal of Contemporary Psychotherapy, 34,* 7–22.

Sartre, J.-P. (1956). *Being and nothingness.* Trans. by Hazel Barnes from the French original of 1943. New York: Washington Square Press.

Schlimme, J. E. (2011). Self-determination and the suicidal experience: A phenomenological approach. Retrieved December 7, 2012 from http://www.ncbi.nlm.nih.gov/pubmed/22042597

Shneidman, E. S. (1973). *On the nature of suicide.* San Francisco, CA: Jossey-Bass.

Shneidman, E.S. (1993). *Suicide as psychache: A clinical approach to self-destructive behavior.* Northvale, NJ: Jason Aronson.

Steinbock, A.J. (2007). The phenomenology of despair. *International Journal of Philosophical Studies, 15,* 435–451.

Toadvine, T. (2011). *Reason and life: The responsibility of philosophy.* World Conference on Phenomenology, Segovia, Spain.

Webb, D. (1971). The many languages of suicide. Retrieved December 7, 2012, from http://www.jungcircle.com/DWebb.html

3

The Ethics of Suicide: Philosophical and Religious Perspectives[1]

Margaret P. Battin

I s suicide wrong, always wrong, or profoundly morally wrong? Or is it almost always wrong, but excusable in a few cases? Or is it sometimes morally permissible? Is it not intrinsically wrong at all, although perhaps often imprudent? Is it sick? Is it a matter of mental illness? Is it a private or a social act? Is it something the family, community, or society could ever expect of a person? Or is it solely a personal matter, perhaps a matter of right, based in individual liberties, or is it even a fundamental human right?

This spectrum of views about the *ethics* of suicide—from the view that suicide is profoundly morally wrong to the view that it is a matter of a basic human right, and from the view that it is primarily a private matter to the view that it is largely a social one—lies at the root of contemporary practical controversies over suicide. These practical, often overlapping controversies include at least four specific matters of high current saliency:

- *Physician-assisted suicide in terminal illness,* the focus of intense debate in parts of the world with long life expectancies and high-tech medical systems, particularly the Netherlands, the United States, England, Canada, Switzerland, Belgium, Germany, and Australia.
- *Hunger strikes, self-immolations, and suicides of social protest,* as in Turkey, Northern Ireland, wartime Vietnam, China, Tibet under Chinese rule, and the Middle East following the 2010 self-immolation of a Tunisian fruit vendor that touched off the "Arab Spring."
- *Religious and ritual practices that lead to death,* for example, some occasions of *sati* or widow-burning, voluntary live burial, and ritual "fasting unto death," called *samadhi, santhara,* or *sallekhana,* as practiced in Jain and other communities in India.

- *Suicide bombings* and related forms of self-destruction employed as military, guerilla, or terrorist tactics, including kamikazi attacks in wartime Japan; suicide missions by groups from Tamil separatists to al-Qaeda; and suicide bombings in the conflicts in Israel, Palestine, Iraq, and elsewhere.

Beneath these specific practical issues lies the question of suicide itself, and how it should be regarded from an ethical point of view. For much of the 20th century and on into the 21st century, at least in the West and in regions affected by Western colonialism, thinking about suicide has been normatively monolithic. Suicide has come to be seen by the public, and particularly by health professionals, as primarily a matter of mental illness, perhaps compounded by biochemical and genetic factors and social stressors, the sad result of depression or other often treatable disease—a tragedy to be prevented. With the exception of the debate over suicide in terminal illness, the only substantive discussions about suicide in current Western culture have concerned whether access to psychotherapy, improved suicide-prevention programs, or more effective antidepressant medications should form the principal lines of defense.

Indeed, suicide very often is a tragedy, and depression or other mental illness is often in play. However, a full exploration of historical and cross-cultural thought concerning suicide must also explore the many additional ways in which the phenomenon of self-destruction has also been understood—some of them bizarre, but many of them profound. A full exploration seeks to broaden the current rather monolithic view, not replace it, and to provide a much wider context for understanding contemporary issues about self-caused death.

HISTORICAL AND CULTURAL BACKGROUNDS

The Western record of discussion and dispute about the morality of suicide begins some three millennia ago with a rather personal dialogue between a man and his soul, a dialogue dating from the First Intermediate Period of ancient Egypt. Writing on suicide continues with the early Hebrew texts that record (without ethical comment) a handful of suicides, including Samson (who pulled the temple down upon himself as well as the Philistines), Saul, and Saul's armor bearer. In a different culture, ancient Greece, Plato developed a somewhat inchoate classification of acceptable and unacceptable suicides, including those subject to burial restrictions (like the Athenian practice of burying the hand apart from the body) and those that were not. In the following centuries, the Greek and Roman Stoics came to celebrate suicide as the act of the wise man, while the Christian Church, from the time of Augustine through the time of Thomas Aquinas, increasingly and vigorously condemned suicide as a sin. Some Enlightenment writers defended suicide; some Romantic writers glorified it; and some writers during these eras repudiated it. What is remarkable is the huge variety of accounts these writers give, both religious and secular, of what makes suicide right, ethically neutral, or wrong.

Debate in the Western tradition continued apace until roughly the time of Durkheim and Freud, at the beginning of the 20th century, with their theories of suicide as socially conditioned and as pathological, respectively. These thinkers in effect silenced the ethical debate, since they saw suicide as socially or psychiatrically caused rather than chosen. This laid the foundation for the view that, because suicide is not voluntarily chosen in any robust sense, it cannot be said to be culpable—not morally wrong, not sinful, and not criminal. While debate over individual responsibility for suicide still continues, it has until recently been largely obscured by the dominant professional view that suicide is a product of mental illness, committed by people in the grip of depression or otherwise incapable of reasoning clearly, and that, therefore, there really is no *ethical* issue here.

At the same time, views about self-caused and self-willed death have been evolving in the East and the Middle East, beginning with ancient Hinduism, Buddhism, Jainism, Confucianism, and Islam, in India, early China, Southeast Asia, and Japan. These views have been carried forward within different religious and cultural traditions, often modified and exaggerated, but nevertheless each typically preserving a characteristic, unique, fundamental ethical stance.

In addition, over long spans of time, oral cultures in the Arctic, Africa, Oceania, and North, Central, and South America have been evolving, often including practices involving suicide and related forms of self-caused, self-willed death. From the practices of these cultures, it is possible to infer (although such inferences always involve a considerable degree of conjecture) the background normative views on which they rest. These views, and the practices in which they are exhibited, are often strikingly different from those of the literate cultures of the East and West. To be sure, reliance on historical accounts is far more problematic in the oral traditions than it is in the literate cultures able to preserve first-hand documents over long stretches of time. For traditional oral cultures, contact with indigenous practices concerning suicide, and the background worldviews and belief systems in which they are embedded, is to a considerable degree filtered through Western eyes, since the written records from which the views of oral cultures can be distilled have become available only with the incursion of explorers, missionaries, conquistadors, adventurers, and ethnographers, themselves largely from Western cultures. Just the same, the older sources from these cultures are invaluable since, despite their distortions, they depict societies comparatively innocent of Westernized attitudes about suicide.

Of course, it cannot be assumed that views of all the members of the various eras and cultures about suicide, whether in Western, Eastern, or traditional oral cultures, were or are alike. Cultures are rarely homogenous groups, but rather living collections of people whose views may differ considerably, although they may appear uniform when contrasted with the views of members of other cultures.

THE EVOLUTION OF VIEWS AND PRACTICES OVER TIME

In order to understand the evolution of these perspectives over time, one might examine, for example, the development of thinking in Judaism, from the Hebrew Bible and its origins in the 12th to 9th centuries BC, through Josephus in the first century AD to the rabbinic writers and the Babylonian Talmud of the third to sixth centuries AD, to the 10th-century Karaite writer Ya'qub al-Qirqisani, the Tosafist writers of the 12–14th centuries, and on to Luria in the 16th century, Margoliouth in the 19th century, and Smul Zygielbojm in the 20th century, whose wrenching suicide note in May of 1943 offers his own death in protest against the Allied indifference to the evolving holocaust for Polish Jews. Or one might examine the Japanese tradition, beginning with Daidoji Yuzan's portrait of medieval Japan's *Bushido* military and chivalric culture; then Chikamatsu's plays and the developing tradition of love-suicide; then Lord Redesdale's account of *hara-kiri*; and finally the letters from kamikaze pilots written just before their final missions in World War II. Or one might explore the entwined traditions of Hinduism, Buddhism, and Jainism, beginning with the ancient Vedas and Upanishads of the 15th to 5th centuries BC; the Dharmashastra law codes of the seventh century BC to first century AD; the writings associated with Buddha's contemporary Mahavira, revered as the founder of Jainism; the *Questions of King Milinda,* an interchange between the Indo-Greek king Menander and the Buddhist monk Nagasena, dating from roughly 100 BC to 200 AD; the Lotus Sutra, composed sometime during the first several centuries AD; Bana, from the late sixth century to early seventh century AD; the anonymous late-19th-century Hindu widow describing *sati* or widow-burning; and on to figures of the 20th century, Gandhi and Thich Nhat Hanh—both concerned, although in quite different ways, with self-sacrifice as a form of social protest. These traditions continue in occasional modern instances of ritual self-starvation in Jain communities and frequent instances of self-immolation elsewhere. These are long, rich traditions of reflection on this issue.

Although the various historical traditions develop initially independently, they have come to interact and often mirror each other over time. For example, reflection on suicide within Judaism begins long before such reflection within Christianity, but in the Talmudic period and during the Middle Ages, Judaism's view of suicide appears to have evolved in part in tandem with that of Christianity. Both exhibit an intensifying condemnation and prohibition of suicide, even though the specific details never fully coincide. Islam first arises several centuries after the Augustinian view that suicide is always wrong had pervaded both Christianity and to some extent Judaism; Islam's view remains comparatively uniform over time. But such mirroring is rarely perfect. While Islam's repudiation of suicide in many ways parallels that of Judaism and Christianity, the distinction it draws between suicide and martyrdom, which also is an issue in Judaism and Christianity, seems to fall in a rather different place.

On another continent, the evolution of Hindu spirituality and its fusion with Buddhist views about the illusoriness of life affect thinking about suicide in Confucian China, and in turn contribute to the *Bushido* military and chivalric culture of medieval Japan that lionized suicide, which in turn played a major role in Japan's military tactics in World War II. On still other continents, late-medieval Catholic attitudes about the sinfulness of suicide were brought to the central and southern parts of the New World by the Spanish conquistadors and the missionaries who traveled with them, while Protestant attitudes, no more tolerant of the sin they saw in suicide than that of the Catholics, were imported into Africa, India, North America, and other places colonized largely by Protestant nations.

CONCEPTUAL ISSUES: SIMILARITIES AND DIFFERENCES

There are many apparent parallels in thinking about suicide. For example, Greek and Roman Stoics saw suicide as rational and responsible in some circumstances, as did the *Bushido* tradition in Japan, Jainism, which sees death by religious fasting as an ideal, and at least one strain in Buddhism, where taking one's own life is not wrong as long as it is not done in hate, anger, or fear. Of course, these are loose parallels, and there are many differences among the views of these traditions as well. It is important to remain sensitive to background differences in cultural assumptions about metaphysical, epistemological, and religious issues, as well as quite different systems of morality, even while noting striking parallels among texts and practices.

Nevertheless, similar elements and common problems are numerous, even across distant traditions. For example, for some traditions, like Talmudic Judaism, the early Christianity of St. Ignatius, and later Christian theologians, and both traditional as well as contemporary Islam, the line between suicide and martyrdom (one prohibited, the other permitted and indeed celebrated) is very finely drawn, although in subtly different ways. Similarly, the line between the desire to die and suicide is also very finely drawn. This is true for writers from St. Paul and Angela of Foligno to Gandhi. Some writers and cultures think it ignoble to die in bed, deteriorating from illness. For the Vikings, the Yoruba in Nigeria, *Bushido* warriors, and Iglulik Eskimo, death by violence, including death by suicide, is the more noble way.

Then, too, writers in very different cultures have been concerned with quelling fashions for suicide. Plutarch, for example, describes an ingenious method of stopping the fad among the maidens of Miletus. Similarly, Huang Liu-hung, a 17th century provincial Chinese administrator, and Caleb Fleming, a fiercely conservative 18th century English divine, both thought exposing the naked body of a suicide in a public place was the most effective deterrent. The founder of Methodism, John Wesley, spoke for shaming by public hanging of the body of "every self-murderer, Lord or peasant," although he did not insist that the body be unclothed. On the other hand, some writers have been accused of fomenting fashions for suicide—for example, the playwrights Chikamatsu and Goethe—whether for thwarted love or to avoid descent into an ordinary, mundane existence. Roman generals, *Bushido* warriors, and kamikaze pilots have been alike in seeing military defeat as an occasion for suicide. Cultures in China, Africa, native North America, the Inca Empire, Viking-controlled northern Europe, and in precolonial and colonial India have seen suicide and/or voluntary submission to being killed as an appropriate part of funerary customs, especially for wives and the retainers of kings and nobles. While such parallels are never exact, they are instructive nevertheless.

There are conceptual similarities and differences among traditions as well. The distinction between killing and letting die, between self-killing and being killed, between being killed at one's request and killing one-self, or between self-killing and provoking another into killing oneself, makes an enormous difference in some cultures (Judaism, Christianity, and Islam), but little in others (Viking culture and Buddhism). Politically motivated suicide may look very different in the East than in the West, partly because political systems are so different and partly because assumptions about what a person would accomplish by committing suicide are different. Different authors and cultures have sharply different views about whether concerns about the impact of a suicide on surviving family members or one's society are important. Some think suicide is largely an individual matter—for example, the Roman philosopher Seneca, who in his famous Letter 70 wrote that "Every man ought to make his life acceptable to others besides himself, but his death to himself alone," and Paul-Louis Landsberg, who died in the Oranienburg concentration camp in 1943. For others, for example, those in kin-based societies, where the suicide of a young or middle-aged person breaks up social networks but the suicide of an elderly person who has ceased to play such roles docs not—suicide is a social issue.

The scope of suicide prohibitions also varies widely, as does the matter of whether exceptions are ever to be made. Then there are group suicides, for example, the mass suicide at Masada described by Josephus, the ritual self-disembowelment of the 47 Ronins, or even the ultimate mass suicide of the whole human race, imagined by Novalis and by Eduard von Hartman. There are suicides of protest and social protest in many times and places and for many politically diverse reasons: Lucretia, Cato, Thich Quang Doc, and Yukio Mishima. Contemporary hunger strikers, suicide bombers, and those who immolate themselves to defend political or religious freedom may also belong in these categories. In some cultures, especially in Africa, suicide is understood as revenge while, in others, it is conceptualized primarily as altruistic, even when some self-killings are clearly egocentric. In some cultures, suicide is understood as a matter of individual choice, however socially plausible the choice of death in that person's specific circumstances may seem to be.

THE ISSUE OF DEFINITION AND LINGUISTIC ISSUES

To note such similarities and differences raises the issue of definition. Exactly what counts as *suicide*? Some definitions are extremely narrow. They count only cases in which a person has knowingly and voluntarily acted in a way that directly causes his or her own death, with the intention that death results. Others are more flexible, including cases of semi-intentional self-killing, semi-accidental self-killing, self-harm which results in the extinction of cognitive capacities although not the physical body, self-killing in which the person acts knowingly and voluntarily but does not want to die or wants to achieve some other goal, and so on. It can be argued that terminological differences often serve to mark views about the morality of self-killing in various circumstances or for various reasons, and that the wide range of terms used in cases of voluntary, intentional causation of one's own death serves this purpose. "Suicide" is normally differentiated (in English) from "self-sacrifice," "martyrdom," "acquiescence in death," "aid-in-dying," "victim-precipitated homicide," "self-deliverance," and a variety of other terms, but these differences will vary in other languages and indeed other speakers. Examples include not only Lactantius' insistence that the death of Cato, the Stoic example *par excellence* of praiseworthy suicide, was actually homicide, and Mao Zedong's view that the death of Miss Zhao, a young peasant woman in China in1919 who slit her own throat rather than submit to an arranged marriage, was actually murder; but also, equally unconventional, John Donne's claim that the death of Jesus Christ, the Christian example *par excellence* of an unjust execution, was actually a suicide.

Linguistic issues also arise in attempts to refer to the performance of the act of suicide. The expression *commit suicide* has been common. Contemporary suicidologists typically use a variety of less stigmatizing alternatives, including "suicided," "completed suicide," and "died by suicide." Depending on the background view of the ethics of suicide, these variant descriptions disguise much—or little.

Problems of definition also arise as a product of translation from one language to another. Just as English had no unique term for suicide until 1651, when Walter Charleton used it in his *Ephesian and Cimmerian Matrons* ("to vindicate oneself from inevitable Calamity, by Suicide is not . . . a Crime"), many other languages refer to this phenomenon in different ways. Greek, Latin, and other European languages did not have an explicit, unique term for suicide, although they had a wide variety of locutions. While English has just one principal term for suicide, "suicide," German has four—*Selbstmord, Selbsttötung, Suizid,* and *Freitod,* the first three of which have varyingly negative or neutral connotations, but the last of which has generally positive ones. This means that German speakers can talk about suicide in a range of ways that English-speakers cannot. Wider exploration would no doubt reveal differences among other languages as well.

Issues of definition are also important in examining the practices of traditional cultures. The only available early reports of practices in oral cultures, especially those made by clerics, conquistadors, and others not trained in ethnography, may distort the meanings of native words considerably. For example, in the Seneca myth called the *Code of Handsome Lake,* Edward Cornplanter speaks of "sin" and of the "Great Spirit"; these are probably imported concepts and mistranslations influenced by European sources, even if there is no adequate correct translation in English. On the other hand, some traditional practices that are not apparently conceptualized as suicide might meet contemporary Western definitions, insofar as they involve the knowing, voluntary taking of an action intended to bring about one's own death. For example, the practice of the Ga people of western Africa of holding individuals accountable for dying at times or in ways that are impermissible suggests that these deaths are understood as a matter of voluntary choice. So are the *sallekhana* or *santhara* deaths by ritual fasting that form the central austerity of the Jains, said to be practiced over 200 times a year in contemporary India. These are not understood as suicide by the group in question, but might well be by outside observers, as for instance in contemporary court challenges to the practice on the grounds that it is "unconstitutional," a violation of Indian law prohibiting suicide. Then again, some practices which are apparently conceptualized as suicide and, given the group's beliefs, would meet common Western definitional criteria, are nevertheless strikingly at odds with Western categories, such as the Mohave belief that stillborn infants are suicides, beings who (knowingly) surveyed the world into which they were about to enter but (voluntarily, deliberately) decided against it.

NEGATIVE CASES

Also of importance in understanding suicide is the significance of *negative* cases—the writings or accounts of individuals who did not consider suicide (like Angela of Foligno), although it might have been a plausible consequence of their reasoning; individuals who considered suicide but did not do it (like Job); authors who did not discuss it or address it directly (especially John Stuart Mill, who, given his views about liberty and impairment, could have been expected to do so far more fully than in his few scattered remarks); texts where it is hinted at, if at all, only by implication (Sophocles' *Oedipus at Colonus*); cultures (e.g., the Tiv of Central Africa), where it was apparently not practiced; and religious traditions where it was not mentioned at all (e.g., Shinto). This is a tricky matter, but important, if the full range of thought about suicide is to be displayed. What is not thought, not done, and not said about this issue can play an immense role in reflection and action about life and death as well.

THE BACKGROUND PHILOSOPHICAL ISSUES

Even in the seemingly most isolated cases, the act of suicide is necessarily connected with background views about the meaning of death, the value of life, the relationship between the individual and the community, the nature of suffering, the significance of punishment, the existence of an afterlife, the nature of the self, and many other deep philosophical questions. The issue of suicide challenges all of these. As Camus is often quoted, "There is but one truly philosophical question, and that is the issue of suicide." Just one thing is clear. A full understanding of suicide cannot *start* with the assumption that all suicide is pathological, that it can be attributed either to pathological mental states or mental illness, that it is a matter of biochemical abnormality, that it is always wrong, or that there are no real ethical issues about suicide. These views are to be explored, not presupposed. To be sure, the history of reflection on the ethics of suicide will be a continuing history, as cultural conceptions of suicide and related issues like self-sacrifice, heroism, social protest, self-deliverance, martyrdom, and so on in each of these contexts evolve but, in an increasingly global world in which once-independent traditions interact more and more fully and in the process shape and reshape each other, it is important to be able to view the deeper roots of these issues.

NOTE

1. This chapter is drawn from the Introduction to Margaret Pabst Battin, ed., *The Ethics of Suicide: A Comprehensive Historical Sourcebook.* New York: Oxford University Press, in preparation, 2014 (used by permission). An earlier version of this essay, framed as a hypothetical project, appears in Margaret Pabst Battin, *Ending Life: Ethics and the Way We Die.* New York: Oxford University Press, 2005, pp. 163–174.

4
The Suicidal Mind

Danielle R. Jahn

In 1996, the founding father of suicidology, Edwin Shneidman, published a book entitled *The Suicidal Mind*. He wrote about how suicidal people think and feel and provided interesting interviews with patients to demonstrate how these topics look in real life. It has been over a decade since this seminal book was published, and a variety of theories have been developed since 1996 to describe the suicidal mind. This chapter explores how suicidal people think and feel and provides examples of the thinking patterns that suicidal people often use.

CONSTRICTION

To begin, consider this hypothetical scenario of a patient who recently attempted suicide and what her thought patterns were at the time she attempted to kill herself.

Chelsea is a 20-year-old woman who attends a large public university. She began seeing Dr. B, a psychologist, approximately three months ago, after she attempted to kill herself by overdosing on pills. When Chelsea first started seeing Dr. B, she told him that she had attempted suicide because of her poor grades and pressure from her family to succeed in her premed studies. Chelsea told Dr. B that she had done well in her coursework during her first year of college, but began struggling with some of the more difficult classes during her second year. After she failed one course in the fall of her sophomore year and received grades of C in two other classes, her parents threatened to stop paying her tuition and force her to move back to her hometown. Chelsea did not want to leave the university, where she had made friends and begun to establish her independence. Moving back in with her parents seemed like an intolerable option because she knew that she would not be treated like an adult and would have to follow many strict rules enforced by her parents.

In the spring of her sophomore year, Chelsea continued to struggle in her courses and became very worried about her parents' threat to force her to move back in with them. She realized that she was not as interested in her premed major as she had originally thought, and was having difficulty understanding some of the topics in her chemistry courses. She considered changing majors, but recognized that this would be a disappointment to her parents, who wanted her to become a doctor. At that point, Chelsea felt trapped. She thought that she had two options: she could drop out of school and move back in with her parents, or she could kill herself. She simply did not see any other choices.

This sort of "tunnel vision" is very common among suicidal people. Shneidman (1996) coined the term *constriction* to describe the idea that people who are thinking about suicide have a very constricted or narrow view of the world and the choices they have. Suicidal people truly believe that their only option to avoid a situation that they consider intolerable is suicide. Shneidman discussed one of the clues to constriction—the word *only*. In fact, Dr. B picked up on this clue as Chelsea first talked to him about why she tried to kill herself. He noticed that she frequently made statements such as, "There was *only* one thing I could do when I found out I failed another chemistry test" and "My *only* option to avoid moving back in with parents was to kill myself." Chelsea's use of the word *only* made it very clear to Dr. B that she was experiencing constriction.

In order to help Chelsea reduce the constriction she was experiencing, Dr. B encouraged her to come up with more options, even if they were not options she thought to be reasonable. Chelsea thought of options such as ending her relationship with her parents and paying for college on her own, talking to her parents about switching to a major that she enjoyed more and could succeed in, paying for a tutor to help her with her coursework, and staying in her college town and working for a few years before getting her college degree. Then, Dr. B asked her to rank these options from "least unacceptable" to "most unacceptable." Chelsea chose talking to her parents about switching her major as the least unacceptable option, and so Chelsea and Dr. B explored this option. Chelsea expressed some fear about having the conversation with her parents and the potential repercussions of it. However, after weighing the pros and cons of this option and role-playing the conversation with Dr. B, Chelsea talked with her parents. While they were slightly disappointed that Chelsea's goal was no longer to be a doctor, because this had been her dream since she was five years old, they were supportive of her decision because they wanted her to get a college degree and have a career that would make her happy. Chelsea ultimately decided to major in elementary education and has been doing well in her classes and in her student teaching since changing her major. She is looking forward to becoming a third-grade teacher and has not had any thoughts of suicide since talking to her parents about changing her major.

ESCAPE

Constriction is very common among suicidal people, but many other ideas also occur in the suicidal mind. For example, people may become suicidal because of an awareness of their failures and a desire to escape this awareness (Baumeister, 1990). When people have high standards for themselves and do not meet these standards, they may feel like failures. If people think that they are the only cause of their failures, they may begin to feel badly about themselves, and this is called *negative self-awareness*. Negative self-awareness can lead to depression, anxiety, hopelessness, and other negative emotions, especially when people continue to compare their failures to their standards.

In general, people want to avoid or escape negative self-awareness and negative emotions, so they begin to experience something similar to constriction, called *cognitive deconstruction* (Baumeister, 1990). Cognitive deconstruction involves focusing on only immediate goals, not thinking about the past or the future (and, therefore, feeling hopeless about the future), and trying to detach themselves from negative self-awareness and negative emotions. People who experience cognitive deconstruction often do not think clearly, cannot come up with new ideas, and are not flexible in their thinking. Cognitive deconstruction can help people escape from their negative self-awareness and negative emotions, but it is not completely effective. Cognitive deconstruction also has an unintended effect of reducing people's inhibitions because they are focused only on the present and their only goal is trying to reduce negative self-awareness and negative emotions. Because cognitive deconstruction is not completely effective in escaping negative self-awareness, and because people who are experiencing cognitive deconstruction may not have inhibitions against suicide, they may become suicidal at this point. To people who cannot tolerate their negative self-awareness and negative emotions, suicide seems like the best option for escape.

Yet, sometimes people experience failures or do not meet their own standards, but do not become suicidal. What makes them different? There are a few possibilities. Baumeister discussed the importance of coping and finding meaning when personal standards are not met, as well as the role of differences in attribution. In terms of attribution, for example, when people fail to meet their standards, they may either attribute that failure to the situation or to themselves. In general, if people think that a situation caused a failure, and the failure was not a result of something they did, they are less likely to become suicidal. However, even if people attribute the failure to themselves, but find meaning in the failure or use the failure to grow as a person, they are similarly less likely to become suicidal.

It is also important to think about the standards people have set for themselves. Some people do not have especially high standards, or do not consider these standards to be very important. Thus, even if they fail to meet these standards, they will not be particularly upset. However, people who are perfectionists (i.e., who have very high standards for themselves that are essential to them) are more likely to fail to meet their standards because the standards are so high. Not meeting these standards, perfectionists are more likely to attribute failure to themselves, resulting in negative self-awareness and negative emotions. Research has shown that perfectionism may be a risk factor for suicidal behavior (O'Connor, 2007), providing some support for the idea that the type of standards people hold may increase their suicide risk.

To illustrate this point, consider the hypothetical story of Joe, a 45-year-old married man with two children.

Joe had been married for nearly 20 years, and he and his wife had a 10-year-old daughter and a 6-year-old son. His wife stayed at home and took care of their children while Joe worked as a successful business executive. Joe had always been described as a perfectionist. He graduated from high school as the valedictorian, and then graduated from his undergraduate university with a bachelor's degree in business and a 4.0 grade point average. He also received a master's degree in business administration and was consistently ranked at the top of his class in business school. Joe was heavily recruited for jobs during business school. Immediately after graduation, he was offered an entry-level job at a prestigious business firm, where he quickly moved up to a management-level position working primarily in the operations division of the company. He was successful in reducing operating costs and increasing profits in his division, and had always been lauded as an effective and highly competent manager.

Joe took great pride in providing for his family. One of Joe's most important standards for himself was to earn enough money to provide for his family financially. However, with the downturn of the economy, Joe was laid off from his job. Joe attributed his layoff to himself, his inability to work hard enough to reduce operating costs, and his failure to come up with creative ways to increase profits even more than he had already (as opposed to attributing the layoff to the poor economy). As Joe began receiving unemployment benefits and looking for new jobs, he constantly compared his current financial situation to his standards for providing for his family financially. This created negative self-awareness, and Joe began feeling depressed and hopeless about finding a good job in the future. He could not find any positive aspects to his layoff, such as his opportunity to spend more time with his family or the fact that he was not feeling as stressed by work-related demands.

Because Joe was experiencing negative self-awareness and negative emotions, he began experiencing cognitive deconstruction. He started focusing only on his goals of feeling less depressed and hopeless and began drinking large amounts of alcohol. He could not see his past successes or think about potential positive events in the future, such as watching his children grow up. The cognitive deconstruction and alcohol use reduced his inhibitions, and he became suicidal. He made a serious suicide attempt, driving his car into a telephone pole at high speed, after which he was hospitalized for his injuries and received psychiatric care.

After his release from the hospital, he began seeing a therapist and taking antidepressant medications. He felt that the medication significantly improved his mood and made him feel less depressed. In therapy, he and his therapist agreed on a number of goals that he wanted to achieve. First, he wanted to restructure his thinking to attribute his layoff to the economic situation instead of his perceived failures, and he spent considerable time and effort working toward this goal. In addition, Joe and his therapist brainstormed to find new standards for him to value. Joe began to view his role as an emotionally supportive father as an important standard. In addition, he focused on helping his wife in the house more and creating a standard for himself of supporting his wife in her role at home. Finally, Joe began looking at options for careers in which he could earn enough to provide for his family while also spending more time with his wife and children and creating less stress for himself. Over time, Joe worked through these issues and no longer had thoughts of suicide.

Joe's situation provides one example of how the desire to escape from negative self-awareness and negative emotions can lead to thoughts of suicide and suicide attempts. Research has also provided support for the theory. For example, a study conducted in Canada showed that unusual thinking (such as having trouble concentrating or feeling as if the mind is blank—signs of cognitive deconstruction) was associated with greater suicidal intent (Mendonca & Holden, 1998). This study examined only one aspect of the theory (the link between cognitive deconstruction and thoughts of suicide). However, other research has successfully tested many of the links proposed by the theory (not meeting standards leading to negative self-awareness, which creates negative emotions, which then causes cognitive deconstruction and eventually suicidal ideation).

For example, research has indicated that problems with health, that is, representing a failure to meet a standard of good self-care and good health, led to negative self-awareness as indicated by negative self-esteem (Reich, Newsom, & Zautra, 1996). Lower self-esteem then led to cognitive deconstruction, and ultimately to thoughts of suicide. Dean and Range (1999) focused on perfectionism, a predisposition to having very high standards and experiencing failure to meet these standards. They proposed that this was associated with depression (a negative emotion) which would lead to hopelessness and suicide ideation. Overall, these studies supported Baumeister's contention that thoughts of suicide can serve as a form of escape from negative self-awareness and negative emotions.

AVAILABILITY AND ATTENTION

Joe's case above provides a good example of suicide being an escape from negative self-awareness and negative emotions. We can also see how his cognitive deconstruction is similar to Chelsea's constriction. In both cognitive deconstruction and constriction, thoughts of suicide become more readily available. If a negative event occurs but people are not experiencing cognitive deconstruction or constriction, they may not think of suicide as one of their first options. However, if they are experiencing cognitive deconstruction or constriction, suicide is more likely one of the first thoughts that comes to mind.

Researchers have examined why thoughts of suicide might come to mind more easily for some people than others. Nock et al. (2010) found that thoughts of suicide were more available (came to mind more easily) in people who had previously attempted suicide than in people who were upset or depressed but who had not made a suicide attempt in the past. In general, people who had attempted suicide associated thoughts of suicide with their sense of self, and this association made it easier for them to think about and attempt suicide in the future. Thus, when people were upset and began thinking about themselves or their difficulties, thoughts of suicide were activated because suicide and thoughts of self had become associated. Nock's research found a strong association between thoughts of suicide and self-predictions of future suicide attempts. Thus, even though people may not always be aware of the link between self-evaluations and thoughts of suicide, these links occur and may be useful in differentiating people who will attempt suicide or die by suicide from those who will not.

Recent studies from Europe have investigated the relations between suicide as escape from negative self-awareness and negative emotions and the availability of suicidal thoughts. Chatard and Selimbegovic (2011) found that, when people failed to meet the standards that they had set for themselves, thoughts of suicide became more accessible (i.e., suicidal thoughts came to mind faster than other thoughts). These studies indicate that, when people felt that there was a large discrepancy between themselves and their standards, suicide-related thoughts were more accessible. It is also interesting that the researchers found that thoughts of escape were also more accessible (similar to thoughts of suicide), thus providing support for the availability of suicidal thoughts in suicidal people, as well as supporting the theory of suicide as escape from negative self-awareness and negative emotions.

People also have changes in their attention that can contribute to suicide (Wenzel, Brown, & Beck, 2009) and increase the availability of suicide-related thoughts. Generally, when people experience stressful events, they are able to pay attention to both the positive and negative aspects of the events. For example, if a person gets into a minor automobile accident, he or she will be upset about the damage to the car and the inconvenience, but will likely be grateful that no one was hurt and that the accident was not more serious. Suicidal people, however, tend to focus only on the negative aspects of situations and interpret information and events in an overly negative way. They may not be able to see the positive aspects of a minor automobile accident (e.g., no injuries), and instead overly focus on the negative factors of the situation (e.g., the cost of repairs or the likelihood of death). Thus, they selectively attend to the negative and ignore the positive.

Suicidal people also focus on suicide as their only option to end the negativity. They do not think about other, more positive ways to end their difficulties or consider their reasons for living. As demonstrated in the case of Chelsea, she was unable to think of any options other than suicide to avoid moving back in with her parents. She also did not think about any other reasons for living, such as her friendships with others. Chelsea's case shows how these changes in attention are similar to constriction and cognitive deconstruction, in that suicidal people narrow their focus and experience tunnel vision. Attention is narrowed to only negative things, with no focus on the positive aspects of the self, a situation, a recent event, or life in general.

Suicidal people also tend to focus on more general memories rather than on specific memories; that is, they have difficulty recalling specific events from the past and instead recall general time periods from their lives, such as when they were in high school, or events that occurred repeatedly, such as going to camp each summer (Wenzel et al., 2009). This lack of attention to detail makes it difficult for them to think of specific positive events from the past. This over-general memory and lack of attention to detail also extends to their current functioning, as well as to future functioning. Without specific positive memories from the past to rely on, suicidal people may have difficulty identifying reasons to live. Related to this, they also seem to have difficulty envisioning positive events in the future as a function of their inability to recall positive past events.

Consider Joe's case in relation to difficulties with attention. He was able only to focus on the negative aspects of his layoff and could not think of any positive consequences, such as reduced work-related stress and more time to spend with his wife and children. He was also unable to see any options to end his negative awareness other than suicide. He did not consider options such as changing his career or having his wife work while he stayed at home with the children. In addition, he did not see his children and wife as reasons to stay alive. Finally, he was unable to recall specific positive events from his past that might help him have hope for a positive future. His difficulty in focusing attention on positive events allowed suicidal thoughts to be more immediately available.

PROBLEM-SOLVING

In addition to changes in attention and constriction, poor problem-solving skills are also common in suicidal people (Wenzel et al., 2009). Both Joe and Chelsea experienced difficulties in their ability to solve the problems they encountered. Poor problem-solving can contribute to thoughts of suicide in a number of different domains, including problems with other people, problems in social situations, or problems within the self (such as intolerable sadness or hopelessness). In general, there are three steps to effective problem-solving (Pettit & Joiner, 2006). The first step is recognizing and identifying the problem. The second step is identifying alternative options to solve the problem, and the third step is evaluating the pros and cons of each of those options, culminating in a choice. People who become suicidal generally can identify the problems they are having, but often have difficulty generating solutions. They may not have the skills needed to come up with creative solutions that would solve the problem and reduce their negative feelings. For example, Chelsea could not figure out how to solve her problem of disliking her major and doing poorly in school without disappointing her parents. She could not see an option in which she would be happy and her parents would not be angry. Chelsea did not consider the option of talking to her parents about changing her major and explaining to them why she was doing poorly in school. Ultimately, this is what she and her therapist decided was the best option, and this option solved her problem without any significant negative consequences. She was also unable to come up with other solutions on her own, but with her therapist was able to identify additional possibilities (such as getting a tutor or paying for college on her own). By herself, she saw only two solutions—agree to her parents' demands or die by suicide.

People who are suicidal may also have difficulty with the third step in effective problem-solving, which is weighing the pros and cons of each alternative. Even if they can think of alternative solutions, they tend to weigh the pros of suicide very heavily and ignore the cons, while they weigh the cons of other options more heavily than the pros. In Chelsea's case, she was able to generate two alternative solutions on her own (drop out of school and move back in with her parents or die by suicide). However, as she was weighing these options, she only saw the benefits of suicide, such as escaping her depression and confusion. She also only saw the negative aspects of moving back in with her parents, including being forced to live under their rules, moving away from her friends, and not attending a university that she enjoyed. She thought very little about the cons of suicide or pros of moving back in with her parents. It is clear that Chelsea had substantial difficulties solving her problem because of her inability to generate solutions to her problem, as well as her biased consideration of the pros and cons for each alternative. This bias in her thinking is similar to the constriction and changes in attention that we have discussed previously, as she was only able to attend to the negative aspects of one of her solutions, and was overly focused on what she viewed as the positive aspects of suicide as a solution. She developed tunnel vision and saw no other way out of her problem.

When suicidal people are faced with problems that they do not know how to solve, they feel stressed and upset about themselves and their situation. They also often experience hopelessness about the resolution of the problem in the future. Chelsea certainly felt like a failure because she was not able to solve her problem, and felt hopeless because she did not know when or how the problem would resolve. Her inability to solve the problem, along with her distress and hopelessness, led her to attempt suicide. However, when she was no longer in crisis and was working with her therapist, she was able to find better solutions to her problem and weigh the alternatives in a less biased manner.

Joe was also unable to see a solution to his problem, which was his unemployment and inability to provide financially for his family. Like Chelsea, Joe was able to identify his problem, but was unable to come up with many solutions. When he could not find a job as a business executive, he thought his only solution was suicide. He did not see other options, such as continuing to receive unemployment benefits, finding a new career field, or his wife going to work while he stayed at home with his children. When he thought of suicide, he focused only on the pros of the solution (not feeling anxious and depressed anymore, not letting his family down by not being able to find a job) and did not consider the cons (his children not having their father, his wife missing her husband). He felt stressed about his inability to find a job and hopeless about his prospects in the future, and subsequently began thinking about suicide. As we can see from these examples, poor problem-solving is an important issue in the suicidal mind.

PERCEIVED BURDENSOMENESS AND THWARTED BELONGING

A variety of issues that occur in the suicidal mind have been presented so far, primarily focused on thoughts that relate to the self or the future and their influence on suicidal behavior. However, there are also thoughts about other people that can increase suicidal thoughts. For example, suicidal people are often concerned that they are a burden on important people in their lives which is referred to as *perceived burdensomeness* (Joiner, 2005). Perceived burdensomeness is a thought or belief held by the suicidal person, although others do not necessarily feel burdened. People who think that they are a burden on others often feel a sense of self-hatred, experience low self-esteem, and believe that they are a liability in the lives of others (Van Orden et al., 2010). They believe their deaths would be worth more than their lives to other people, and so they consider suicide. Suicidal people who are experiencing perceived burdensomeness often feel expendable and blame themselves for others' problems, as well as their own.

Joe's case provides an example of perceived burdensomeness. After Joe was laid off from his job, he blamed himself for the layoff and for the resulting changes in his family's lifestyle because of his lack of income. He experienced extremely low self-esteem because his job had provided so much meaning in his life. In addition, he felt expendable in his family because he was not fulfilling his role as the financial provider. Since he no longer filled a role that he viewed as primary, he did not think that he was needed in his family. He began to hate himself for not fulfilling his role and for not finding a new job in a timely manner. These feelings of self-hatred began to develop into feelings of liability to his family. He felt that they would be better off without him because they would receive his life insurance policy payout, and they would have one less person to feed and care for. He perceived that he was a burden to his wife and children, and at this point Joe became suicidal.

Another thought that suicidal people may experience is the belief that they do not belong or fit in with the people in their lives. Joiner (2005) calls this *thwarted belongingness*. Again, it is important to remember that people who are experiencing thwarted belongingness may in fact have social support and strong social groups, but they do not believe that they fit in. This makes thwarted belongingness something that occurs in the suicidal mind, not necessarily in social relationships. When people experience thwarted belongingness, they do not feel supported by others nor do they feel like they are a part of social groups and relationships that they value. As a result of these beliefs they feel disconnected, lonely, and uncared for (Van Orden et al., 2010).

Chelsea is a good example of how thwarted belongingness can influence suicidal thoughts. When Chelsea was faced with her problems of doing poorly in classes and disappointing her parents, she began to experience thwarted belongingness. Although she valued her relationship with her parents, she felt that, if she disappointed them, they would not truly care about her well-being. She believed that conflict between her needs and their expectations would lead to her being rejected by her family. In addition, while she had friends at her university, she felt that they could not understand what she was going through because of her parents' demands on her, so she also felt disconnected from her friends. This led to feelings of loneliness and abandonment, which increased her sense of hopelessness and exacerbated her thoughts of suicide.

Joe and Chelsea demonstrate how thwarted belongingness and perceived burdensomeness may develop in suicidal people. Research has examined the roles of thwarted belongingness and perceived burdensomeness and found that each is associated with thoughts of suicide and death by suicide (Van Orden et al., 2010). For example, when major events occur that pull communities together (i.e., reducing thwarted belongingness), suicide rates go down. These events can be negative, such as a terrorist attack, or positive, such as a football team winning a national championship. Notes left by people who died by suicide also more often contain themes of perceived burdensomeness and thwarted belongingness when compared to notes left by people who attempted suicide but did not die. In addition, perceived burdensomeness has been shown to differentiate between people who had made a suicide attempt and people who had not, and has been linked to an increased risk for death by suicide. This research supports the theoretical prediction that perceived burdensomeness and thwarted belongingness are common occurrences in the suicidal mind.

MENTAL PAIN

Thus far, the discussion has focused primarily on the thoughts and thought patterns that occur in the suicidal mind, and the patterns of thinking or coping with situations. However, emotions are also relevant to the suicidal mind, such as when negative self-awareness leads to negative emotions. Shneidman (1993) discussed the impact of negative emotions on the suicidal mind, and he coined the term *psychache* to describe this mental pain. According to Shneidman, psychache is a term describing intolerable mental pain such as shame, guilt, depression, or anxiety, hypothesized to be the result of unmet psychological needs. For example, achievement is generally thought of as a basic psychological need that all humans have. In Joe's case, this need was thwarted when he was laid off from his job and unable to find another. Joe's unmet need for achievement created intolerable feelings of depression and anxiety or, in Shneidman's terminology, psychache, for which a commonly considered solution is death by suicide.

According to Shneidman, there are a number of factors that combine to create psychache, including a desire to escape from negative self-awareness and negative emotions and the occurrence of life events perceived as negative and painful, coupled with the sense that the pain is unbearable. In addition, there is the recognition that ending consciousness through suicide will end the pain. For people with a low tolerance for psychache, this pain is too intense to continue living, and so they decide that ending the pain through suicide is the best option. Chelsea's situation shows one way in which these factors may develop and create psychache. Her negative life event was her poor performance in classes and her parents' ultimatum to either perform better or move back in with them. She had an unmet need of autonomy. She wanted to make decisions about her major and career based on what she was truly interested in, but feared repercussions from her parents if she made this decision autonomously. Chelsea perceived this unmet need as overwhelmingly negative and painful. She felt that the pain was unbearable and viewed suicide as a means to escape.

Research has provided support for mental pain as a risk factor for suicide attempts. For example, Levi and colleagues (2008) assessed mental pain in people who had attempted suicide and compared it to mental pain in people who had not attempted suicide or thought about suicide. They found that people who had made suicide attempts had higher levels of depression, hopelessness, and general mental pain than people who were not suicidal. Depression has also been identified as a common form of mental pain in suicidal people, as has anxiety (Westefeld et al., 2000).

Hopelessness, in particular, is a form of mental pain that is often experienced in the suicidal mind. Researchers have found that suicidal people tend to have more severe hopelessness than people who were not suicidal (Mendonca & Holden, 1998). In fact, hopelessness appears to be more important than depression as a risk factor for suicidal behavior (Weishaar & Beck, 1992). Hopelessness has been linked to current thoughts of suicide, and it also predicts who will experience thoughts of suicide and die by suicide in the future (Weishaar & Beck, 1992). It is important to note that hopelessness is not only a form of mental pain, but can also be a sign of cognitive deconstruction, as previously discussed, and can act as a worldview, or schema, through which events are interpreted. Overall, theories and research regarding mental pain or psychache indicate that it is one of the most common experiences within the suicidal mind.

PRESS, PERTURBATION, AND PAIN

In addition to Shneidman's work on psychache and constriction, he also developed a larger model of suicidal behavior. This model is referred to as the cubic model of suicide with three components, each forming an axis of a cube. The first component of this model is mental pain or *psychache,* conceptualized in the model as represented on a continuum from little or no pain to intolerable or unbearable pain. *Perturbation,* the second axis of the cube, is the term that Shneidman (1993) used to measure how upset or distressed a suicidal person is feeling, how impulsively a suicidal person is acting, and how much constriction a suicidal person is experiencing. Perturbation is conceptualized on a continuum similar to pain, with low levels of perturbation representing a relatively calm, clear-thinking person, whereas high levels of perturbation represent agitation, impulsivity, and constriction. The final component of the cubic model is *press*. Press encompasses the negative events that occur in life that may lead a person to think about suicide, and is similarly rated on a continuum from low to high.

When a person is at the highest level of all three of these dimensions, they may be at the highest risk for suicidal behavior. At lower levels, people may be unhappy, but they are less likely to attempt suicide. We can think about Chelsea and Joe in terms of this model. Chelsea's press was her poor grades and her parents' threat to make her move back in with them. Her perturbation was a result of the constriction that occurred as she became more focused on the negative aspects of her situation and her sense of urgency to resolve the situation. Her psychache, in the form of depression and hopelessness, was created by her inability to solve her problem. However, even though Chelsea had been experiencing press for an extended period of time, and her perturbation and pain developed over time, she did not attempt suicide until all three of these components were at the highest end of their respective continuums.

Similarly, Joe attempted suicide when his press, pain, and perturbation were at their highest levels. His press was being laid off from his job, his inability to find another job, and his failure to provide for his family financially. His perturbation was his negative self-awareness and cognitive deconstruction, which made his thinking unclear and lowered his inhibitions, increasing his impulsivity. Finally, his pain was related to his sense that his anxiety and depression were intolerable. According to the cubic model, these three things at their highest levels led him to attempt suicide.

There has not been much research examining the cubic model of suicide, but Jobes (2006) used these concepts to develop a questionnaire and interview to assess suicide risk. This is called the Suicide Status Form and is used as part of a therapeutic approach known as the Collaborative Assessment and Management of Suicidality. The questionnaire and interview form is an effective way to identify suicidal people, and this type of therapy has been shown to successfully reduce suicide risk.

COGNITIVE MODEL

Just as mental pain fits into the larger cubic model of suicidal behavior, many of the processes discussed fit similarly into another broad model known as the cognitive model of suicidal acts (Wenzel et al., 2009). This model uses a general cognitive approach to understand suicidal people. In this model, there are two concepts that influence a person's thinking—negative events and negative schemas. Schemas are the ways in which people interpret the world or events that occur. They generally develop early in life and provide structure for and understanding of previous events. This structure is then used to understand later events. Events, in combination with schemas, lead to thoughts and interpretations, which then create emotions. In particular, these thoughts and interpretations are often negative and focus on three primary themes: negative thoughts about the self, negative thoughts about other people and the world, and negative thoughts or hopelessness about the future. These three themes integrate the previous concepts that have been identified. Negative thoughts about the self are similar to the negative self-awareness component that people try to escape through suicide. Negative thoughts about other people and the world are similar to perceived burdensomeness and feelings of thwarted belongingness. Finally, hopelessness and negative thoughts about the future are cognitive constructs that fit in this model as well.

From the perspective of the cognitive model, traits like perfectionism and poor problem-solving can influence suicide risk in the face of negative events by creating a predisposition for suicide-related schemas. These schemas often relate to hopelessness about the future and rigid and high expectations, coupled with a limited set of problem-solving skills to draw upon.

When negative life events or stressors occur, these schemas are activated and result in the experience of cognitive constriction, changes in attention, or cognitive deconstruction. Thus, thinking changes or breaks down, leading to negative emotions. These negative emotions can then lead to more negative thinking and constriction, creating a cycle of negative thoughts and emotions that feeds into suicide-related schemas. When these schemas, thoughts, and emotions are activated, it is difficult for people to refocus their attention on options other than suicide, and they enter a suicidal crisis.

This model can be used to understand how both Chelsea and Joe became suicidal. Chelsea had a number of dispositional traits that increased her risk for becoming suicidal. First, she had a difficult time with problem-solving. This created a significant amount of stress when she was faced with a problem regarding her parents' expectations for her major and career being in conflict with her interests. Chelsea's problem-solving difficulties, in combination with her school-related problems, activated suicide-related schemas for her. In particular, she felt hopeless about being able to solve her problem, and also felt that her life was unbearable because of the consequences she faced (dropping out of school and moving back in with her parents). These schemas of hopelessness and unbearableness then began to alter her thinking and way of approaching her problem. She began focusing her attention on the negative aspects of her life and situation, to the exclusion of positive aspects. This is when she experienced the constriction described previously. These negative thoughts led Chelsea to experience the negative emotions of sadness and depression, which led to further negative thinking. This cycle further activated her schemas of hopelessness and unbearableness, which were increased by her attention only to negative and suicide-related information. She eventually felt that her hopelessness and life's unbearableness were intolerable, and she began to think of suicide as a solution to this intolerability and her crisis. It was at this point that she attempted suicide.

Similarly, Joe's previously discussed risk factors also fit into the cognitive model of suicide as well. Joe had predispositions toward poor problem-solving and perfectionism, and he encountered a significant life stressor when he was laid off from his job. Because of his perfectionism, this layoff was extremely upsetting to him. In addition, the layoff combined with his perfectionism to activate his schema of failure. This schema led to changes in thinking about himself and his abilities, which created depression and anxiety. As he thought about himself as a failure and attributed his failure to his shortcomings, he experienced worry about his abilities to get a job in the future and feelings of sadness regarding his current unemployment. As Joe's failure schema was activated and increased his negative thinking and emotions, his suicide-related schemas also became activated. In particular, he felt incredibly hopeless about the future. As his attention became more focused on the negative and he could not figure out a way to solve his problem, he felt that he could not tolerate his hopelessness anymore and began thinking about suicide. These case examples show that the cognitive model incorporates a number of cognitive risk factors for suicide and is thus an effective way to understand the suicidal mind.

FUTURE DIRECTIONS

A number of aspects of the suicidal mind have been explored in this chapter including constriction, escape from negative self-awareness and negative emotions, availability of suicidal thoughts, changes in attention to focus on only negative aspects of a situation, poor problem-solving, perceived burdensomeness, thwarted belongingness, and mental pain. These cognitive risk factors fit into larger models of suicide including the cubic model and the cognitive model of suicidal acts. Yet, work in this area is not finished. Some of the risk factors discussed have not been researched in detail. For example, there is research support for parts of the theory that explains suicide as escape from negative self-awareness and negative emotions, but not all of the proposed constructs have been tested together. There is little, if any, research on the cubic model of suicide. In addition, the cognitive model has not received support from research that has examined all parts of the model. It is essential to test the complete models discussed previously to assess their validity and utility for understanding suicidal people.

Work must also focus on the potential for theoretical integration in this area as opposed to the current fragmented approach to understanding suicidal behavior. The cognitive model of suicidal acts incorporates many of the other risk factors for suicide, but still does not provide a complete understanding of suicide risk. It is especially important to think about dispositional traits that may increase risk for suicide or the development of suicide-related schemas and to integrate a consideration of these traits into existing theories to better understand and recognize people who are thinking about suicide.

CONCLUSION

A variety of things may occur in the suicidal mind. These include mental pain, such as psychache and hopelessness, and thoughts, such as perceived burdensomeness and thwarted belongingness. Thought patterns may also change when people become suicidal, and they may experience cognitive deconstruction, constriction, and changes in their attention. Concepts such as poor problem-solving and perfectionism can increase the likelihood of these changes in thinking. In addition, people sometimes think of suicide as an escape from negative self-awareness and negative emotions. People who are suicidal may associate thoughts of suicide with their sense of self, which can lead to increased availability of suicide-related thoughts and thus increased suicide risk in the future. The cubic model of suicide accounts for some of these risk factors as pain, press, and perturbation. In addition, many of these risk factors fit into a cognitive model of suicidal acts, which also includes suicide-related schemas, to provide a comprehensive approach to understanding the suicidal mind.

The suicidal mind is complex, and there is not one single cause of suicidal behavior. This can make it difficult to recognize people who are thinking about suicide but, as we create more theories, conduct research into more risk factors, and integrate the theories and risk factors that we know, we may be able to develop a better understanding of how suicidal people think and feel. Using our understanding of the suicidal mind, we can work to identify people who are at risk for suicide and assist them to reduce their suicidal thinking. In this way, we will be able to prevent suicide and ultimately lower suicide rates.

REFERENCES

Baumeister, R. F. (1990). Suicide as escape from self. *Psychological Review, 97,* 90–113.

Chatard, A., & Selimbegovic, L. (2011). When self-destructive thoughts flash through the mind: Failure to meet standards affects the accessibility of suicide-related thoughts. *Journal of Personality and Social Psychology, 100,* 587–605.

Dean, P. J., & Range, L. M. (1999). Testing the escape theory of suicide in an outpatient clinical population. *Cognitive Therapy & Research, 23,* 561–572.

Jobes, D. A. (2006). *Managing suicidal risk: A collaborative approach.* New York: Guilford.

Joiner, T. E., Jr. (2005). *Why people die by suicide.* Cambridge, MA: Harvard University Press.

Levi, Y., Horesh, N., Fischel, T., Treves, I., Or, E., & Apter, A. (2008). Mental pain and its communication in medically serious suicide attempts: An "impossible situation." *Journal of Affective Disorders, 111,* 244–250.

Mendonca, J. D., & Holden, R. R. (1998). Interaction of affective and cognitive impairments in the suicidal state: A brief elaboration. *Acta Psychiatrica Scandinavica, 97,* 149–152.

Nock, M. K., Park, J. M., Finn, C. T., Deliberto, T. L., Dour, H. J., & Banaji, M. R. (2010). Measuring the suicidal mind: Implicit cognition predicts suicidal behavior. *Psychological Science, 21,* 511–517.

O'Connor, R. C. (2007). The relations between perfectionism and suicidality: A systematic review. *Suicide & Life-Threatening Behavior, 37,* 698–714.

Pettit, J. W., & Joiner, T. E., Jr. (2006). Cognitive vulnerability to suicide. In L. B. Alloy & J. H. Riskind (Eds.), *Cognitive vulnerability to emotional disorders,* pp. 125–154. Mahwah, NJ: Lawrence Erlbaum.

Reich, J. W., Newsom, J. T., & Zautra, A. J. (1996). Health downturns and predictors of suicidal ideation: An application of the Baumeister model. *Suicide & Life-Threatening Behavior, 26,* 282–291.

Shneidman, E. S. (1993). *Suicide as psychache: A clinical approach to self-destructive behavior.* New York: Rowman & Littlefield.

Shneidman, E. S. (1996). *The suicidal mind.* New York: Oxford University Press.

Van Orden, K. A., Witte, T. K., Cukrowicz, K. C., Braithwaite, S. R., Selby, E. A., & Joiner, T. E., Jr. (2010). The interpersonal theory of suicide. *Psychological Review, 117,* 575–600.

Weishaar, M. E., & Beck, A. T. (1992). Hopelessness and suicide. *International Review of Psychiatry, 4,* 177–184.

Wenzel, A., Brown, G. K., & Beck, A. T. (2009). *Cognitive therapy for suicidal patients: Scientific and clinical applications.* Washington, DC: American Psychological Association.

Westefeld, J. S., Range, L. M., Rogers, J. R., Maples, M. R., Bromley, J. L., & Alcorn, J. (2000). Suicide: An overview. *The Counseling Psychologist, 28,* 445–510.

5
The Neurophysiology of Suicide

Maurizio Pompili and Gianluca Serafini

S uicide is a complex human phenomenon resulting from several factors, including psychiatric, biological, and environmental factors. Many biological processes are involved in determining suicidal behavior, and this presents a great challenge for the science and clinical practice of suicidology.

A genetic background may play role in the precipitation of suicide and, according to a stress diathesis model, both genetic makeup and acquired susceptibility contribute to a person's predisposition to suicidal acts in stressful situations (Mann, 2003). It is well established that there is a substantial genetic contribution to suicidal behavior involving serotonergic dysfunction. Despite several convincing reports noting that most suicides were suffering from psychiatric disorders (Cavanagh, Carson, Sharpe, & Lawrie, 2003; Harris & Barraclough, 1997), particularly depression and bipolar disorders, having a mental disorder is not a sufficient or necessary condition for increased suicide risk. Many studies measuring the incidence of psychiatric disorder in suicides employ only after-the-fact diagnosis and are constrained by the limitations of psychological autopsy study procedures. However, prospective biological studies suggest that HPA-axis dysfunctions have some predictive power for suicidal behavior in mood disorders (Jokinen & Nordstrom, 2008), with HPA-axis hyperactivity a risk factor for suicide both in patients with major depression and in those without a clear psychiatric diagnosis (Nemeroff, Owens, Bissette, Andorn, & Stanley, 1988). The aim of this chapter is to review the current literature and shed light on some neurophysiological dysregulations underlying suicidal behavior.

SEROTONIN ABNORMALITIES ASSOCIATED WITH SUICIDAL BEHAVIOR

Serotonergic function has been reported to be altered both in patients with major depressive disorder and those who die by suicide (Purselle & Nemeroff, 2003). Abnormalities in serotonergic activity have been found in patients with violent and aggressive behaviors (Mann, 1998) as well as in violent suicidal behavior (Lester, 1995). Therefore, serotonergic dysfunction appears to be a well-established substrate for suicidal behavior, a relationship apparently mediated by increased aggressivity in mood disorders (Oquendo et al., 2006). Moreover, serotonin (5-HT) activity fluctuations might be associated with the transition from a less lethal suicidal behavior to a more lethal suicidal behavior (van Heeringen, Audenaert, Van de Wiele, & Verstraete, 2000). At a molecular level, postmortem studies have documented impaired signal transduction in the serotonergic system in suicides (Pandey et al., 1999). Specifically, a reduction in the brain in protein and mRNA[1] expression of two specific protein kinase A (PKA) subunits[2] may be associated with the pathogenesis of teenage suicide. However, whether these changes in PKA subunits are a *cause* of suicidal behavior or a *result* of suicide is still a matter of debate. In addition, an association between basal reduction of 5-HT_{2a} receptor binding in the prefrontal cortex and some personality traits (such as aggression, anger, and a dominant personality pattern characterized by lower novelty seeking and harm avoidance) has been found in suicide attempters (Lauterbach et al., 2006).

Other biological abnormalities have been found in subjects with a history of suicide attempts. Pompili et al. (2007) found an increased incidence of white matter hyperintensities (WMHs) in patients with a major affective disorder and a history of suicide attempts. After controlling for risk factors (such as comorbid substance abuse), the presence of WMHs was a marker for past suicide attempts in patients with major depression and also in patients with bipolar disorder. These findings have been replicated in a sample of patients with major affective disorders (Serafini et al., 2011). Roughly 48 percent of the patients had periventricular WMHs, and 39 percent of them had deep WMHs. Also, patients with higher dysthymia scores and lower hyperthymia scores on an inventory measuring temperament were more likely to have higher Beck Hopelessness Scale scores, more WMHs, higher suicide risk on the Mini International Neuropsychiatric Interview, and more recent suicide attempts. Serafini et al. suggested that different temperament profiles may be associated with differences in the subcortical structures of the brain in those with a history of suicide attempts.

The association between relatively milder forms of aggressive behavior and serotonergic dysfunction was found both in suicidal patients with Axis-I disorders and in suicidal patients with a low concentration of cerebrospinal fluid levels of 5-hydroxyindoleacetic acid (CSF 5-HIAA) which is related to aggressive behavior (Stanley et al., 2000). The reduced concentration of CSF 5-H1AA, the major degradation product of serotonin (5-HT), is one of the major biochemical 5-HT abnormalities associated with suicidal behavior. A meta-analytic study of 27 reports, including both prospective and retrospective studies, found that suicide attempters, particularly those who use violent methods, had low CSF 5-HIAA when compared to psychiatric controls, contributing to a 4.5-fold increase in suicide risk (Mann, Brent, & Arango, 2001).

It has also been observed that postsynaptic $5HT_{1A}$ and $5HT_{2A}$ receptors are up-regulated in the prefrontal cortex of suicides as a compensatory mechanism in response to low serotonergic activity (Mann, 2003). The increased up-regulated levels of $5HT_{1A}$, mainly localized in the ventral prefrontal cortex (which plays a major role in behavioral and cognitive inhibition), together with low serotonergic input in this area, may result in impaired inhibition of aggressive, impulsive, and suicidal behaviors (Mann, 2003).

Other studies have confirmed the existence of dysfunctions in the serotonergic system. Rao, Hawellek, Papassotiropoulos, Deister, and Frahnert (1998) found that the blood concentration of 5-HT was significantly lower in suicidal patients than normal subjects. They also demonstrated that the B_{max} of $5-HT_{2a}$ receptors (a measure of receptor density) of the suicidal patients was up-regulated compared to that of healthy controls. This finding suggests the existence of an imbalance in the serotonergic system, and the increase in the B_{max} of $5-HT_{2a}$ receptors in the blood platelets of acutely suicidal patients may be a compensation for the low blood and platelet 5-HT levels. Moreover, it has been reported that the B_{max} of the $5HT_{2a}$ receptors was significantly higher in depressed suicidal patients and in suicide attempters compared to nonsuicidal depressed patients and normal controls. Rao et al. (1998) suggested that these patients had fluctuations in blood 5-HT concentrations which modified their psychopathology. In fact, immediately after the suicide attempt, there was an increase of approximately 70-fold in the blood 5-HT concentrations of these patients even though these values remained low compared to those of normal controls. Therefore, changes in 5-HT turnover may be a result of suicidal impulses.

Some studies have found that there is a correlation between the levels of platelet monoamine oxidase (MAO) and the type of suicide attempt (Schalling, Asberg, Edman, & Oreland, 1987). Low levels of platelet MAO have been detected in patients with high levels of impulsivity and a psychosomatic reaction to anxiety and irritability (Tripodianakis,

Markianos, Sarantidis, & Leotsakou, 2000). The relationship between suicidal behavior and impulsiveness has been investigated particularly in patients with borderline personality disorder, for whom MAO activity is negatively associated with impulsive behavior and a loss of inhibition. Interestingly, platelet MAO activity is thought to reflect central serotonergic activity (Oreland et al., 1981). Tripodianakis et al. (2000) reported that a low level of platelet MAO activity characterized patients who attempted suicide more impulsively and with less planning. Therefore, these findings support the hypothesis of an association between impulsiveness (both as a personality trait and as a characteristic of suicide attempts) and a lower serotonergic turnover.

Overall, several lines of evidence suggest the existence of serotonergic dysfunctions in patients with major depressive disorder, in suicide attempters, and in suicides. Future longitudinal studies will establish whether these abnormalities are merely associated with suicidal behavior or whether they *cause* suicidal behavior.

THE ROLE OF SPECIFIC CANDIDATE GENES IN PSYCHIATRIC DISORDERS AND SUICIDAL BEHAVIOR

Considering that suicide has been associated with reduced serotonergic neurotransmission, research has investigated the contribution of specific genes affecting serotonergic neurotransmission. Without doubt, genetically based alteration of the serotonergic system may predispose patients to both psychiatric disorders and suicidal behavior. However, studies investigating suicide in families have demonstrated that suicide may be transmitted in families independently of the presence of psychiatric disorders (Brent & Mann, 2005).

We do not yet know the specific genes associated with suicidal behavior, but candidate genes related to suicide include tryptophan hydroxylase,[3] the 5-HT transporter, and the 5-HT$_{1B}$ and 5-HT$_{2A}$ genes. The 5-HT transporter regulates 5-HT turnover and concentration acting at the synaptic level (Lesch et al., 1996). Roy (1999) suggested a reduced affinity of the 5-HT transporter for 5-HT in suicidal patients with major depression compared to nonsuicidal patients with major depression and with healthy controls. Caspi et al. (2003) examined the association over time between stressful life events and depression in subjects with 5-HT transporter genotype variants. They found that the long form of the 5-HT transporter genotype may reduce the probability of major depressive disorder episodes, while the short form of the 5-HT transporter gene was associated with adverse (stressful) life events and with a modest efficacy of paroxetine in elderly depressed patients (Murphy, Hollander, Rodrigues, Kremer, & Schatzberg, 2004). Therefore, polymorphisms in the promoter region of the 5-HT transporter gene may influence both antidepressant efficacy and tolerability.

Several studies have described the possible role of the promoter region of the 5-HT transporter gene (5-HTTLPR) polymorphism in the emergence of suicidal behavior. Bondy, Erfurth, de Jonge, Kruger, and Meyer (2000) suggested that the S allele (short form) of the 5-HT transporter gene was significantly associated with violent completed suicide, and other authors, such as Courtet et al. (2004), have shown that it is significantly associated with violent suicide attempts and repeated suicide attempts. It is important to note that the frequency of the S allele is not increased in nonviolent suicide attempters (Courtet et al., 2003) and that it is not associated with suicidal ideation.

A meta-analysis by Anguelova, Benkelfat, and Turecki (2003) of 12 studies (with a total of 2,539 suicide attempters, completed suicides, and healthy controls) found a significant association between the S allele of the 5-HTTLPR and suicidal behavior. In a recent meta-analysis, Li and He (2007) replicated these findings, suggesting the existence of a strong positive association between the S allele of the 5-HTTLPR and suicidal behavior. In another meta-analytic study, although no association between 5-HTTLPR and suicidal behavior was found in general, Lin and Tsai (2004) reported that the presence of the S allele appeared significantly more often in suicide attempters as compared to non-attempters, independent of psychiatric diagnosis, and that the S allele was significantly associated with violent suicide (but not with nonviolent suicide). Hung et al. (2011) provided preliminary evidence for a potential gender-specific role for a "high-expression" 5-HTTLPR polymorphism in susceptibility to suicide in Chinese patients with schizophrenia. They showed that men with the L allele of 5-HTTLPR polymorphism were at a higher risk of suicide, although the lack of a significant association in women may have resulted from the small sample size. On the contrary, no gender effect was found for violent suicide attempts. Wasserman et al. (2007) suggested that the presence of the S allele was associated with the emergence of violent aggression or with a strong intent to die by suicide which partially explains the use of more lethal methods for attempting suicide.

To summarize, several research studies and meta-analyses have shown that 5-HTTLPR polymorphism is a component of genetic susceptibility to suicide and that the S allele of the 5-HT transporter is associated with violent suicidal behavior. In addition, subjects with the S allele may experience poor impulse control and aggression, choose highly lethal methods of suicide, and engage in violent behavior (Lin & Tsai, 2004). Since no association has been reported between nonviolent suicide and the 5-HTTLPR polymorphism, it is possible that the causes of nonviolent suicide are more heterogeneous than the causes of violent suicide.

Not all studies have reported a positive association between 5-HTTLPR polymorphism and suicidal behavior. However, the existence of contradictory findings could be explained by the fact that many studies investigating the characteristics of suicidal behavior use small and heterogeneous samples and patients with diverse suicidal behaviors.

5-HTTLPR polymorphisms have been reported to be associated not only with suicidal behavior but also with unipolar depression (Clarke, Flint, Attwood, & Munafo, 2010), although not all research confirms these findings (Risch et al., 2009). One of the most interesting questions at this point is whether different brain regions are involved in determining depression and suicidal behavior. Alterations in 5-HT transporter binding specific to suicide as opposed to major depression seem to be concentrated in the ventral prefrontal cortex (Arango, Underwood, Gubbi, & Mann, 1995), whereas 5-HT transporter density reduction is more widespread in major depression (Mann et al., 2000), with some studies even reporting increased 5-HT transporter density in major depression (Wrase, Reimold, Puls, Kienast, & Heinz, 2006).

Finally, another candidate gene related to suicide must be mentioned. The brain-derived neurotrophic factor (BDNF) gene, which is implicated in the regulation of the development of serotonergic neurons, may play a crucial role in suicidal behavior. Vincze et al. (2008) found that one BDNF functional polymorphism (a gene variation that codes for BDNF) was associated with suicidal behavior and antidepressant-induced suicidal ideation.

Mann et al. (2009) suggested that no single candidate gene might completely describe complex multifaceted behaviors such as suicidal behavior and nonlethal suicide attempts, and a more useful approach might be to identify possible biological and clinical endophenotypes. An endophenotype is any hereditary characteristic that is normally associated with some condition but is not a direct symptom of that condition. An appropriate endophenotype should be associated with the illness in the population, quite heritable (at least 20%), state-independent, and present in non-affected family members more frequently than in the general population. Mann et al. (2009), in a recent review article, proposed the existence of some endophenotypes for suicidal behavior such as impulsive-aggressive traits, early onset of major depression, impaired neurocognitive function, and increased cortisol response to social stress. However, although identifying those endophenotypes for suicidal behavior allows clinicians to handle the heterogeneity and complexity of the phenotype, Mann et al. admitted that methodological challenges in identifying important genes and clarifying their causal pathways still remain. Clearly, further studies investigating the possible role of other candidate genes in the emergence of suicidal behavior as well as their possible interaction with the 5-HT transporter gene are required.

EPIGENETICS AND SUICIDE

Transmission of specific genes through a direct generation-to-generation mechanism may not be the only way in which genetic factors impact suicidal behavior. A genetic vulnerability may also be transmitted through early environmental epigenetically induced changes determining abnormalities in neurobiological functions.

Epigenetics is the science that investigates how the environment influences the genome. Studying epigenetic changes allows us to understand the impact of life adversity, negative environmental factors, and stressors on the human gene pool. Epigenetic changes are non-DNA coding processes able to modify the gene expression, including those chemical and physical modifications (histone modifications, DNA methylation, and noncoding RNA silencing) within the DNA structure which alter the ability of a gene to create coded mRNA. Epigenetic modifications, although reversible, may persist for a long time. Early adverse life events could activate, through specific cellular signaling, enzymes involving in the chromatin sculpture, producing long-lasting DNA changes that impact mental and physical health (Pompili et al., 2011). There are at least two types of evidence that epigenetic factors play a role in psychiatric disorders: (1) the existence of discordance in monozygotic twins and (2) the existence of discordance for psychiatric illness in twins having different DNA methylation.

It has been demonstrated that some epigenetic changes in gene expression determined by childhood adversity may increase the vulnerability of individuals to suicidal behavior. McGowan et al. (2008) suggested that the promoters of the genes encoding ribosomal RNAs (rRNAs) were more highly methylated in the hippocampi of suicides as compared to controls. A reduced, epigenetically regulated ability to synthesize specific proteins which are crucial in learning and memory processes may be involved in suicidal behavior.

Important dysfunctions in one of the most relevant components of neuroendocrine influence and stress response have been hypothesized to determine both the epigenetically induced short-term and long-term neuronal adaptations. McGowan et al. (2008, 2009) suggested that parental care may regulate the expression of the glucocorticoid receptor gene promoter in the rat hippocampus during early postnatal development. While early stress and childhood adversity may determine the hypermethylation of the glucocorticoid receptor gene promoter, early and later social experiences may mitigate the effect induced by stress responses, suggesting a protective role for good parental care. McGowan et al. suggested that hypermethylation of the glucocorticoid receptor gene promoter may be found in suicides having a history of abuse in childhood and severe neglect but not in controls or in suicides without a history of childhood abuse or severe neglect. Therefore, they proposed the existence of an association between psychopathology and methylation of the glucocorticoid receptor gene promoter. The increased methylation of the rRNA promoter may result in decreased rRNA gene expression in suicides.

Research findings are consistent with this hypothesis, namely that early life events may alter the epigenetic status of candidate genes mediating relevant neural functions and contributing to individual differences in the risk for suicide. Childhood adversity or severe neglect might alter the development of a system regulating stress responses such as the hippocampal glucocorticoid receptor expression or the activity of the HPA axis and increase suicidal risk by influencing the vulnerability to psychopathology.

HPA-AXIS[4] DYSFUNCTIONS IN SUICIDAL BEHAVIOR

Several lines of evidence suggest the association between HPA-axis dysfunctions and suicidal behavior. Prospective biological studies suggest that HPA-axis dysfunctions have some predictive power for suicide in patients with mood disorders (Jokinen & Nordstrom, 2008), and HPA-axis hyperactivity may be a relevant risk factor for suicide both in subjects with major depression and in those without a clear psychiatric diagnosis (Nemeroff et al., 1988), as well as for nonfatal suicidal behavior (Westrin, Ekman, Regnell, & Traskman-Bendz, 2001) and for completed suicide (Jokinen & Nordstrom, 2008) in general. In addition, higher cortisol levels in the dexamethasone suppression test (DST) (a clinical measure of

HPA-axis hyperactivity) may indicate an increased risk of suicide by as much as 14-fold (Coryell & Schlesser, 2001) and an elevated cortisol response to the dexamethasone/CRH test[5] is associated with a 4- to 6-fold higher risk for depressive relapse (Zobel et al., 2001).

Increased pituitary gland volume (Pariante et al., 2004), a measure of HPA-axis activation, is associated (in animal studies) with increased levels of corticotropin-releasing hormone (CRH), subsequent increased size and number of pituitary corticotrophs (adrenocorticotropic hormone [ACTH]-producing cells), and increased levels of circulating cortisol (Axelson et al., 1992). Further evidence is provided by the association of suicide with larger adrenal glands and less CRH binding in the prefrontal cortex (Mann, 2003). However, studies in high-risk patients with major depression showed that abnormalities in HPA-axis function exist *prior* to the onset of the clinical symptoms, and these abnormalities may merely precipitate depressive episodes (Holsboer, 2000). There is also evidence of HPA-axis hypoactivity in the physiology of stress-related and fatigue-related disorders.

Banki and Arato (1983) and others have found a positive correlation between increased levels of post-dexamethasone cortisol and low 5-HIAA. In the stress-diathesis model, Mann (2003) focused on two candidate biomarkers for suicidal behavior—low CSF 5-HIAA and non-suppression in the DST (a marker of HPA-axis dysfunction). The question is whether CSF 5-HIAA and non-suppression in DST are associated or whether they are independent risk factors. Mann et al. (2001) proposed that non-suppressors in the DST had more than a 4-fold increased risk of suicide compared with suppressors. Most studies have found that non-suppressors were at higher risk for future suicide regardless of CSF-5-HIAA levels and psychiatric diagnosis (Westrin et al., 2001). Fawcett, Busch, Jacobs, Kravitz, and Fogg (1997) found a positive correlation between low CSF 5-HIAA and DST non-suppression in suicide attempters, but Jokinen et al. (2007) found that low CSF 5-HIAA was a predictor of short-term suicide risk (within 1 year) while DST non-suppression was a long-term (after 1 year) suicide predictor in six male suicides.

Considering the possible contribution of both serotonergic and HPA dysfunctions in suicidal behavior, what is the relationship between serotonin (5-HT) and the HPA axis? Roy, Jimerson, and Pickar (1986) suggested that 5-HT plays an excitatory role in the regulation of the release of CRH. CRH neurons stimulate the secretion of ACTH[6] in the anterior pituitary, and in the central amygdala they are connected to brain nuclei such as the locus coeruleus and raphe nuclei (Meijer & de Kloet, 1998), the major source of serotonergic projections involved in the stress response (Owens & Nemeroff, 1991). The hippocampus is important for HPA-feedback mechanisms as demonstrated in rats where hippocampal lesions result in increased circulating corticosterone (Herman et al., 1989). Also, animal studies showed that corticosteroids may alter several elements of serotonergic neurotransmission.

PITUITARY ABNORMALITIES AND HPA-HYPOACTIVITY IN SUICIDAL BEHAVIOR

Pituitary microadenomas and adrenal enlargement, clinical as well as sub-clinical, are relatively frequent in completed suicides (Furgal-Borzych et al., 2007). In a retrospective study, they found pituitary microadeno-mas in 48 percent of completed suicides compared to only 18 percent in the nonsuicidal group. After a logistic regression analysis, they showed that microadenomas represented an independent risk factor for suicide. The immunohistochemical phenotyping revealed a higher percentage of immunopositive (secreting) microadenomas in the nonsuicidal group compared to the suicidal group (80% vs. 59%) and a predominance of growth hormone-secreting microadenomas in both groups. Some post-mortem changes, such as in pro-opiomelancortin (the precursor mole-cule for ACTH), were found in the pituitaries of the completed suicides, both as mRNA and peptide content and as an indication of chronic acti-vation of the HPA axis.

Finally, not all studies have found a positive association between HPA-axis hyperactivity and suicidal behavior. Heim and Nemeroff (2001) found evidence of HPA-axis hypoactivity in stress-related disorders. An-tonijevic (2006) found low HPA-axis activity in patients who have depres-sion with atypical features and in patients with multi-episodic and chronic depressive disorders. Westrin et al. (2001) found that suicide attempters with Axis-II personality disorders displayed lower cortisol levels than those without such a diagnosis. Lindqvist, Isaksson, Traskman-Bendz, and Brundin (2008) followed up attempted suicides and nonsuicidal con-trols for 12 years and found that the level of evening salivary cortisol was lower in the suicide attempters compared to the controls. Low cortisol levels at follow-up were associated with severe psychiatric symptoms. They also found a negative association between suicidal intent and post-dexamethasone blood cortisol levels among suicide attempters with major depression, indicating an inverse relationship between suicidal behavior and HPA-axis activation. Low 24-hour urinary cortisol is associated with adverse events during the early life of similar patients (Sunnqvist, Westrin, & Traskman-Bendz, 2008). Confirming these results, other studies have also demonstrated that suicidal patients may show decreased levels of cortisol (Pfennig et al., 2005).

Overall, the present findings indicate an association between low HPA-axis activity and suicidal behavior and are probably due to long-lasting and severe psychiatric morbidity which, in turn, has exhausted the HPA axis. Clinicians should focus more carefully on the potential role of HPA-hypoactivity and hypocortisolism in suicidal behavior.

CONCLUSIONS

Several studies have reported an association between neurophysiological abnormalities and suicidal behavior in vulnerable subjects. There might be an interplay between underlying biological factors and psychosocial factors, leading to suicidal behavior in vulnerable patients with psychiatric disorders (Pompili et al., 2010). Combined genetic factors (genetic vulnerability) and physiological abnormalities, involving the serotonergic system as well as the HPA axis, determine this biological vulnerability to stressful life events and may predispose people to engage in suicidal behavior. The psychosocial factors (psychosocial vulnerability) may involve early negative childhood experiences (abuse or severe neglect) which induce epigenetic modifications, leading to the emergence of psychopathology and suicidal behavior. Those factors, taken together, may influence neuroendocrine factors (the HPA axis), neurochemical factors (particularly serotonin), and clinical factors (aggression, impulsivity, neuroticism, and hopelessness) that increase the risk of suicidal behavior (Pompili et al., 2010).

HPA-axis hyperactivity represents a common finding in a large sub-population of depressed subjects, although HPA-hypoactivity and hypocortisolism have been also reported. Abnormalities in the 5-HT and HPA systems, as well as the presence of the S allele of the 5-HT transporter, have been identified both in completed suicides and in patients with affective disorders without suicidal behavior. An interesting question is whether those biological abnormalities found in completed and attempted suicides are characteristic of only some subgroups of patients (e.g., patients with affective disorders), or whether they may be considered to be neurobiological predictors common to all suicides.

Further additional studies are required in order to understand whether neurophysiological dysfunctions are critical elements in determining suicidal behavior, as well as a poor outcome in some vulnerable subgroups of patients, or whether they may be merely considered to be an epiphenomenon of the suicidal state.

NOTES

1. Messenger RNA (ribonucleic) acid.
2. An enzyme found in cells.
3. An enzyme involved in the synthesis of serotonin.
4. Hypothalamic-pituitary-adrenal axis.
5. Corticotrophin-releasing hormone.
6. Adrenocorticotropic hormone.

REFERENCES

Anguelova, M., Benkelfat, C., & Turecki, G. (2003). A systematic review of association studies investigating genes coding for serotonin receptors and the serotonin transporter: II. Suicidal behavior. *Molecular Psychiatry, 8,* 646–653.

Antonijevic, I. A. (2006). Depressive disorders. *Psychoneuroendocrinology, 31,* 1–15.

Arango, V., Underwood, M. D., Gubbi, A. V., & Mann, J. J. (1995). Localized alterations in pre- and postsynaptic serotonin binding sites in the ventrolateral prefrontal cortex of suicide victims. *Brain Research, 688,* 121–133.

Axelson, D. A., Doraiswamy, P. M., Boyko, O. B., Rodrigo Escalona, P., McDonald, W. M., Ritchie, J. C., Patterson, L. J., . . . Krishnan, K. R. (1992). In vivo assessment of pituitary volume with magnetic resonance imaging and systematic stereology: Relationship to dexamethasone suppression test results in patients. *Psychiatry Research, 44,* 63–70.

Banki, C. M., & Arato, M. (1983). Amine metabolites and neuroendocrine responses related to depression and suicide. *Journal of Affective Disorders, 5,* 223–232.

Bondy, B., Erfurth, A., de Jonge, S., Kruger, M., & Meyer, H. (2000). Possible association of the short allele of the serotonin transporter promoter gene polymorphism (5-HTTLPR) with violent suicide. *Molecular Psychiatry, 5,* 193–195.

Brent, D. A., & Mann, J. J. (2005). Family genetic studies, suicide, and suicidal behavior. *American Journal of Medical Genetics C: Seminar in Medical Genetics, 133,* 13–24.

Caspi, A., Sugden, K., Moffitt, T. E., Taylor, A., Craig, I. W., Harrington, H., et al. (2003). Influence of life stress on depression: Moderation by a polymorphism in the 5-HTT gene. *Science, 301,* 386–389.

Cavanagh, J., Carson, A. J., Sharpe, M., & Lawrie, S. (2003). Psychological autopsy studies of suicide: A systematic review. *Psychological Medicine, 33,* 395–405.

Clarke, H., Flint, J., Attwood, A. S., & Munafo, M. R. (2010). Association of the 5-HTTLPR genotype and unipolar depression: A meta-analysis. *Psychological Medicine, 40,* 1767–1778.

Coryell, W., & Schlesser, M. (2001). The dexamethasone suppression test and suicide prediction. *American Journal of Psychiatry, 158,* 748–753.

Courtet, P., Buresi, C., Abbar, M., Baud, P., Boulenger, J. P., Castelnau, D., et al. (2003). No association between non-violent suicidal behavior and the serotonin transporter promoter polymorphism. *American Journal of Medical Genetics B: Neuropsychiatric Genetics, 116B,* 72–76.

Courtet, P., Picot, M. C., Bellivier, F., Torres, S., Jollant, F., Michelon, C., et al. (2004). Serotonin transporter gene may be involved in short-term risk of subsequent suicide attempts. *Biological Psychiatry, 55,* 46–51.

Fawcett, J., Busch, K. A., Jacobs, D., Kravitz, H. M., & Fogg, L. (1997). Suicide: A four-pathway clinical-biochemical model. *Annals of the New York Academy of Sciences, 836,* 288–301.

Furgal-Borzych, A., Lis, G. J., Litwin, J. A., Rzepecka-Wozniak, E., Trela, F., & Cichocki, T. (2007). Increased incidence of pituitary microadenomas in suicide victims. *Neuropsychobiology, 55,* 163–166.

Harris, E. C., & Barraclough, B. M. (1997). Suicide as an outcome for mental disorders. *British Journal of Psychiatry, 170,* 205–228.

Heim, C., & Nemeroff, C. B. (2001). The role of childhood trauma in the neurobiology of mood and anxiety disorders: Preclinical and clinical studies. *Biological Psychiatry, 49,* 1023–1039.

Herman, J. P., Schafer, M. K., Young, E. A., Thompson, R., Douglass, J., Akil, H., et al. (1989). Evidence for hippocampal regulation of neuroendocrine neurons of the hypothalamo-pituitary-adrenocortical axis. *Journal of Neuroscience, 9,* 3072–3082.

Holsboer, F. (2000). The corticosteroid receptor hypothesis of depression. *Neuropsychopharmacology, 23,* 477–501.

Hung, C. F., Lung, F. W., Chen, C. H., O'Nions, E., Hung, T. H., Chong, M. Y., et al. (2011). Association between suicide attempt and a tri-allelic functional polymorphism in serotonin transporter gene promoter in Chinese patients with schizophrenia. *Neuroscience Letters, 504,* 242–246.

Jokinen, J., Carlborg, A., Martensson, B., Forslund, K., Nordstrom, A. L., & Nordstrom, P. (2007). DST non-suppression predicts suicide after attempted suicide. *Psychiatry Research, 150,* 297–303.

Jokinen, J., & Nordstrom, P. (2008). HPA axis hyperactivity as suicide predictor in elderly mood disorder inpatients. *Psychoneuroendocrinology, 33,* 1387–1393.

Lauterbach, E., Brunner, J., Hawellek, B., Lewitzka, U., Ising, M., Bondy, B., et al. (2006). Platelet 5-HT2A receptor binding and tryptophan availability in depression are not associated with recent history of suicide attempts but with personality traits characteristic for suicidal behavior. *Journal of Affective Disorders, 91,* 57–62.

Lesch, K.P., Bengel, D., Heils, A., Sabol, S.Z., Greenberg, B.D., Petri, S., et al. (1996). Association of anxiety-related traits with a polymorphism in the serotonin transporter gene regulatory region. *Science, 274,* 1527–1531.

Lester, D. (1995). The concentration of neurotransmitter metabolites in the cerebrospinal fluid of suicidal individuals: A meta-analysis. *Pharmacopsychiatry, 28,* 45–50.

Li, D., & He, L. (2007). Meta-analysis supports association between serotonin transporter (5-HTT) and suicidal behavior. *Molecular Psychiatry, 12,* 47–54.

Lin, P. Y., & Tsai, G. (2004). Association between serotonin transporter gene promoter polymorphism and suicide: Results of a meta-analysis. *Biological Psychiatry, 55,* 1023–1030.

Lindqvist, D., Isaksson, A., Traskman-Bendz, L., & Brundin, L. (2008). Salivary cortisol and suicidal behavior: A follow-up study. *Psychoneuroendocrinology, 33,* 1061–1068.

Mann, J.J. (1998). The neurobiology of suicide. *Nature Medicine, 4,* 25–30.

Mann J.J. (2003). Neurobiology of suicidal behavior. *Nature Reviews: Neuroscience, 4,* 819–828.

Mann, J.J., Arango, V.A., Avenevoli, S., Brent, D.A., Champagne, F.A., Clayton, P., et al. (2009). Candidate endophenotypes for genetic studies of suicidal behavior. *Biological Psychiatry, 65,* 556–563.

Mann, J.J., Brent, D.A., & Arango, V. (2001). The neurobiology and genetics of suicide and attempted suicide: A focus on the serotonergic system. *Neuropsychopharmacology, 24,* 467–477.

Mann, J.J., Huang, Y.Y., Underwood, M.D., Kassir, S.A., Oppenheim, S., Kelly, T.M., et al. (2000). A serotonin transporter gene promoter polymorphism (5-HTTLPR) and prefrontal cortical binding in major depression and suicide. *Archives of General Psychiatry, 57,* 729–738.

McGowan, P.O., Sasaki, A., D'Alessio, A.C., Dymov, S., Labonté, B., Szyf, M., et al. (2009). Epigenetic regulation of the glucocorticoid receptor in human brain associates with childhood abuse. *Nature Neuroscience, 12,* 342–348.

McGowan, P.O., Sasaki, A., Huang, T.C., Unterberger, A., Suderman, M., Ernst, C., et al. (2008). Promoter-wide hypermethylation of the ribosomal RNA gene promoter in the suicide brain. *PLoS One, 3(5),* e2085.

Meijer, O.C., & de Kloet, E.R. (1998). Corticosterone and serotonergic neurotransmission in the hippocampus: Functional implications of central corticosteroid receptor diversity. *Critical Reviews of Neurobiology, 12,* 1–20.

Murphy, G. M., Jr., Hollander, S. B., Rodrigues, H. E., Kremer, C., & Schatzberg, A. F. (2004). Effects of the serotonin transporter gene promoter polymorphism on mirtazapine and paroxetine efficacy and adverse events in geriatric major depression. *Archives of General Psychiatry, 61,* 1163–1169.

Nemeroff, C. B., Owens, M. J., Bissette, G., Andorn, A. C., & Stanley, M. (1988). Reduced corticotropin releasing factor binding sites in the frontal cortex of suicide victims. *Archives of General Psychiatry, 45,* 577–579.

Oquendo, M. A., Russo, S. A., Underwood, M. D., Kassir, S. A., Ellis, S. P., Mann, J. J., et al. (2006). Higher postmortem prefrontal 5-HT2A receptor binding correlates with lifetime aggression in suicide. *Biological Psychiatry, 59,* 235–243.

Oreland, L., Wiberg, A., Asberg, M., Träskman, L., Sjöstrand, L., Thorén, P., et al. (1981). Platelet MAO activity and monoamine metabolites in cerebrospinal fluid in depressed and suicidal patients and in healthy controls. *Psychiatry Research, 4,* 21–29.

Owens, M. J., & Nemeroff, C. B. (1991). Physiology and pharmacology of corticotropin-releasing factor. *Pharmacology Review, 43,* 425–473.

Pandey, G. N., Dwivedi, Y., Pandey, S. C., Teas, S. S., Conley, R. R., Roberts, R. C., et al. (1999). Low phosphoinositide-specific phospholipase C activity and expression of phospholipase C beta1 protein in the prefrontal cortex of teenage suicide subjects. *American Journal of Psychiatry, 156,* 1895–1901.

Pariante, C. M., Vassilopoulou, K., Velakoulis, D., Phillips, L., Soulsby, B., Wood, S. J., et al. (2004). Pituitary volume in psychosis. *British Journal of Psychiatry, 185,* 5–10.

Pfennig, A., Kunzel, H. E., Kern, N., Ising, M., Majer, M., Fuchs, B, et al. (2005). Hypothalamus-pituitary-adrenal system regulation and suicidal behavior in depression. *Biological Psychiatry, 57,* 336–342.

Pompili, M., Ehrlich, S., De Pisa, E., Mann, J. J., Innamorati, M., Cittadini, A., et al. (2007). White matter hyperintensities and their associations with suicidality in patients with major affective disorders. *European Archives of Psychiatry & Clinical Neuroscience, 257,* 494–499.

Pompili, M., Innamorati, M., Venturini, P., Serafini, G., Lester, D., & Girardi, P. (2011). Child abuse as a risk factor for suicide in life: A selective overview. *Minerva Psichiatrica, 52,* 61–69.

Pompili, M., Serafini, G., Innamorati, M., Möller-Leimkühler, A. M., Giupponi, G., Girardi, P., et al. (2010). The hypothalamic-pituitary-adrenal axis and serotonin abnormalities: A selective overview for the implications of suicide prevention. *European Archives of Psychiatry & Clinical Neuroscience, 260,* 583–600.

Purselle, D. C., & Nemeroff, C. B. (2003). Serotonin transporter: A potential substrate in the biology of suicide. *Neuropsychopharmacology, 28,* 613–619.

Rao, M. L., Hawellek, B., Papassotiropoulos, A., Deister, A., Frahnert, C. (1998). Upregulation of the platelet serotonin2A receptor and low blood serotonin in suicidal psychiatric patients. *Neuropsychobiology, 38,* 84–89.

Risch, N., Herrell, R., Lehner, T., Liang, K. Y., Eaves, L., Hoh, J., et al. (2009). Interaction between the serotonin transporter gene (5-HTTLPR), stressful life events, and risk of depression: A meta-analysis. *Journal of the American Medical Association, 301,* 2462–2471.

Roy, A. (1999). Suicidal behavior in depression: Relationship to platelet serotonin transporter. *Neuropsychobiology, 39,* 71–75.

Roy, A., Jimerson, D. C., & Pickar, D. (1986). Plasma MHPG in depressive disorders and relationship to the dexamethasone suppression test. *American Journal of Psychiatry, 143,* 846–851.

Schalling, D., Asberg, M., Edman, G., & Oreland, L. (1987). Markers for vulnerability to psychopathology: Temperament traits associated with platelet MAO activity. *Acta Psychiatrica Scandinavica, 76,* 172–182.

Serafini, G., Pompili, M., Innamorati, M., Fusar-Poli, P., Akiskal, H. S., Rihmer, Z., et al. (2011). Affective temperamental profiles are associated with white matter hyperintensity and suicidal risk in patients with mood disorders. *Journal of Affective Disorders, 129,* 47–55.

Stanley, B., Molcho, A., Stanley, M., Winchel, R., Gameroff, M. J., Parsons, B., et al. (2000). Association of aggressive behavior with altered serotonergic function in patients who are not suicidal. *American Journal of Psychiatry, 157,* 609–614.

Sunnqvist, C., Westrin, A., & Traskman-Bendz, L. (2008). Suicide attempters: Biological stressmarkers and adverse life events. *European Archives of Psychiatry & Clinical Neuroscience, 258,* 456–462.

Tripodianakis, J., Markianos, M., Sarantidis, D., & Leotsakou, C. (2000). Neurochemical variables in subjects with adjustment disorder after suicide attempts. *European Psychiatry, 15,* 190–195.

van Heeringen, K., Audenaert, K., Van de Wiele, L., & Verstraete, A. (2000). Cortisol in violent suicidal behavior: Association with personality and monoaminergic activity. *Journal of Affective Disorders, 60,* 181–189.

Vincze, I., Perroud, N., Buresi, C., Baud, P., Bellivier, F., Etain, B., et al. (2008). Association between brain-derived neurotrophic factor gene and a severe form of bipolar disorder, but no interaction with the serotonin transporter gene. *Bipolar Disorders, 10,* 580–587.

Wasserman, D., Geijer, T., Sokolowski, M., Frisch, A., Michaelovsky, E., Weizman, A., et al. (2007). Association of the serotonin transporter promotor polymorphism with suicide attempters with a high medical damage. *European Neuropsychopharmacology, 17,* 230–233.

Westrin, A., Ekman, R., Regnell, G., & Traskman-Bendz, L. (2001). A follow up study of suicide attempters: Increase of CSF somatostatin but no change in CSF-CRH. *European Neuropsychopharmacology, 11,* 135–143.

Wrase, J., Reimold, M., Puls, I., Kienast, T., & Heinz, A. (2006). Serotonergic dysfunction: Brain imaging and behavioral correlates. *Cognitive, Affective and Behavioral Neuroscience, 6,* 53–61.

Zobel, A. W., Nickel, T., Sonntag, A., Uhr, M., Holsboer, F., & Ising, M. (2001). Cortisol response in the combined dexamethasone/CRH test as predictor of relapse in patients with remitted depression: A prospective study. *Journal of Psychiatric Research, 35,* 83–94.

6

Examining the Role of Adverse Life Events and Daily Hassles in Suicide

Jeff Klibert and Dorian A. Lamis

An estimated one million individuals around the world kill themselves annually, which is higher than the number of world deaths from war and homicide combined (World Health Organization, 2004). Moreover, cross-national data suggest that suicide rates are either stabilizing or increasing in most countries, but not decreasing. These statistics are both alarming and tragic. In light of these trends, suicidologists target the underlying components of suicide to better understand how such behaviors are developed, maintained, and exacerbated across time. Unfortunately, the dynamics and structure of suicidal behaviors vary across age and maturation, culture, and vulnerability factors, making it extremely difficult to establish standardized means of preventing and treating individuals who are at risk. However, it is universally accepted that suicidal behaviors are often preceded as well as accompanied by stressful or adverse live events (Van Praag, 2004).

At some point, external conditions generate stress for everyone. Furthermore, most individuals successfully navigate through stressful situations with few, if any, lasting psychological consequences. So an intriguing question may be, "What types of adverse life events precipitate the desire and willingness to engage in suicidal behaviors?" To date, researchers have identified numerous stressful life experiences that are predictive of suicidal behaviors. Some occur in childhood and adolescence, including parental loss and emotional, physical, and sexual abuse, whereas others occur immediately prior to the suicidal act, such as the breakup of an intimate relationship, legal problems, and work-related and financial problems. In this chapter, we will discuss the role that life experiences play in predisposing an individual to be at an increased risk for engaging in suicidal behaviors, as well as in triggering suicidal acts.

THE CONCEPT OF STRESS

While the concept of stress has historical roots, it was not until the 1960s that stress and its associated components became a focal point in how we conceptualize and treat psychological difficulties. However, one major drawback in focusing on stress to develop theoretical models that explain the onset of psychopathology is the lack of a clear and concise definition. According to the current literature, stress can be defined in any number of ways across various fields of study. For a more detailed review of this topic, see Cooper and Dewe (2004).

Broadly, stress reflects attempts to adapt to impinging demands. However, such a definition is limited as it does not consider the factors and processes that underlie the experience of stress. For instance, the above definition does not clarify the conditions (internal vs. external demands) that perpetuate stress, how stress is experienced (cognitively vs. physiologically), and what types of individual characteristics contribute to a heightened vulnerability to stress. Thus, finding a definition that adequately considers all of the previously noted components is a complex and time-consuming challenge. In the context of this essay, we use Ingram and Luxton's (2005) interpretation of stress, which is defined as adverse life events that disrupt an individual's ability to maintain physiological, emotional, and cognitive stability.

Additionally, researchers often examine adverse life events through two dimensions: intensity and timing. In general, intensity refers to the perceptual impact (major vs. minor) of stressful life events on an individual's homeostatic functioning. Major life events are universally stressful and often viewed as out of one's control. They substantially impact one's ability to function and require major adjustment efforts that extend over long periods of time. Traumatic abuse, divorce, legal problems, loss of a loved one, natural disasters, and loss of employment are a few examples of major live events. In contrast, minor life events or daily hassles are less traumatic in nature. Daily hassles are often associated with feelings of irritation, frustration, and distress in managing common obstacles embedded within the maintenance of specific life roles and interpersonal relationships. Losing one's keys, having an argument with your child, waiting in long lines, having your parents spend the week at your house, and feeling lonely are all examples of daily hassles. Individually, daily hassles seem manageable. However, the combined effect of repeated and co-occurring daily hassles can have a profound effect on an individual's physical and mental health.

In this chapter, timing refers to the temporal closeness between a life event and a specific mental health outcome (e.g., depression, suicide, etc. [Martin & Martin, 2002]). Proximal life events are experiences that not only precede, but occur relatively close to the outcome under investigation. Examples of proximal life events to suicide may include interpersonal conflicts, relationship breakdowns, loss of employment, and loss of a loved one. Distal life events also precede outcomes, but they often reach further into the personal histories of individuals. Considering that life events are incorporated in one's sense of self in childhood and adolescence, some researchers argue that distal life experiences are the most robust in regard to predicting future mental health outcomes. Some salient, distal life events that influence adult suicidal behavior are childhood physical and sexual abuse, parent–child conflicts, and bullying. In the following sections, we discuss how the intensity and timing of stressful life events contributes to the onset and exacerbation of suicidal behaviors.

DEFINING AND ASSESSING SUICIDE

Suicide is a complex and not a very well understood behavior, which is why it is important to move beyond a simple and clear definition. Accordingly, most researchers and mental health professionals view suicide as a process that can be measured along a continuum. The process of suicide is often activated by thoughts of death or dying, which can develop into more serious life-threatening behaviors that may include self-injury and suicide attempts, eventually culminating into death by suicide. Moreover, suicidologists have established a litany of suicide markers (e.g., suicide gestures, suicide proneness, suicide ideation, parasuicide, etc.) that estimate the degree to which an individual is suicidal. Interestingly, different markers of suicide risk are associated with different dynamics, defenses, and intentions and may provoke different responses and social attitudes from others. As a result, a careful assessment of where an "at risk" individual lies on the continuum is the first step in selecting and implementing prevention strategies that protect against future suicidal acts.

Considering the various degrees of suicidal risk, it is important that we have a diverse set of instruments to help us understand the dynamics behind why individuals choose to kill themselves. Fortunately, there are a number of surveys and interviews that help us elicit important information from individuals who are thinking about or planning a suicide attempt. Detailed reports are also available from individuals who have survived a suicide attempt. However, the psychological autopsy is our most powerful instrument as it allows suicidologists to uncover psychologically rich data about a person who *has* died by suicide. The psychological autopsy combines data obtained through interviews with those closest to the deceased, with corroborating evidence from sources such as health, criminal, and legal records, to form the most comprehensive picture about the emotional and physical functioning of the victim (Cavanagh, Carson, Sharpe, & Lawrie, 2003). One of the more revealing sources of information within the psychological autopsy is the suicide note.[1] Although suicide notes represent the last words of emotionally burdened individuals, they also offer an opportunity to glean important information concerning adverse life events that led up to the suicidal act and potential interpersonal, emotional, and cognitive processes that may have triggered the act. Below is an example of a fictitious suicide note.

Dear Mom and Dad,

I am not strong, thus the reason for my action against myself. I have failed miserably at each stage of my life despite your best efforts to make me into a good person. I am unlovable, shamed, and tainted. I cannot stand to be shunned or looked at differently anymore. All I want to do is escape this life into a void of numbness. I know you have tried to encourage me to be strong but I cannot possibly think that I will ever be strong enough. I will never be able to overcome the shame of not getting into college, disgracing my best friend, and getting arrested. All of those actions should demonstrate to you how weak I am. There is no hope for me, I will never be able to see myself as a good person and I am sure that you have your own doubts about my goodness. Considering my acts in life, I hope that you eventually find comfort that I will not be a burden on you for much longer. You have both been great. I wish I would have listened and acted more like you. I will love you always even from whatever hell I am sending myself to.

Stephanie

Plainly, there are a number of pieces within the suicide note that contribute to our understanding of why Stephanie took her own life. By deconstructing Stephanie's suicide note, we obtain information regarding her situational (e.g., getting arrested), emotional (e.g., shame), and cognitive (e.g., belief that she is unlovable) processes that are associated with her decision to kill herself. Using information derived from suicide notes and other supplemental data obtained through psychological autopsies, suicidologists may begin to understand the process of how one becomes suicidal.

In Stephanie's case, we have to determine how negative life events, her emotional responses to these events, and her underlying thought patterns fit together to form the best explanation for her suicide. Variables that contribute to a suicide can be integrated in many ways to produce a diverse range of suicide theories. In the following sections, we will review some long-standing and validated theories of suicide, paying close attention to the role of adverse life events and/or daily hassles in each.

ADVERSE LIFE EVENTS AND SUICIDE

Based on the results of many psychological autopsies, we believe quite certainly that adverse life events are associated with a predisposition toward suicide. However, can we identify an individual who is at high risk for suicide by simply assessing the effects of adverse events? For example, consider John, a middle-aged man who recently experienced the loss of his job and will have to move his family to another state to search for new employment opportunities. Is he likely to engage in suicidal behavior? While the answer to this question is dependent upon factors outside of our purview, it highlights the complexity inherent within the relationship between stressful life events and suicide. In order to facilitate a more accurate understanding of this relationship, it is important to differentiate between risk and vulnerability factors to suicide.

The distinction between risk and vulnerability factors is important as it determines how we understand and treat suicidal behaviors. Risk factors are variables that are used to predict suicidal behavior within specific individuals (Ingram, Miranda, & Segal, 1998). Variables such as age, gender, socioeconomic status, homosexuality, and physical illness are some well-established risk factors to suicide. However, risk factors provide little information in regard to the processes that provoke suicidal behavior. Instead they merely imply an increased probability that one may have thoughts about suicide or engage in suicidal behaviors. Similarly, risk factors provide limited information to clinicians who are attempting to highlight natural points of interventions for individuals who are actively suicidal.

In contrast, vulnerability factors are a special subset of variables that provide details about the mechanisms that precipitate future suicidal behaviors. According to Ingram and colleagues (1998), vulnerability factors are stable (enduring or ever-present traits), latent (are not easily observable), and endogenous (reside within an individual) constructs that facilitate insights into the processes behind one's desire and capability to engage in suicidal behavior. The information provided from such constructs may guide the process of selecting and implementing appropriate treatment interventions for individuals at risk for suicide.

Considering that most stressful events are fleeting, observable, and heavily influenced by outside factors, adverse life events and general levels of perceived stress are ill-suited to be vulnerability factors for suicide. Moreover, research has indicated that about half of the individuals who experience adverse life events *do not* report symptoms or problem behaviors concurrent with mood difficulties (Monroe & Hadjiyannakis, 2002), suggesting that a substantial number of people can either successfully navigate through, or at least tolerate, the burden of stress without significant psychological impairment. Overall, findings such as these limit the usefulness of adverse life events in determining why someone may have chosen to end his or her life. Consequently, the relationship between adverse life events and suicide needs to be understood within the context of more general vulnerability theories, meaning that the pathway to which adverse life events promote risk for suicide needs to be understood through specific vulnerability factors. A possible diagram of the relationship between stressful life events and suicide is depicted in Figure 6.1.

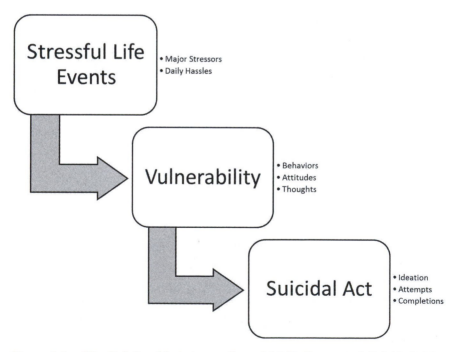

Figure 6.1. The Relationship between Stressful Life Events and Suicide Is Not Direct and Best Understood through a Vulnerability Factor.

Although adverse life events may not directly cause the suicidal act, they may still play an integral role in the emergence of suicidal behavior. Suicide is a complex behavior that is marked by breakdowns in multiple emotional, cognitive, and stress response systems. As a result, it is unlikely that any one particular risk or vulnerability factor causes a death by suicide. Instead, it is common practice for suicidologists to espouse interactional approaches (multifactorial) to explain the onset and exacerbation of suicidal behavior. In the following sections, we discuss specific theories and how they integrate proximal and distal adverse events, which may confer risk for suicide. In addition, we will also indicate possible links between daily hassles and suicide behaviors.

PROXIMAL LIFE EVENTS AND ESCAPE THEORY

Approximately 80 percent of individuals who take their own lives report at least one recent adverse life event in the three months prior to their suicide (Heikkinen, Aro, & Lönnqvist, 1994). Adverse life events that are most likely to trigger the process of initiating or exacerbating one's risk for suicide include job-related problems, marital and family conflicts, divorce, physical illness, and death of a loved one. Moreover, during certain developmental periods, specific adverse life events may have a substantial influence on one's desire to die. For instance, the suicide notes of adolescents and young adults often carry themes of interpersonal turmoil stemming from either a recent breakup of an intimate relationship or the loss of a close friend. In addition, adverse life events that reduce one's sense of purpose and competence are clearly apparent in the suicide notes of older adults. Taken together, it appears that recent life events that entail a loss of a valued resource (e.g., friend, spouse, job, skill, etc.) may be particularly associated with suicidal acts (Wenzel, Brown, & Beck, 2009).

For individuals who attempt suicide or die by suicide, adverse life events often reflect setbacks and disappointments that contribute to negative appraisals about one's sense of worth and meaning. According to Baumeister's Escape Theory of Suicide (1990), the act of suicide will occur when one has the desire to escape meaningful awareness from recent life stress and the concurrent implications about the self. In this context, suicide is not a simple act but instead a product of complex interactions between stressful life events and specific vulnerability factors. Accordingly, Baumeister's Escape theory is presented in a causal chain (see Figure 6.2) where recent negative life events, emotional states, and cognitive factors are highlighted in the prediction of suicide. In order to get a better understanding of Baumeister's Escape theory, we present a case illustration of a hypothetical scenario.

Lori is an 18-year-old student who is about to begin her college career at a prestigious university. Lori's parents promised that they would pay Lori's tuition for four years if she would agree to maintain a 3.5 GPA and pursue a degree in pre-law. Lori accepted her parent's terms and entered college with an optimistic attitude. About a month into her college career, Lori took her first criminal justice exam. Despite studying hard, Lori earned a failing grade. Needless to say, Lori's grade did not fall in line with her own or her parents' expectations. As she processed factors that contributed to her failing grade, Lori began to think of herself as incompetent, underserving, and laughable. These appraisals were reinforced by her performance in subsequent examinations. Specifically, despite spending an extraordinary amount of hours studying per week, the highest grade Lori could obtain in her criminal justice course was a B. After two-thirds of her first semester, Lori began to feel depressed and hopeless about her future as a lawyer. In order to avoid thinking about her future, she started to drink large amounts of alcohol daily. For Lori, drinking alcohol generated a feeling of physical and mental numbness which she particularly desired given the overwhelming amount of stress she faced on a daily basis. Unfortunately, right before finals Lori decided to consume a large quantity of her antianxiety medications with a fifth of vodka. Approximately 10 minutes later, a roommate found Lori unconscious on the floor of their dorm room barely breathing. Her roommate called 911 and Lori was rushed to the hospital. Lori eventually recovered.

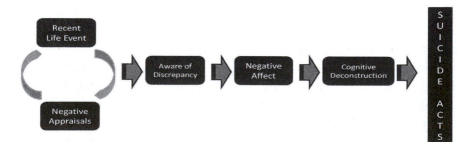

Figure 6.2.   The Causal Chain Process Embedded within Baumeister's Escape Theory of Suicide

Clearly, Lori was experiencing a substantial amount of inner turmoil when she attempted suicide. According to Baumeister's Escape Theory, the suicidal process is generally triggered by a severe and stressful experience that is unanticipated given one's expectations. In the instance of Lori, she may have been anticipating an A on her first criminal justice exam considering the amount of hours she had studied. Instead, she received an F which was an outcome that fell substantially below her expectations. In reaction to receiving a failing grade, Lori began to make negative internal attributions concerning her competence, worthiness, and appearance as a college student. This is consistent with Baumeister's second stage of escape, where at-risk individuals begin to perceive and imply negative characteristics toward themselves based on recent adverse life events. Moreover, these attributions are often maintained and exacerbated through subsequent adverse life events. For Lori, an inability to achieve an A on future exams reinforced the idea that she was incompetent and undeserving.

If the interaction between stressful life events and negative self-appraisals persists, at-risk individuals become acutely aware of the discrepancy between where they are and where they think should be. This discrepancy is reflected in Baumeister's third step of escape. Consistent with this idea, after two months into her college career, Lori became demoralized by the realization that she was falling short of the standards needed to gain entrance into law school. In his fourth step of escape, Baumeister indicated that a keen awareness of one's shortfalls often precipitates aversive states of negative affect. In our case illustration, Lori appears to exhibit depressive symptoms (e.g., hopelessness) in response to the realization that she is underperforming. In addition, Lori attempted to manage and alleviate her depressive and hopeless feelings by consuming alcohol. At this point, her actions appear to be reflective of Baumeister's fifth step of escape, where at-risk individuals engage in some form of cognitive deconstruction. Cognitive deconstruction is represented by a shift in focus away from meaningful thought and toward more concrete physical or bodily sensations. For Lori, drinking alcohol served as a coping mechanism that allowed her to replace meaningful thoughts concerning her failures with immediately pleasing feelings of numbness. According to Baumeister, at-risk individuals will often cycle between ruminating about shortfalls and patterns of cognitive deconstruction which inevitably foster a more permanent means of escaping one's problems. Moreover, frequent use of alcohol often disinhibits the body's self-preservation instincts making it easier for an individual to die by suicide (Joiner, 2005). As a result, Lori's suicide attempt was most likely facilitated by a desire to escape her problems and depleted levels of physiological self-preservation instincts.

Although Baumeister's Escape Theory encompasses a number of interrelated components, the influence of negative life events is quite clear and powerful in predicting future suicidal behaviors. Particularly, in the case illustration, negative life events played a number of roles that contributed to Lori's suicide attempt. Specifically, Lori's first negative life event fostered the development of vulnerability factors (e.g., thoughts of being incompetent) that increased her risk for suicide. Moreover, subsequent life stressors appeared to have bolstered or even exacerbated her negative self-appraisals (e.g., "I am worthless") and negative affect symptoms (e.g., depression and hopelessness). Overall, Baumeister's Escape Theory has been validated in many studies and currently remains one of the most robust theories of suicide.

DISTAL LIFE EVENTS AND COGNITIVE THEORIES

During childhood and adolescence, we encounter a diverse range of challenges that inevitably shape the person we are today. At least in part, one can make the case that our identity is cultivated through our early life experiences. In a perfect world, all of us would have the capability and resources to confront obstacles that threaten our overall sense of well-being with optimism, skill, and resilience. However, unfortunately, adverse life events such as physical abuse, bullying, and the loss of a parent may overwhelm children's resources, disrupting psychological foundations that are still in construction. In addition, if these children were denied opportunities to develop a stable set of psychological resources (e.g., secure parental attachments, safe and warm family environments, etc.), the impact of traumatic life events may damage their sense of identity, security, and self-worth (Wheaton & Gotlib, 1997). The realization that some children may enter crucial developmental stages (e.g., the transition from middle school to high school) with an unstable sense of self is disheartening, but ultimately may explain how the effects of childhood adversities precipitate self-harm behaviors in adulthood.

Again, stressful life events are generally not considered vulnerability factors to suicide. As such, to explain the relationships between adverse childhood conditions and adult suicidal behavior, suicidologists must identify mechanisms through which adverse life events exert their influence on the desire and capability to die by suicide. Beck (1967) suggests that traumatic events in childhood are responsible for initiating and stabilizing the development of maladaptive schemas. Schemas are cognitively based structures that dictate how we organize information, make decisions, and focus our attention. Our schemas are comprised of memories, emotions, cognitions, and bodily sensations that were generated through our life experiences (Young, Klosko, & Weishaar, 2003) and serve as the lenses through which we view the world (Wenzel et al., 2009). Based upon the amount and degree of adversity faced in childhood and adolescence, our schemas can be either adaptive or maladaptive. If our childhood and adolescent experiences were marked by adversity, we are at a greater risk for developing early maladaptive schemas.

Early maladaptive schemas are defined as enduring, cognitive themes or patterns concerning oneself and one's relationships with others that are destructive to an individual's self-concept (Young et al., 2003). They originate from negative childhood and adolescent experiences that strip individuals of their basic needs (e.g., nurturance, sense of identity, creativity, etc.) and are perpetuated into adulthood. Thus, adverse life events play an integral role in cultivating and reinforcing the growth of maladaptive schemas. In part, the strength in which an individual adheres to a maladaptive schema depends upon the frequency with which one encounters adverse life events.[2] To demonstrate the importance of adverse life events in cultivating and reinforcing maladaptive schema growth, we present a vignette of a hypothetical scenario.

Tim lost both of his parents in a car accident at the age of seven. Because he did not have any living relative who could care for him, Tim was placed in a foster home. At the foster home, Tim was provided with shelter, food, and clothes. However, his foster parents were not warm and nurturing. He was able to make some friends with his foster brothers and sisters, but realized that most of his friendships were temporary as his foster brothers and sisters were often adopted quickly. Every time one of his foster brothers and sisters was adopted, Tim felt even more lonesome. He tried to connect with his foster mother and father when he felt lonely, but they often ignored him. Tim even tried to impress them by showing them his skills in sports, academics, and painting, but his foster parents never seemed interested in getting to know him. As a result of the inability to connect with his foster parents, Tim began to harbor negative feelings about himself. Specifically, he began to think of himself as unlovable and useless. By the age of 12, Tim stopped trying to befriend other children in the foster home because he knew that he would just wind up alone in the end. He also lost any hope of being adopted since he believed no one would be interested in adopting someone who was damaged. In middle school, Tim tried to form relationships with some of his classmates. However, he had difficulty approaching other kids his age, which made him feel awkward and foolish. Over time, Tim stopped trying to connect with others. Tim also tried to isolate himself from his high school classmates because he was afraid of being rejected or embarrassed. As a result, he rarely explored any of his interests during high school. By his junior year, Tim felt as if he was destined to be alone because no one had ever expressed any interest in getting to know him. When Tim finally graduated from high school, he felt depressed and hopeless about his future because he had no idea of who he was or where he belonged. Unlike his classmates who appeared excited about their future opportunities, Tim could only ruminate about what future failures he was destined to encounter and how suicide could be a means to end his misery and strife.

Tim's story is sad and tragic, but demonstrates the process in which a disconnection and rejection schema is developed and reinforced. Tim's basic needs of stability, nurturance, and acceptance were thwarted by numerous adverse conditions. The tragic loss of his parents, subsequent loss of friends, and the inability to connect with his foster parents converged in a way that promoted internalized and self-destructive attitudes that were consistent with a disconnection and rejection schema (Young et al., 2003). Whenever Tim encountered a stressful situation, his disconnection and rejection schema was activated and strengthened. By the age of 12, Tim had already defined himself by terms such as unlovable and useless. In addition, these schema-consistent attitudes deprived him of opportunities to develop psychological resources that are essential in overcoming the inherent conflicts within adolescence. Specifically, Tim had not cultivated a diverse set of coping strategies that could help him creatively find resolutions to his difficulties. Tim approached problems by either surrendering to them or actively avoiding them. His inability to generate a creative repertoire of coping strategies impinged upon his ability to solve complex and abstract challenges in later adolescence. Furthermore, Tim's desire to socially isolate himself from others was severely restricting opportunities to develop needed social skills. In the future, Tim may have difficulty creating and establishing social and intimate relationships that will foster a higher quality of life. Finally, Tim's reluctance to take risks and experiment with new ideas and interests was negatively affecting his identity development. As a result, Tim may have difficulties in identifying employment opportunities that will pique his interest and in making tough decisions about his life direction. Taken as a whole, the interactive effects between Tim's adverse life events and his outlook on life eliminated the coping resources necessary to prevent future self-harm behaviors.

Considering that an infinite number of maladaptive schemas can emerge from childhood adversity, it is important for researchers to identify those that are specific to the process of suicide. According to Abramson, Alloy, and Metalsky (1989), depressogenic vulnerabilities marked by three inferential styles (tendencies to attribute adverse conditions to stable and global causes, predict that negative consequences will inevitably follow from current negative events, and inferring the occurrence of negative life events as indications that one is defective, ineffective, and worthless) are hypothesized to contribute to the development of core hopelessness symptoms including suicide ideation and attempts.

Some of the inferential styles that precipitate hopelessness can be detected in Tim's process of suicidal ideation. For instance, based upon his previous life experiences and disposition toward the future, he does not appear to be optimistic about a change in fortune. On the contrary, Tim seems overly preoccupied by his negative expectations for the future, ruminating about failures that he was destined to encounter. Moreover, Tim attributed his inability to elicit praise and warmth from his foster parents as an indication that he is characteristically flawed—unlovable, useless, and damaged. These attributions ("I am unlovable, useless, and damaged") closely resemble themes found in many suicide notes. For Tim, these inferential styles work in concert to produce a sense of pessimism and helplessness, which influence his thought process of viewing suicide as a viable option.

In sum, childhood adversities may initiate a process whereby an individual may become suicidal. However, understanding the mechanisms through which childhood adversities exert their influence on adult suicidal behaviors is crucial. In the model presented, we examined aspects from Young and colleagues' Schema Theory and Abramson and colleagues' Hopelessness Theory of Suicide. To obtain a concise description of the integrated causal chain presented in this section, please see Figure 6.3.

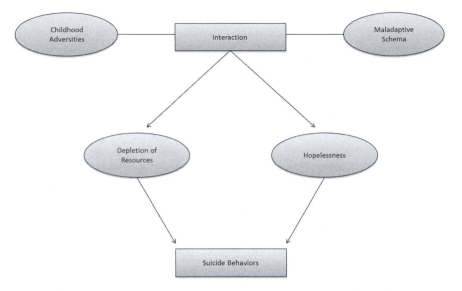

Figure 6.3.   Causal Chain Depicting the Interaction of Childhood Adversities and Thought Processes Contributing to Suicidal Behaviors

DAILY HASSLES AND SUICIDE

Unlike major life stressors, there is a dearth of research examining the relationship between daily hassles and suicidal behaviors. While the lack of a connecting theory is a problem, it is most likely attributable to difficulties in identifying distinct features between major life events and daily hassles. For instance, researchers have noted that individuals who encounter major life stressors are more vulnerable to experiencing a higher rate of daily hassles. Such findings suggest that major life events and daily hassles are part of the same process and distinguishing between them would provide few benefits for theory development. Alternatively, several researchers argue that daily hassles generate more explanatory power in associated emotional distress symptoms and problems behaviors compared to major life stressors (for a review, see Bolger, DeLongis, Kessler, & Schilling, 1989). Wherever the truth may lie, it is important that we consider the possibility that daily hassles may offer a unique perspective in explaining how a person may become suicidal.

During any given week, a person may expect to experience a handful of daily hassles concerning work, family roles, social relationships, and other personal responsibilities. Although each type of daily hassle has the potential to impinge upon an individual's well-being, research has indicated that nonfamily interpersonal conflicts contribute most to emotional and physical dysregulation. Nonfamily interpersonal conflicts may include frustrating or confrontational interactions with coworkers, neighbors, and friends. Why are nonfamily conflicts more detrimental to one's sense of well-being compared to other daily hassles? The answer is complex and still under investigation. However, the available research suggests that interpersonal conflicts may alter one's belongingness status, which in turn may negatively affect people's impression of their relational value within a work environment or social network. Moreover, frequent and repeated interpersonal conflicts may become detrimental to the functioning of the group as a whole. Overall, the proposed connection between interpersonal daily hassles and a sense of connectedness within a group is intriguing and fits well within Joiner's (2005) Interpersonal-Psychological Theory of Suicide (see Figure 6.4).

Think back to any dramatic or romantic movie you have watched recently and ask yourself how a happy and pleasant ending is portrayed. One of the more common features of a fulfilling ending includes the protagonist finding a sense of security, acceptance, and belongingness within a specific relationship or group. Moreover, if you were asked to think about a time in high school and write about an embarrassing or hurtful experience, you would most likely choose to write about a circumstance where you were rejected or alienated from a certain person, group, or event.

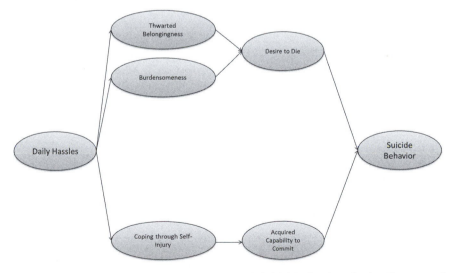

Figure 6.4. Daily Hassles Contributing to Suicidal Behaviors in the Context of Joiner's (2005) Interpersonal-Psychological Theory of Suicide

Hopefully, by participating in these mental exercises you are able to understand the value of belongingness and how it influences one's sense of personal meaning and well-being.

In terms of psychological needs, the desire to belong to a valued group is among the most powerful. As humans, we strive for life meaning through our connections with others (Baumeister & Leary, 1995). As a result, a stable sense of belongingness often provides us with a diverse range of effective "tools" that we can use to cope with stress, conflict, and inner turmoil. Belongingness also instills a sense of hope for the future, generates positive appraisals regarding one's self-concept, and fosters a better understanding of our personal identity, all of which are key ingredients to increasing our overall quality of life. Conversely, when belongingness is thwarted, individuals are at a greater risk of experiencing declines in their overall self-worth, work performance, and ability to regulate their emotions. In severe cases, those who perceive themselves as having low levels of belongingness may feel rejected and begin to question the meaningfulness of their life to a point in which they may consider suicide. Overall, it seems that the interaction between interpersonal conflicts and one's sense of belongingness is important in understanding one's desire to die.

Similarly, a wider range of daily hassles can negatively influence one's sense of purpose. Much like belongingness, purposiveness is another psychological need that is associated with life satisfaction. To better understand the relationship between purposiveness and happiness, think about how one obtains the "good life." More than likely, you entertained thoughts of winning the lottery or finding the formula to build a time machine. However, if you were to identify and interview someone who was content with their life, you might discover that their path to happiness is directly related to their willingness and desire to invest themselves in activities that promote the betterment of a specific group or community (Seligman, 2002). For these individuals, proactively pursuing goals that potentially enhance the quality of the group experience for all members instills a dynamic sense of purpose that underlies life fulfillment.

In contrast, consider a life where a sense of purposiveness cannot be developed adequately due to barriers and obstacles that are outside of an individual's control. Although the images you envision may appear troubling and uncomfortable, many people navigate through these situations in their daily lives. For example, trying to find a stable job with a decent salary to support one's family is becoming a difficult and stressful endeavor in today's economy. An individual who was just recently laid off will need to enter a limited marketplace and may apply for a wide range of job openings with little consideration of relevant interests and experiences. This process is likely wrought with daily hassles, some of which include filling out applications, waiting for call backs, findings ways to reduce the family's spending, and managing ambiguity regarding one's future prospects as an employee. The culminating effects of the daily hassles associated with job loss and recovery may lead to a sense of self-hate and perceived ineffectiveness concerning one's ability to meet family needs. If these hassles persist, one may view the situation as permanent and un-changeable. This negative attributional style may exacerbate feelings of self-hate and perceived ineffectiveness, ultimately culminating in a state of burdensomeness whereby an individual may feel that he or she is a drain on the family's resources. This sentiment is often conveyed in suicide notes. Individuals considering suicide often report that they are conflicted about the value of their life in regard to the overall functioning of their social support network (e.g., family, friends, etc.). For some individuals who die by suicide, the desire to take their own life is the product of their perception that they are a burden to their loved ones.

In combination, it appears that daily hassles can influence one's desire for death through interpersonal constructs such as thwarted belongingness and perceived burdensomeness. However, a significant number of individuals who desire death are incapable of going through with the act of killing themselves. This is, in large part, due to the human body's de-fense system, where our most basic instinct, self-preservation, disrupts our ability to inflict serious harm upon ourselves. Unfortunately, some irregular and self-destructive behaviors can help individuals work up to the act of suicide by diminishing the response system associated with self-preservation. Most notably, repeated practice of self-injurious behavior (e.g., cutting, body carving, and burning) are conceptualized as habitu-ation experiences that increase one's tolerance and sense of fearlessness toward pain and provocation. Although the intent of self-injury may not be related to a desire to kill oneself, inevitably the injurious acts temper one's response to threatening and pain-inducing behaviors, creating the acquired capability to enact lethal self-injury (Joiner, 2005). Given that the motiva-tions often underlying self-injurious behaviors are to alleviate emotional distress, understanding how one copes with persistent daily hassles is im-portant when assessing one's capability to kill himself or herself.

The purpose behind initiating coping processes is to permanently al-leviate a threatening conflict or hassle, while concurrently helping an in-dividual reestablish a healthy sense of well-being. However, based on the time, intensity, and conditions in which daily hassles are experienced, some coping strategies may impede or exacerbate rather than promote positive health behaviors. For instance, daily hassles can contribute to feelings of emotional distress and a lack of control over one's environment. For some individuals, daily hassles can be described as a constant source of intense and uncomfortable emotional pain. Individuals who are in desperate need of relief may turn to self-injury as a means to cope. Those who self-injure often report that cutting and other forms of direct self-harm have a distracting, pain-relieving quality that allows them to take back control over their lives (Walsh, 2006). However, engaging in self-injury as a coping response is dangerous since self-injurers seemingly become overly reliant on using self-harm behaviors to find relief from daily hassles. Research has indicated that those who self-injure do so at a high rate, approximately 20–100 times per year. Clearly, self-injuring at such high rates can have adverse effects on an individual's physical and emotional functioning. Moreover, self-injuring incidents are likely to deplete one's self-preservation instincts, placing individuals at an increased risk for suicide, particularly when their sense of belongingness, purposiveness, and effectiveness becomes threatened.

To summarize, daily hassles may influence one's desire to die and capability to commit suicide. In particular, daily hassles, in the form of interpersonal conflicts, may perpetuate instabilities in one's sense of belongingness and effectiveness to the point where individuals may perceive suicide as a viable means of ending their own suffering as well as the suffering they believe that they inflict on others. Further, in response to daily stressors, distressed individuals may turn to self-harm behaviors to recover a sense of control and stability over their environment. Consequently, such behaviors cause individuals to habituate to high levels of pain, which in turn make them susceptible to more lethal and life-threatening forms of self-harm. If these two processes work in concert, an individual is at a greater risk of dying by suicide. Finally, it is important to emphasize that the theoretical and scientific literature suggesting a unique relationship between daily hassles and suicide is limited. However, based on Joiner's work regarding the interpersonal and physiological components of suicide, it may be important for future researchers to examine the influence of specific daily hassles on the desire to die and the capability to enact lethal self-injury.

EXPLORING THE RELATIONSHIP BETWEEN STRESS AND SUICIDE IN CLINICAL WORK

From a clinical standpoint, examining individuals' experiences with stress provides opportunities to determine what types of vulnerabilities are contributing to their suicidal thoughts and behaviors. Recall that most vulnerability factors are latent, meaning that they are not easily observed through one's normal self-presentation. In fact, most suicidologists believe that vulnerability factors to suicide lie dormant, residing outside of one's conscious awareness. Activation of an individual's vulnerability to suicide is dependent upon their experience of stress whether through major life events or through the accumulation of several daily hassles (Wenzel et al., 2009). As a result, vulnerabilities to suicide may be detected by a thorough inspection of subjective experience with a stressful life event. Below is a case illustration depicting an interaction between John and his therapist. Within the vignette, John and his therapist process John's suicidal ideation and his most recent encounter with life stress. By just asking a few questions about John's stressful experience, the therapist is able to obtain rich information pertaining to the mechanisms that may be provoking his suicidal thoughts.

Therapist: John, earlier you indicated that you recently thought about killing yourself. Can you talk a little more about that?

John: I don't know. I just felt like my life was not worth living anymore. Thoughts like that seemed to just come on quickly. I am not really sure where they came from.

Therapist: I see. I want you to think back to the last time you had thoughts such as the one you described. What was going on in your life?

John: Well, the last time I remember thinking that my life was not worth living was around the time I got fired from my job and had to tell my family we needed to move. That was an extremely stressful time for me.

Therapist: It seems like those experiences really took a toll on you emotionally?

John: Yes!

Therapist: I see. Given the difficulty associated with those stressful events, what were some emotions or thoughts running through your head?

John: Well, initially I was mad and confused because I really did not think I deserved to be fired. However, after a few moments I felt really sad, like I failed my family or something. In fact, I really could not shake those feelings of failure. It is like I felt broken, like I could not function in even the most basic ways. I remember thinking that I would never be able to get another job because everyone would see me as damaged goods, especially my family. It was hard for me even to look at them after I got fired. I felt so ashamed. I still feel ashamed of myself even today. It is something that I just cannot shake.

Of note, this excerpt highlights the ambiguity that often accompany their understanding of how they became suicidal. Although individuals who present with suicidal thoughts often can extrapolate on their motivations (e.g., to escape emotional pain) for wanting to end their life, they often have a difficult time understanding the stressful life events, emotions, and thoughts that perpetuate their desire. By helping individuals deconstruct their emotional and cognitive responses to a stressful situation, clinicians may be able to help identify and examine specific vulnerabilities that contribute to the development of suicidal thoughts and behaviors. Interestingly, insight into one's own process of suicide can often be therapeutic in itself as it may promote higher levels of awareness and control over one's emotional and cognitive responses to stress.

Overall, viewing stressful life events and vulnerabilities as distinct constructs may limit our ability to understand why individuals kill themselves. Conversely, understanding vulnerabilities through the context of stressful life events may contribute to more accurate conceptualizations of suicide, which are integral in helping individuals obtain insight into their suicide process as well as selecting and implementing psychological interventions targeted toward their identified vulnerabilities.

SUMMARY AND FUTURE DIRECTIONS

In this chapter, we have reviewed the contribution that adverse life events and daily hassles play in the development and persistence of suicidal behavior. Although specific research studies were not described in detail, there is a consensus among suicidologists, researchers, and mental health professionals that encountering negative life events and daily hassles may place individuals at an increased risk of having thoughts about suicide and engaging in suicidal behaviors. As discussed, negative life events may act as distal (e.g., childhood abuse) or proximal (e.g., interpersonal disruptions) risk factors, both of which frequently precede a suicidal act. Moreover, daily life hassles (e.g., dissatisfaction with work), while often less severe, also confer a heightened risk for suicide. There is a wealth of literature suggesting that the way in which individuals appraise situations and events can affect levels of stress, depression, and suicide risk. There are several theories and models that attempt to explain the causal chain of events from experiencing stressful life events to considering suicide and ultimately engaging in a suicidal or life-threatening behavior. The majority of these theoretical frameworks are in agreement that the events that cause stress in peoples' lives are mediated by a host of maladaptive cognitions and appraisals, in turn promoting risk for suicide. Although the environment can create stress, not all individuals respond identically to this stress. Thus, it will be important for suicidologists in the future to investigate specific life events in prospective developmental studies from early childhood experiences to subsequent adulthood encounters while considering self-appraisals, coping strategies, and attributional styles. Conducting such research may aid in the identification of mechanisms that underlie the complex association among adverse life events and suicidal behavior. The current state of the literature provides a solid framework to expand upon, which may guide basic research and inform applied work to reduce suicidal behaviors in individuals experiencing stress due to negative life events and daily hassles.

Mental health professionals and prevention specialists could use the models described in this chapter to effectively identify and treat individuals who may be at risk for suicide. Accordingly, individuals who report experiencing several life stressors may need to be assessed for suicidal behaviors on a regular basis or referred to treatment. In addition to assessment, treatment strategies should be tailored to address the *nature* of the relationship between adverse life events and suicide risk for individuals who present with stress-related issues and suicidal behavior. This relation can be examined both directly and indirectly by assessing individuals for the specific stressors found to contribute to suicide risk using techniques such as functional analysis (Haynes, Leisen, & Blaine, 1997) or behavior chain analysis (Linehan, 1993). These highly individualized treatment strategies involve the generation of individualized models of the etiology and maintenance of stress, coping strategies, and suicide-related behaviors. Typically, functional analysis involves the examination of chronic processes, whereas behavior chain analysis focuses on acute behaviors. In terms of the latter, a clinician would conduct a behavior chain analysis on a specific instance of targeted behaviors (e.g., interpersonal loss on February 4, 2012), rather than the targeted behavior in general (e.g., interpersonal loss and suicidal behavior as an accumulated process). The effectiveness of a chosen treatment strategy for a particular client likely depends on the nature of the adverse life event–suicidal behavior association. Moreover, preventive intervention programs that target identified stressful events as well as the moderators and mediators underlying suicidal behavior should be designed and implemented specifically for individuals who have experienced life stressors in their past (e.g., childhood abuse) or in the present (e.g., divorce). In terms of clinical care and treatment, mental health professionals should directly address the specific risk factors which are generating high levels of stress incorporated in the models of suicidal behavior described in this chapter. It is our hope that by providing a better understanding of the association between adverse life events, daily hassles, and suicidal behaviors, more effective prevention efforts may be developed.

NOTES

1. About 30 percent to 40 percent of suicides leave a note.
2. Psychological resources that are established and stabilized during a child or adolescent's development may also affect the growth of maladaptive schemas. However, for the purposes of this chapter we will emphasize the role of *adverse life events*.

REFERENCES

Abramson, L. Y., Metalsky, G. I., & Alloy, L. B. (1989). Hopelessness depression: A theory-based subtype of depression. *Psychological Review, 96,* 358–372.

Baumeister, R. F. (1990). Suicide as escape from self. *Psychological Review, 97,* 90–113.

Baumeister, R. F., & Leary, M. R. (1995). The need to belong: Desire for interpersonal attachments as a fundamental human motivation. *Psychological Bulletin, 117,* 497–529.

Beck, A. T. (1967). *Depression: Causes and treatment.* Philadelphia: University of Pennsylvania Press.

Bolger, N., DeLongis, A., Kessler, R. C., & Schilling, E. A. (1989). Effects of daily stress on negative mood. *Journal of Personality & Social Psychology, 57,* 808–818.

Cavanagh, J. O., Carson, A. J., Sharpe, M. M., & Lawrie, S. M. (2003). Psychological autopsy studies of suicide: A systematic review. *Psychological Medicine, 33,* 395–405.

Cooper, C. L., & Dewe, P. (2004). *Stress: A brief history.* Malden, MA: Blackwell.

Haynes, S. N., Leisen, M. B., & Blaine, D. D. (1997). Design of individualized behavioral treatment programs using functional analytic clinical case models. *Psychological Assessment, 9,* 334–348.

Heikkinen, M. E., Aro, H. M., & Lönnqvist, J. K. (1994). Recent life events, social support and suicide. *Acta Psychiatrica Scandinavica, 89,* 65–72.

Ingram, R. E., & Luxton, D. D. (2005). Vulnerability-stress models. In B. L. Hankin & J. Z. Abela (Eds.), *Development of psychopathology: A vulnerability-stress perspective,* pp. 32–46. Thousand Oaks, CA: Sage Publications.

Ingram, R. E., Miranda, J., & Segal, Z. V. (1998). *Cognitive vulnerability to depression.* New York: Guilford.

Joiner, T. E., Jr. (2005). *Why people die by suicide.* Cambridge, MA: Harvard University Press.

Linehan, M. M. (1993). *Cognitive-behavioral treatment of borderline personality disorder.* New York: Guilford.

Martin, P., & Martin, M. (2002). Proximal and distal influences on development: The model of developmental adaptation. *Developmental Review, 22,* 78–96.

Monroe, S. M., & Hadjiyannakis, K. (2002). The social environment and depression: Focusing on severe life stress. In I. H. Gotlib & C. L. Hammen (Eds.), *Handbook of depression,* pp. 314–340. New York: Guilford.

Seligman, M. E. P. (2002). *Authentic happiness.* New York: Free Press.

Van Praag, H. M. (2004). Stress and suicide are we well-equipped to study this issue? *Crisis, 25,* 80–85.

Walsh, B. W. (2006). *Treating self-injury: A practical guide.* New York: Guilford.

Wenzel, A., Brown, G. K., & Beck, A. T. (2009). *Cognitive therapy for suicidal patients: Scientific and clinical applications.* Washington, DC: American Psychological Association.

Wheaton, B., & Gotlib, I. (1997). Trajectories and turning points over the life course: Concepts and themes. In I. Gotlib & B. Wheaton (Eds.), *Stress and adversity over the life course: Trajectories and turning points.* New York: Cambridge University Press.

World Health Organization (2004). Deaths by cause, in WHO Regions, estimates for 2004. Retrieved December 29, 2011, from http://apps.who.int/ghodata/?vid=10012

Young, J. E., Klosko, J. S., & Weishaar, M. E. (2003). *Schema therapy: A practitioner's guide.* New York: Guilford.

7

The Role of Psychiatric Disorder

Lars Mehlum

A mong all known risk factors for suicide, mental illness represents the strongest and most consistent. A diagnosable psychiatric disorder is present in at least 90 percent of suicides (Cavanagh, Carson, Sharpe, & Lawrie, 2003), although this proportion may vary somewhat across geographical regions, cultures, and population subgroups. Data from Danish registers have demonstrated that the population attributable risk (PAR) for suicide, the proportion of suicides in the population that could be removed if the risk factor could be removed, associated with lifetime psychiatric hospitalization, is about 40 percent (Qin, Agerbo, & Mortensen, 2003). Although the majority of suicides are generally not in psychiatric treatment at the time of their death, a large proportion of individuals in the general population who die by suicide have had inpatient psychiatric care in the year before their death. The strong association between suicide and psychiatric disorders makes effective psychiatric treatment and care central components of suicide prevention. According to estimates from the World Health Organization (Bertolote, Fleischmann, De Leo, & Wasserman, 2003), as many as 165,000 lives could possibly be saved worldwide annually if adequate psychiatric treatment for major psychiatric disorders were provided. Knowledge about what psychiatric disorders carry the highest risk and about the specific risk profiles of different psychiatric disorders is, however, important as a basis for developing and implementing targeted and systematic preventive measures. The scope of this chapter is to provide a review of suicide risk factors associated with specific psychiatric disorders. Only major diagnostic groups and high-risk potentials will be addressed in this chapter. Although many treatment-relevant aspects of psychiatric disorders and suicide risk will be mentioned, a systematic presentation of treatments or prevention falls outside the scope of this chapter.

DEPRESSIVE DISORDERS

Case Example

Alec was a 55-year-old male admitted to the emergency medical department after having been found in a comatose condition by his landlord. Alec was divorced and lived alone, and he had very few social contacts. In the past he had been repeatedly admitted to psychiatric hospital because of major depressive episodes. His depressive symptoms had returned two weeks earlier, and almost immediately he had developed strong suicidal thoughts. Finally, he ingested all the pills he had available and went to bed after having written a letter of farewell to his younger brother. Waking up at the medical ward, he seemed very depressed, but also angry because he did not die. He appeared shut off, and the doctors were unable to establish any therapeutic alliance with him.

Depressive disorders are among the most prevalent of any disorder, somatic or psychiatric, although prevalence figures vary depending on population characteristics and on how depression is defined and assessed. Adopting DSM-IV or ICD-10 criteria, however, at any given point in time, about 5 percent of the adult general population will have a diagnosable major depression, whereas the lifetime prevalence has been found to be about 15 percent. Recurrent thoughts of death, recurrent suicidal ideation, a suicide plan, or a suicide attempt are diagnostic criteria for major depressive disorder, and among individuals with this disorder the life time risk of suicide has been found to be 6 percent (Inskip, Harris, & Barraclough, 1998). The risk is, however, strongly increased in patients with additional psychiatric disorders, such as substance abuse, borderline personality disorder, or posttraumatic stress disorder (PTSD). The risk is also increased in the subgroup of patients who have more intense depressive symptoms, psychotic symptoms, melancholia, more sleep disturbance, weight loss, stronger feelings of worthlessness or guilt feelings, and stronger suicidal ideation. Within the large population of people who have been depressed, suicide risk is also strongly increased among those who have been in psychiatric treatment, have received psychopharmacological treatment, or have been psychiatrically hospitalized, all of which are factors usually indicating that the patients have a more severe depressive disorder. Depression is strongly associated with suicide risk in all age groups in the population. Among elderly people, however, depression is a particularly important, but often not detected, risk factor. Although depressive disorders are more prevalent in the elderly, they are often not diagnosed because symptoms may be confused with dementia or even normal signs of aging. The elderly also have more additional somatic and psychiatric disorders which may complicate the diagnostic evaluation.

Of all psychiatric disorders, depression is probably the most closely linked to suicide. About half of suicides have had depression according to several estimates. For serious but nonfatal suicidal behavior, the PAR for depression is as high as 80 percent (Beautrais et al., 1996). The association becomes apparent also when considering the nature of the disorder. Depressed mood or loss of interest or pleasure (anhedonia) leading to significant impairment of at least two weeks' duration is a core aspect of an episode of major depression. In addition to this, depressive individuals generally have repetitive, unintended, and not readily controllable negative thinking about themselves, the world, and the future. Such negative thinking seems to be closely linked to excessive feelings of guilt, helplessness, and hopelessness. The latter has been found to be a particularly strong predictor of suicidal behavior. Finally, depressive individuals frequently experience information processing distortions or biases which make their attention, perception, and memory more selective. This may further strengthen negative thinking and hopelessness and give rise to a sense of entrapment.

Depressive disorders often follow a relapsing and life-long course. Approximately 60 percent of individuals who have had an episode of major depression will eventually have a second one, and the risk of future episodes increases for every new episode, mounting to an average number of 4, each of approximately 20 weeks duration (Judd, 1997). In many cases the diagnosis of depression is, however, made several years after the first episode, and treatment is, therefore, substantially delayed. Screening procedures and programs to identify individuals with depressive disorders is an important suicide prevention strategy as are initiatives to enhance healthcare providers' competence in the early detection and treatment of depression. Adequate management of depression, which could include both psychotherapeutic and pharmacological intervention, must deal with both acute episodes and relapse prevention and also address the many possible comorbid or concomitant problems predisposing for depression and suicidal behavior.

Case Example, Continued

Based on an assessment of the medical lethality of Alec's suicide attempt and his expressed suicidal intent, the doctors considered the risk of further suicidal behavior to be strong. To save his life, Alec was therefore involuntarily admitted to the hospital's psychiatric inpatient unit. Suicide risk was immediately reevaluated upon Alec's arrival at the psychiatric unit and continuous observation was instigated. Alec was medicated with a selective serotonin reuptake inhibitor (SSRI) and, as his depressive symptoms started to recede, he was also engaged in a physical training program and received supportive psychotherapy. His doctor helped Alec contact his brother who was happy to help him start solving some of his problems of daily life functioning.

BIPOLAR DISORDER

Case Example

Judy, a 23-year-old female college student who had had two previous episodes of major depression as a teenager was brought by the police to the psychiatric emergency unit after having been arrested for reckless driving. Her behavior had changed dramatically over the last few days. She had stayed up all night, had been much more energetic, talkative, aggressive, and sexually active than usual, and she had spent a lot more money than she could afford. She was very angry and upset over being brought to the hospital and refused to receive any treatment or medication.

Bipolar disorder is associated with strong shifts in mood, energy, cognitions, and behavior—from mania at one extreme, to depression at the other. Bipolar disorder has a lower prevalence than major depression, but the risk of suicide associated with this disorder is equally high or even higher (Inskip et al., 1998), although risk estimates vary widely depending on what samples or populations have been studied. Previous suicide attempts, hopelessness, a family history of suicide, early illness onset, frequent illness relapse, rapid mood cycles, and substance abuse are all factors leading to an increased risk of suicide in patients with bipolar disorder (Hawton, Sutton, Haw, Sinclair, & Harriss, 2005). Some of the traditional risk factors for suicide, such as male gender, unemployment, marital status, and early losses have, however, not been found in individuals with bipolar disorder.

Bipolar disorder is typically episodic. Individuals with both depressive and manic episodes (Bipolar I) and individuals with depressive and hypomanic episodes, but no full-blown manic episodes (Bipolar II) seem to have equally high suicide risk (Hawton et al., 2005). The presence of mixed emotional states (both depressive and manic symptoms present simultaneously) is, however, associated with a particularly high risk. Suicide in individuals with bipolar disorder typically occurs within the first years after illness onset, often in a depressive phase or in connection with psychiatric hospitalization and after discharge (Qin & Nordentoft, 2005).

A large proportion of bipolar patients who have ended their lives through suicide have been in psychiatric treatment, but they have often received inadequate treatment or they have been noncompliant with the treatment. In view of the chronic relapsing nature of bipolar disorder, clinicians should provide long-term mood stabilizing medication, psychoeducation and supportive psychotherapy, and help patients make necessary lifestyle adjustments to reduce risk factors. Lithium prophylaxis has been shown to be effective in the prevention of suicide and suicide attempts in patients with mood disorders (Cipriani, Pretty, Hawton, & Geddes, 2005).

Case Example, Continued

Judy's condition was diagnosed as bipolar disorder type I and, despite the fact that she strongly refused, she was treated in a closed psychiatric ward where she received medication. After a few days her manic symptom had disappeared, and she could be transferred to an open ward. Judy was, however, very unhappy when learning and thinking about her manic behavior and soon developed strong depressive symptoms as well as feelings of hopelessness and suicidal ideation. Recognizing that Judy might be at risk of suicide, her psychiatrist provided supportive psychotherapy and arranged for Judy to be followed up in a specialized treatment program after discharge for patients with bipolar disorder.

SCHIZOPHRENIA

Case Example

Scott, a 28-year-old engineer who still lived in his parental home, developed strong paranoid symptoms and auditory hallucinations after some minor conflict at his work place. He felt that his boss and the colleagues were plotting to have him killed and, therefore, stayed home and in bed. His mother tried to make him see a doctor for these problems, but he refused. His condition deteriorated within a few days to the extent he had to be involuntarily admitted to a psychiatric hospital where he was treated for six months. On medication many of Scott's psychotic symptoms gradually diminished, but they were replaced by depressive feelings and a strong sense of hopelessness. Two weeks after he was discharged from hospital, Scott was found dead from suicide in his home.

The lifetime risk of suicide in individuals with schizophrenia has been reported to be 5 percent–6 percent (Inskip et al., 1998). The risk may, however, have increased over the past two to three decades; a systematic literature review by Saha, Chant, and McGrath (2007) indicated that individuals with schizophrenia now have a suicide risk 12 times greater than expected from the general population. Between 25 percent and 50 percent of patients with schizophrenia have made one or more suicide attempts. The suicide risk is highest in young people and in the first years after illness onset, in particular in those who had a high premorbid level of functioning and where the illness led to a marked drop in the level of functioning. Suicide risk is highest in the active phases of the disorder and related to hospitalization or after discharge from hospital. A history of suicide attempts and suicidal ideation, agitation and restlessness, fear of mental disintegration, recent interpersonal loss experiences, poor treatment compliance, and a high number of hospitalizations are other known risk factors (Hawton, Sutton, Haw, Sinclair, & Deeks, 2005). Compared with suicide attempters in the general population, suicide attempters with schizophrenia on average have stronger suicide intent, make more attempts, and use more lethal methods.

Comorbidity with depressive disorder and substance use disorders (SUDs) are probably the strongest of all known risk factors for suicide in individuals with schizophrenia. Both previous and current depressive episodes, depressive illness in family members, and depression-related features, such as hopelessness and low self-esteem, are associated with an increased risk (Hawton et al., 2005). Despite this, depression has often been ignored or left untreated in patients with schizophrenia (Pompili et al., 2007). This may be a result of difficulties in distinguishing depression from negative symptoms or the side effects of medication. SUDs are highly prevalent among patients with schizophrenia, and both substance abuse and dependence increases suicide risk substantially. In contrast to the general population, this substance use-related risk is associated only with nonalcoholic substances (Hawton et al., 2005).

Among the major psychiatric disorders, schizophrenia seems to be the only one in which higher illness awareness and insight seems to be a risk factor for suicide. It is, however, important to note that insight seems to increase the risk of suicide only when it leads to increased hopelessness (Kim, Jayathilake, & Meltzer, 2002). Research is inconsistent as to how psychotic symptoms may influence suicide risk. Whereas the presence of command hallucinations (where voices encourage the patient to commit suicide) is generally regarded as a clear risk factor (Harkavy-Friedman et al., 2003), delusions seem to reduce the risk. Most psychotic symptoms, however, are not predictive of suicidal behavior. It is rather the strong psychosocial consequences of the incapacitating recurrent positive and negative psychotic symptoms that seem to mediate the major part of the risk. Also, side effects and other negative experiences with the treatment (medication, involuntary admissions, change of therapists, etc.) should be taken into consideration when assessing suicide risk in patients with schizophrenia and planning the treatment. The treatment needs to be planned for the long term and involve key resources such as the psychiatrist, the family doctor, social services, and housing. Patients should receive long-term tailor-made pharmacological treatment for which there is some evidence of effectiveness for preventing suicide (Meltzer et al., 2003). Depressive symptoms and substance abuse should not be overlooked. Also, psychosocial support addressing the many negative secondary effects of the illness is needed, as is sometimes hospitalization to provide increased protection and support.

Inherent in the negative symptoms of schizophrenia is the reduced capacity for feeling joy. Many patients with schizophrenia have not felt good or happy for a very long time and seem to have lost this capacity entirely. Progress has, however, been made in developing treatments to target this problem and help patients recognize and express affects and to alter defeatist beliefs, in order to break the vicious circle leading to more withdrawal and negative behavioral symptoms (Grant, Huh, Perivoliotis, Stolar, & Beck, 2011). Programs for the early detection of psychosis have been shown to reduce the duration of untreated psychosis, which is particularly important for addressing the problem of increased risk in young people with schizophrenia. There are some indications that this may prevent suicidal behavior early in the course of the illness (Melle et al., 2006).

PERSONALITY DISORDERS

Case Example

Grace, a 32-year-old single assistant nurse, was referred to the emergency room after having ingested an unknown number of sleeping pills. She displayed symptoms of depression with suicidal ideation and anxiety and wished to be hospitalized. This was Grace's fourth presentation to the hospital within the last year. Apparently Grace had not been able to comply with the follow-up psychiatric treatment she had been offered after the previous self-harm episodes. This time, after standard overdose treatments had been given, the psychiatrist, who was called, referred Grace to an outpatient program for patients with borderline personality disorder and repetitive suicidal crises, after which her emergency room presentations ceased.

Suicidal behavior is a well-known challenge to many clinicians treating patients with personality disorders. The risk of completed suicide, which is comparable to the risk in major affective disorder, is, however, often underestimated because it may be masked by the presence of one or more of a range of low lethality self-destructive behaviors. In a very large population-based Danish psychiatric case register study of unnatural causes of death over a 20-year period, personality disorders constituted the second most frequent diagnostic category associated with suicide (after affective psychoses) (Hiroeh, Appleby, Mortensen, & Dunn, 2001). Among different categories of personality disorder, borderline personality disorder (BPD) has a particularly high suicide rate (Cheng, Chen, Chen, & Jenkins, 2000), although antisocial, avoidant, and dependent types have also been shown to be independent risk factors for suicide. Sixty to seventy percent of people with BPD attempt suicide at some point in their life (Oldham, 2006).

People with borderline personality disorder constitute a heterogeneous group with regard to symptoms and behaviors. Self-destructive behaviors, a diagnostic criterion of this syndrome, is, however, present in the majority of borderline patients. There is a whole range of such behaviors including self-mutilation, risk-taking behaviors, eating problems, substance abuse, suicide attempts, and completed suicide. It is important to realize that suicidal behavior, at least in the form of suicidal ideation, in borderline patients tends to be linked more to personality traits and less to depressive states. It is present, to some extent, much of the time (Mehlum, Friis, Vaglum, & Karterud, 1994). This does not imply that borderline patients are at equally high risk of suicidal behavior most of the time.

Affective instability, impulsivity and a pronounced sensitivity to environmental stressors are additional characteristics of the borderline syndrome closely linked to suicidal and self-harming behavior. Individuals with borderline personality disorder frequently have additional psychiatric disorders, notably major depression, anxiety disorders, substance abuse, and PTSD, all of which may add to the suicide risk. In borderline patients, completed suicide is often seen relatively late in the course of the illness, frequently after several failed treatment attempts.

Many patients with borderline personality disorder are offered only short-term generic or crisis-oriented treatments, but such approaches to the treatment have the potential to create self-confirming vicious circles, reinforcing dysfunctional behaviors at the cost of the patients' prognosis with regard to suicidal behaviors. Suicidal threats and suicidal behavior in borderline patients are frequently experienced as extremely stressful to their healthcare providers and may provoke anger, anxiety, and burnout in therapists. Irrational decisions, ill-advised hospitalizations, ineffective practice, and treatment failure may then easily result. A number of specialized long-term psychotherapeutic interventions have, however, been developed for patients with borderline personality disorder and several of them have been shown to be efficacious in reducing suicidal and self-harm behaviors (National Institute for Health and Clinical Excellence, 2009).

ANXIETY DISORDERS

Anxiety disorders are extremely common with a one-year prevalence estimated between 15 percent and 25 percent. These disorders are, however, very frequently seen in combination with other psychiatric disorders and, with the exception of PTSD discussed separately below, the risk of suicide attributable to the different diagnoses has been difficult to disentangle. A few studies have indicated that anxiety disorders may be an independent risk factor for suicidal ideation and suicide attempts (Sareen et al., 2005), whereas the evidence for such risk in relation to completed suicide is weaker (McGirr et al., 2006). According to clinical experience, anxiety symptoms and disorders may, however, make life problems and other psychiatric disorders seem unbearable and thus create an action urge toward suicidal behavior, as we have indicated above. There is, therefore, clearly a need for clinicians to take anxiety symptoms into consideration when conducting suicide risk evaluations.

POSTTRAUMATIC STRESS DISORDER

Case Example

Gary, a 24-year-old previously healthy man, was brought to the family doctor by his fiancée who was worried because of his lately escalating depressive symptoms and heavy drinking. The doctor learned that Gary was an army sergeant who had returned from military service in Iraq three months ago. Since then he had increasing problems with readjusting to his job and social life in his home town. He was irritable and restless, had concentration problems, nightmares and sleeplessness, and occasional strong panic anxiety attacks. He told his doctor that he could not stand all of the thoughts and images that "keeps rushing through my head" and that he recently had started thinking that it would be best to put an end to it all by killing himself. He had, however, not made any clear decision or plan for suicide. After a closer assessment, the doctor found that the immediate suicide risk was moderate, but that Gary needed specialized treatment for what was likely a combat-related PTSD. Arrangements were, therefore, made for him to be admitted to an outpatient veterans' psychiatric treatment program.

PTSD, with a lifetime prevalence of around 8 percent, in contrast to other anxiety disorders, has a clear association with both fatal and non-fatal suicidal behavior (Mehlum, 2005). Substantial evidence stems from studies of various groups exposed to traumatic stress. Many studies have shown that childhood adversities, such as childhood physical and sexual abuse, increase the risk of both adolescent and adult self-harm and suicidal behaviors both in community samples (Molnar, Berkman, & Buka, 2001), and in clinical settings (Ystgaard, Hestetun, Loeb, & Mehlum, 2004). Since the prevalence of childhood sexual abuse is high—according to the U.S. National Comorbidity Survey the exposure prevalence is 2.5 percent among men and 13.5 percent among women—it is not surprising that the PAR for child sexual abuse has been estimated to be up to 20 percent for attempted suicide (Molnar et al., 2001). The risk of attempted suicide on the basis of adverse childhood experiences seems to be elevated throughout the lifespan, and the risk of repeated suicidal behavior has been particularly well documented in individuals having been exposed to childhood *sexual* abuse (Ystgaard et al., 2004).

Sadly, there seems to be endless ways individuals may become exposed to trauma. Hence the research literature on the association between traumatic stress exposure and suicidal behavior is rich. Studies have demonstrated an association between trauma such as violence, rape, war, torture, and disasters and subsequent suicidal behavior. The risk of suicidal behavior related to traumatic stress exposure has been especially well documented in military personnel, and this risk seems to persist many years after the service experience (Thoresen, Mehlum, & Moller, 2003). Several important studies on this have been carried out in the American Vietnam veteran population, where a significantly increased risk of both fatal and nonfatal suicidal behavior has been found (Bullman & Kang, 1994).

Whether a diagnosis of PTSD functions as a mediating variable between traumatic exposures and suicidal behavior has been studied in several contexts, for example in Vietnam veterans, where soldiers who had a diagnosis of PTSD (Bullman & Kang, 1994) or had been wounded had a significantly higher suicide risk. PTSD has also been found to mediate the association between traumatic exposure and depression and nonfatal suicidal behavior in inner city youth (Mazza & Reynolds, 1999). The combination of PTSD and major depression, which is common, seems to accentuate the risk of suicide.

Trauma histories are frequently not recognized in patients presenting with suicidal behaviors, and suicide risk is often overlooked in traumatized patients. Although the population of traumatized patients is heterogeneous, there is a general need to integrate suicide risk assessments in the clinical evaluation and treatment planning for all these patients. In cases where the suicide risk is considered moderate to high, the first and most important focus should be put on patient safety and treatment interventions to reduce this risk. Patients who have been stabilized through appropriate first measures may then receive one or more of psychotherapeutic and pharmacological treatments for which there is evidence of effectiveness in individuals with PTSD. For an overview, see Foa, Keane, Friedman, and Cohen (2008).

SUBSTANCE USE DISORDERS

Case Example

Claudia, a 50-year-old widow, sought her doctor because of strong depressive symptoms, memory impairment, and problems of concentrating that was making it very difficult for her to function in her work as a librarian. It turned out that ever since she first lost her husband three years ago, and then her only son one year later, she had been in grief and unrelenting distress. She managed to control her depressive symptoms and her strong suicidal impulses and function at work only by using increasing amounts of alcohol and pills. Recently, she had blackouts and intermittently felt confused and disoriented. Her doctor suspected that Claudia was suffering from complicated grief and also severe mixed SUD. A careful assessment of the acute suicide risk indicated that there was not a need for emergency hospitalization, but that Claudia should receive rapid treatment for both her complicated grief and her SUD.

The lifetime prevalence of abuse or dependence of psychoactive substances (the so-called substance use disorders [SUD]) has been estimated at about 15 percent, of which alcohol accounts for the major part in most contexts. There are, however, large variations across populations according to age, gender, geographical regions, and culture in the prevalence of SUD and in which substances are involved. Despite these variations, SUD seem to represent a major risk factor for suicidal behavior. Individuals with alcohol use disorder have a nearly 10-fold increased risk of suicide compared with the general population, whereas those with opioid use disorder or mixed drug use disorder have about 14-fold and 17-fold increased risk, respectively (Wilcox, Conner, & Caine, 2004). The evidence is, however, unclear as to whether cannabis used as a single substance increases the risk of suicide (Calabria, Degenhardt, Hall, & Lynskey, 2010). Data on the proportion of suicides who had been under substance influence at their time of death, or who had been diagnosed with a SUD, also vary greatly across studies and samples, but as a rough estimate about one-third of all suicides have had a diagnosable SUD. In the majority of these cases, SUD is seen in combination with other psychiatric disorders, and such comorbidity strongly escalates the risk of suicide. The most apparent explanation to this is, of course, the increased burden additional disorders bring to the individual. Another reason may be that the attention of the patient's healthcare providers and their next of kin may be too strongly drawn toward the SUD, and disorders such as depression or PTSD are then overlooked. Substance use also typically complicates suicide risk assessments and management. Finally, patients who appear drunk or intoxicated to healthcare personnel are not perceived as their most attractive clients and may be faced with negative or judgmental attitudes and thus risk receiving poorer quality of care.

The association between SUD and suicidal behavior is complex. People with psychiatric disorders such as depression, anxiety, or PTSD frequently use alcohol or psychoactive drugs to seek symptom relief and even to cope with or reduce suicidal ideation. While this may sometimes be a successful short-term strategy, the long-term price of such self-medication is high. Chronic SUDs, with their plethora of negative consequences to physical health, personal safety, interpersonal relations, and career, often ultimately lead to social isolation and to an accumulation of losses and other negative life events that may increase the risk of suicide. Substance abuse or withdrawal may also induce psychiatric symptoms and secondary psychiatric disorders, such as depression, delirium, delusions, or other psychotic symptoms that may persist long after detoxification. In the short term, substance abuse leads to a series of negative psychological effects impairing judgment and control over affects and impulses. This may increase the risk of suicidal behavior in vulnerable individuals in several ways. Binge drinking is a well-known risk factor for suicide in young people. Since alcohol ingestion generally lowers the threshold for suicidal behavior, it is commonly involved in both fatal and nonfatal suicidal behavior in all age groups. Sometimes alcohol is used intentionally as part of the suicidal act to overcome fears, moral objections, or thoughts that would otherwise prevent the suicidal individual from such behavior.

The association between SUD, particularly alcohol use disorder, and suicidal behavior is, in many ways, neglected both by policy makers and clinicians. At the societal level, the problem of alcohol is so huge that it calls for more active public health interventions such as restricting the availability of alcohol and increasing the availability of alcohol abuse prevention and intervention programs, which have been shown to have a strong suicide preventive potential (Wasserman & Varnik, 1998). When treating intoxicated suicidal patients, clinicians should be alert to the added problems of assessing suicide risk in this context, and undertake appropriate short-term safety precautions. As indicated above, patients with SUD constitute a heterogeneous group. Hence treatment planning should be made according to each patient's substance abuse history, comorbid psychiatric disorders, and other stressors and problems that are probably part of the patient's life situation.

CONCLUSIONS

Most psychiatric disorders imply a substantially increased risk of suicide. Naturally, this does not mean that suicide risk is completely mediated through the development of psychiatric disorder. Variations have been found across cultures and age groups as to what extent suicides have had a diagnosable psychiatric disorder. Clearly, there are many more risk factors than psychiatric disorders that are important to assess and address in suicide research, prevention, and intervention. In this chapter, however, our focus has been the impact of psychiatric disorders, which is huge both on suicide rates and on public health in general. According to European estimates, during one year, nearly 40 percent of the total population will have a fully developed mental illness (Wittchen et al., 2011). In terms of disability-adjusted life years (DALYs), mental illness will account for 23.4 percent of all DALYs in men and 30.1 percent in women, constituting the greatest of all health burdens. To improve treatment for psychiatric disorders is, therefore, an essential component of suicide preventive strategies. In large parts of the world, particularly low-income countries, there is a profound lack of mental health resources. There is a scarcity of hospital facilities, community mental health centers, and adequately trained mental health workers. But even in many high-income countries of North America and Europe, not enough psychiatric treatment resources are available to populations that seem to become increasingly in need of them. From a suicide prevention perspective, there is a universal need to strengthen psychiatric services and to make them more optimally available.

REFERENCES

Beautrais, A. L., Joyce, P. R., Mulder, R. T., Fergusson, D. M., Deavoll, B. J., & Nightingale, S. K. (1996). Prevalence and comorbidity of mental disorders in persons making serious suicide attempts: A case-control study. *American Journal of Psychiatry, 153,* 1009–1014.

Bertolote, J. M., Fleischmann, A., De Leo, D., & Wasserman, D. (2003). Suicide and mental disorders: Do we know enough? *British Journal of Psychiatry, 183,* 382–383.

Bullman, T. A. & Kang, H. K. (1994). Posttraumatic stress disorder and the risk of traumatic deaths among Vietnam veterans. *Journal of Nervous & Mental Disease, 182,* 604–610.

Calabria, B., Degenhardt, L., Hall, W., & Lynskey, M. (2010). Does cannabis use increase the risk of death? Systematic review of epidemiological evidence on adverse effects of cannabis use. *Drug & Alcohol Review, 29,* 318–330.

Cavanagh, J. T. O., Carson, A., Sharpe, M., & Lawrie, S. (2003). Psychological autopsy studies of suicide: A systematic review. *Psychological Medicine, 33,* 395–405.

Cheng, A. T., Chen, T. H., Chen, C. C., & Jenkins, R. (2000). Psychosocial and psychiatric risk factors for suicide. Case-control psychological autopsy study. *British Journal of Psychiatry, 177,* 360–365.

Cipriani, A., Pretty, H., Hawton, K., & Geddes, J. R. (2005). Lithium in the prevention of suicidal behavior and all-cause mortality in patients with mood disorders: A systematic review of randomized trials. *American Journal of Psychiatry, 162,* 1805–1819.

Foa, E. B., Keane, T. M., Friedman, M. J., & Cohen, J. A. (2008). *Effective treatments for PTSD: Practice guidelines from the International Society for Traumatic Stress Studies* (2nd ed.) New York: Guilford.

Grant, P. M., Huh, G. A., Perivoliotis, D., Stolar, N. M., & Beck, A. T. (2011). Randomized trial to evaluate the efficacy of cognitive therapy for low-functioning patients with schizophrenia. *Archives of General Psychiatry, 69 (2), 121–127*.

Harkavy-Friedman, J. M., Kimhy, D., Nelson, E. A., Venarde, D. F., Malaspina, D., & Mann, J. J. (2003). Suicide attempts in schizophrenia: The role of command auditory hallucinations for suicide. *Journal of Clinical Psychiatry, 64,* 871–874.

Hawton, K., Sutton, L., Haw, C., Sinclair, J., & Deeks, J. J. (2005). Schizophrenia and suicide: Systematic review of risk factors. *British Journal of Psychiatry, 187,* 9–20.

Hawton, K., Sutton, L., Haw, C., Sinclair, J., & Harriss, L. (2005). Suicide and attempted suicide in bipolar disorder: A systematic review of risk factors. *Journal of Clinical Psychiatry, 66,* 693–704.

Hiroeh, U., Appleby, L., Mortensen, P. B., & Dunn, G. (2001). Death by homicide, suicide and other unnatural causes in people with mental illness: A population-based study. *Lancet, 358,* 2110–2112.

Inskip, H. M., Harris, E. C., & Barraclough, B. (1998). Lifetime risk of suicide for affective disorder, alcoholism and schizophrenia. *British Journal of Psychiatry, 172,* 35–37.

Judd, L. L. (1997). The clinical course of unipolar major depressive disorders. *Archives of General Psychiatry, 54,* 989–991.

Kim, C. H., Jayathilake, K., & Meltzer, H. Y. (2002). Hopelessness, neurocognitive function, and insight in schizophrenia: Relation to suicidal behavior. *Schizophrenia Research, 60,* 71–80.

Mazza, J. J. & Reynolds, W. M. (1999). Exposure to violence in young inner-city adolescents: Relationships with suicidal ideation, depression, and PTSD symptomatology. *Journal of Abnormal Child Psychology, 27,* 203–213.

McGirr, A., Seguin, M., Renaud, J., Benkelfat, C., Alda, M., & Turecki, G. (2006). Gender and risk factors for suicide: Evidence for heterogeneity in predisposing mechanisms in a psychological autopsy study. *Journal of Clinical Psychiatry, 67,* 1612–1617.

Mehlum, L. (2005). Traumatic stress and suicidal behavior: An important target for treatment and prevention. In K. Hawton (Ed.), *Prevention and treatment of suicidal behaviours: From science to practice,* pp. 121–138. Oxford, UK: Oxford University Press.

Mehlum, L., Friis, S., Vaglum, P., & Karterud, S. (1994). The longitudinal pattern of suicidal behaviour in borderline personality disorder: A prospective follow-up study. *Acta Psychiatrica Scandinavica, 90,* 124–130.

Melle, I., Johannesen, J. O., Friis, S., Haahr, U., Joa, I., Larsen, T. K., . . . McGlashan T. (2006). Early detection of the first episode of schizophrenia and suicidal behavior. *American Journal of Psychiatry, 163,* 800–804.

Meltzer, H. Y., Alphs, L., Green, A. I., Altamura, A. C., Anand, R., Bertoldi, A., et al. (2003). Clozapine treatment for suicidality in schizophrenia: International Suicide Prevention Trial (InterSePT). *Archives of General Psychiatry, 60,* 82–91.

Molnar, B. E., Berkman, L. F., & Buka, S. L. (2001). Psychopathology, childhood sexual abuse and other childhood adversities: Relative links to subsequent suicidal behaviour in the US. *Psychological Medicine, 31,* 965–977.

National Institute for Health and Clinical Excellence (2009). *Borderline personality disorder: Treatment and management.* London, UK: National Institute for Health and Clinical Excellence.

Oldham, J. M. (2006). Borderline personality disorder and suicidality. *American Journal of Psychiatry, 163,* 20–26.

Pompili, M., Amador, X., Girardi, P., Harkavy-Friedman, J., Harrow, M., Kaplan, K., et al. (2007). Suicide risk in schizophrenia: Learning from the past to change the future. *Annals of General Psychiatry, 6,* 10.

Qin, P., Agerbo, E., & Mortensen, P. B. (2003). Suicide risk in relation to socioeconomic, demographic, psychiatric, and familial factors: A national register-based study of all suicides in Denmark, 1981–1997. *American Journal of Psychiatry, 160,* 765–772.

Qin, P., & Nordentoft, M. (2005). Suicide risk in relation to psychiatric hospitalization: Evidence based on longitudinal registers. *Archives of General Psychiatry, 62,* 427–432.

Saha, S., Chant, D., & McGrath, J. (2007). A systematic review of mortality in schizophrenia: Is the differential mortality gap worsening over time? *Archives of General Psychiatry, 64,* 1123–1131.

Sareen, J., Cox, B. J., Afifi, T. O., de Graaf, R., Asmundson, G. J., ten Have, M., et al. (2005). Anxiety disorders and risk for suicidal ideation and suicide attempts: A population-based longitudinal study of adults. *Archives of General Psychiatry, 62,* 1249–1257.

Thoresen, S., Mehlum, L., & Moller, B. (2003). Suicide in peacekeepers: A cohort study of mortality from suicide in 22,275 Norwegian veterans from international peacekeeping operations. *Social Psychiatry & Psychiatric Epidemiology, 38,* 605–610.

Wasserman, D., & Varnik, A. (1998). Suicide-preventive effects of perestroika in the former USSR: The role of alcohol restriction. *Acta Psychiatrica Scandinavica, 98 (suppl 394),* 1–4.

Wilcox, H. C., Conner, K. R., & Caine, E. D. (2004). Association of alcohol and drug use disorders and completed suicide: An empirical review of cohort studies. *Drug & Alcohol Dependence, 76 (suppl),* S11–S19.

Wittchen, H. U., Jacobi, F., Rehm, J., Gustavsson, A., Svensson, M., Jonsson, B., et al. (2011). The size and burden of mental disorders and other disorders of the brain in Europe 2010. *European Neuropsychopharmacology, 21,* 655–679.

Ystgaard, M., Hestetun, I., Loeb, M., & Mehlum, L. (2004). Is there a specific relationship between childhood sexual and physical abuse and repeated suicidal behavior? *Child Abuse & Neglect, 28,* 863–875.

8

Interpersonal Dynamics and Suicide[1]

Kimberly A. Van Orden and Ian H. Stanley

D epression is one of the strongest risk factors for suicide across the
lifespan, and most individuals who die by suicide experience depression, or another mental disorder before their deaths (Nock et al.,
2008). At the same time, the vast majority of those diagnosed with mental disorders will not attempt or die by suicide. These epidemiological
findings suggest that depression (and other mental disorders) play a key
role in elevating risk for suicide but, in order to understand who among
the population of individuals with mental disorders is at risk for suicide, additional risk and resilience factors must be considered. In this
chapter, we make the case that, in order to fully understand and prevent
suicide, we must consider the interpersonal context in which it occurs.
As will be reviewed below, interpersonal factors, including both a lack
of connectedness to others as well as discordant connections, are associated with suicidal ideation, attempts, and deaths across the lifespan. In
our view, considering the presence of both mental disorders and the interpersonal context in which those disorders occur will produce the best
suicide prevention science.

In this chapter, we consider several dimensions of the interpersonal
context of suicide. First, we provide an overview of different indices of
interpersonal functioning that are associated with the risk for suicide, or
conversely, resilience to suicidal behavior. Next, we consider theoretical
perspectives that emphasize interpersonal factors and, where possible, integrate findings discussed in the section on risk and resilience to highlight
how the theories are consistent (or inconsistent) with epidemiological considerations. Next, we consider the interpersonal dynamics between suicidal individuals and both clinicians and those left behind in the wake of a
suicide death (i.e., suicide survivors). Finally, the ultimate goal of any review on suicide is to synthesize the literature in such a way that ultimately

yields insights into methods for improved treatment and prevention efforts. Thus, we conclude the chapter with a discussion of implications for prevention from an interpersonal perspective, as well as a consideration of future directions for research that have the potential to significantly impact both practice and research.

INTERPERSONAL RISK AND RESILIENCE

In this section, we examine interpersonal risk factors for suicide. Our brief review includes studies that examine suicidal ideation, nonlethal attempts, and suicide deaths. When possible, we include studies with samples varying in age, nationality, and race. We propose that interpersonal risk factors can be subsumed under the umbrella of social disconnectedness.[2] Some risk factors involve having or perceiving too few meaningful connections with others (e.g., isolation or loneliness), while others involve having or perceiving discordant connections with others that do not contribute to a sense of positive connectedness. We frame our discussion of these findings within social psychological models that propose that human beings have an innate need to belong to, or feel connected to, valued relationships and groups (Baumeister & Leary, 1995; Cacioppo & Patrick, 2008), and, when that need to belong is unmet, deleterious health outcomes result, including suicide. Thus, for social disconnectedness factors involving too few connections, we use the term belongingness. For social disconnectedness factors involving discordant connections, we use the term discord.

Regarding belongingness, people in a suicidal crisis often report feeling disconnected or isolated from family, friends, neighbors, religious organizations, and the like. They feel as if they do not belong anywhere or with anyone. A lack of belongingness predicts suicide ideation, attempts, and deaths among children, middle age adults, and older adults. Belongingness can be measured with both structural indices (e.g., having few, if any, friends or family members to turn to in times of need) and subjective indices (e.g., feeling as if the friends or family members one does have do not provide positive support). Both subjective and structural indices of belongingness are associated with suicidal ideation, attempts, and deaths. Regarding subjective indices, loneliness and low perceived social support are associated with suicidal ideation, attempts, and deaths among samples varying in age, nationality, and clinical severity (Van Orden et al., 2010). Regarding objective indices, the number of supportive individuals in a person's life is related to suicide risk across the lifespan, with marriage, children, and a greater number of friends and family decreasing risk for suicidal behavior, while living alone and having few social supports elevates risk (Van Orden et al., 2010).

Belongingness has been shown to be associated with increased risk for suicide across studies with varying research designs, including prospective studies and psychological autopsy studies, further underlining the robustness of the association. The psychological autopsy method is a retrospective investigation, utilizing interviews with a next of kin, to determine relevant life stressors, including interpersonal stressors that affected an individual in the days, weeks, and months leading up to their death by suicide. Control groups for psychological autopsy studies are typically individually matched with cases on demographic variables, and interviews are conducted with proxy respondents. In one study that employed this research design, Duberstein and colleagues (2004) found that poor social integration, defined in part as the degree to which one is in contact with nonfamily (i.e., social or community) supports, particularly within one week prior to death (or prior to the interview for controls), conferred increased risk for suicide for adults 50 years and older, even after statistically controlling for active mental disorders. Thus, the researchers found that the relationship between poor social integration and suicide is not fully accounted for by mental disorders and that social connectedness conveys information relevant to suicide risk above and beyond the information provided by mental disorders. Regarding prospective designs, Turvey and colleagues (2002) found that older adults who reported having someone to confide in were significantly less likely to die by suicide over a 10-year period. Thus, both population-based prospective studies and retrospective investigations of individuals who died by suicide converge on the finding that indicators of social disconnectedness elevate risk for suicide.

Interpersonal discord is also associated with the spectrum of suicidal behavior across the lifespan. Indices of discordant relationships that have consistently been linked with suicide are family conflict, domestic violence, childhood abuse, and perceptions that one is a burden on others (Van Orden et al., 2010). Perceiving oneself as a burden on others as a risk factor for suicide is supported by data from academic disciplines outside behavioral health, including sociology and anthropology. For example, likely dating back to the samurai tradition of *seppuku* (i.e., ritualistic suicide that occurred when a samurai was unable to fulfill his duties [Young, 2002]), suicide in Japan may be viewed by some as honorable (Fusé, 1980), especially when an individual dies by suicide in order to demonstrate responsibility for past behaviors (Lifton, Reich, & Shuichi,

1979). Another illustration of perceived burdensomeness comes from a traditional practice of ritual suicide in the Yuit Eskimos of St. Lawrence Island (Leighton & Hughes, 1955). The belief underlying this practice is that becoming too sick, infirm, or old could threaten the survival of the group. In this society, ritual suicide became an explicit and socially sanctioned response to perceptions that one's existence burdened the group. We describe these data, not to invoke the debate as to whether rational suicide exists, but rather to highlight the diversity of the literature indicating a role for perceived burdensomeness in suicidal behavior.

Converging results are found in the psychological literature. Perceiving oneself as a burden on close others is associated with suicidal ideation and attempts among physically healthy adults (from young adulthood through older adulthood [Van Orden et al., 2010]), as well as among those with advanced-stage illnesses (McPherson, Wilson, & Murray, 2007), for whom perceptions of burdensomeness are also associated with desire for euthanasia (Wilson et al., 2007). Feeling like a burden also appears relevant to suicidal behavior among adolescents and children. For example, Rosenthal and Rosenthal (1984) compared the characteristics of 16 preschoolers (2½–5 year of age) who engaged in nonlethal attempts with a group of preschoolers with behavioral problems (but without histories of suicidal behavior) and found that the suicidal children were more likely to come from "unwanted" pregnancies and to have experienced abuse and neglect by their parents. Sabbath (1969) argued that these types of childhood stressors cause children to feel expendable by communicating a "parental wish, conscious or unconscious, spoken or unspoken, that the child interprets as [the parents'] desire to be rid of him, for him to die" (pp. 272–273). Extending this literature to older youth, Woznica and Shapiro (1990) found that suicidal adolescents (compared to psychiatric controls) reported higher scores on a measure of perceived expendability in the family, which included feelings of being unwanted and a burden on the family.

A similar interpersonal construct, expressed emotion, may represent the interpersonal context in which perceptions of burdensomeness develop. Expressed emotion (EE) is the degree to which family members display over-involved, critical, and even hostile attitudes toward a family member with a mental illness. EE is a reliable predictor of early relapse across many mental disorders, including bipolar disorder, schizophrenia, and depression (Butzlaff & Hooley, 1998). Specifically examining suicidal behavior, among adolescents, family EE, particularly parental criticism, is associated with suicide ideation, plans, and attempts (Wedig & Nock,

2007), particularly for adolescents who demonstrate a self-critical cognitive style. Thus, the family environment, especially the degree to which family members engage in EE processes, could either buffer against or contribute to suicidal behavior. Future research should examine whether high EE is associated with suicidal behavior among those prone to self-criticism because individuals come to perceive themselves as a burden on family.

In sum, interpersonal factors appear to play a role in the etiology of suicide ideation, attempts, and deaths among youth, adults, and older adults. Both low belongingness and high discord appear to elevate risk for suicide. These findings are consistent with social psychological theories proposing a human need for connectedness. The idea of a need to feel connected is a theme that emerges in several theories of suicidal behavior, a topic to which we now turn.

THEORETICAL PERSPECTIVES

In this section, we briefly describe and discuss theories of suicide that emphasize interpersonal factors as key etiological forces. While most (if not all) theoretical perspectives on suicide acknowledge the role of interpersonal factors, some emphasize intrapersonal or cognitive factors, and so we do not discuss them in detail here. Another point of note is that, while there may seem to be a great number of theoretical perspectives on suicide by virtue of the fact that we discuss several different perspectives here, few of these theories have received direct empirical investigation, leaving many hypotheses untested. Although many explanations are possible, the fact remains that the field of suicidology has not fully harnessed the scientific power of theory in guiding research. Thus, our aim in presenting these perspectives is not to endorse or "promote" a particular theory, but rather, to raise awareness and suggest that studies testing and comparing theories could promote suicide prevention.

We start with one of the oldest, yet most influential theories of suicide. In 1897 Emile Durkheim presented a sociological theory of suicidal behavior that is still widely cited today (Durkheim, 1897). According to Durkheim, dysregulation of two social forces, social integration and moral integration, results in four types of suicide: egoistic, altruistic, anomic, and fatalistic. The first two types, egoistic and altruistic, result from dysregulation of social integration (i.e., the degree to which an individual is integrated into society). Both too much and too little social integration result in negative outcomes. Durkheim proposed that too little social integration in society leads to an increase in egoistic suicides because individuals lack a connection to something that transcends themselves. They lack a connection with society. Durkheim also proposed that too much social integration in society leads to an increase in altruistic suicides because individuals sacrifice themselves for the larger good of society. The other two types of suicide, anomic and fatalistic, result from dysregulation of moral integration according to Durkheim. This involves the degree to which society regulates the beliefs and behaviors of individuals (e.g., societal norms, the legal system). Too little moral regulation results in anomic suicide, often through economic upheavals, because individuals' needs and abilities to achieve those means are thrown into a state of disequilibrium. Too much moral integration results in fatalistic suicide, the prototypical example, according to Durkheim, being slaves who die by suicide. When examining changes in suicide rates for a population over time, Durkheim's theory could provide explanations for, and facilitate prediction of, patterns and shifts in suicide rates from an interpersonal perspective, but largely ignores individual differences and is unable to explain why not all members of a society exposed to the social forces do not die by suicide.

The next theory we describe takes a more micro-level view of causal factors, but is not fully focused on the individual. It focuses on interpersonal dynamics within families. As described briefly above in the section on discordant connections, Sabbath's (1969) family systems theory of adolescent suicidal behavior emphasizes adolescents' perceptions that they are expendable members of the family. The causal factors leading to adolescent suicidal behavior, according to the theory, are pathogenic parental attitudes toward the adolescent that are interpreted by the adolescent that he or she is not needed in the family and, in fact, that the family would be better-off if the adolescent was dead. Another theory, grounded in sociobiology, also emphasizes perceptions of burdensomeness (de Catanzaro, 1995). The theory attempts to reconcile suicidal behavior, an attempt to overcome self-preservation, with the tenet of natural selection that traits most likely to be passed onto offspring are those that promote survival and reproduction. De Catanzaro's theory proposes that suicide may occur when individuals perceive that they are a burden on family members (i.e., those with whom they share the most genetic material) such that family members may be less likely to reproduce and pass on genetic material. The theory does not address the fact that most individuals with the proposed risk factor (i.e., perceptions of being a burden on family) will not attempt or die by suicide. De Catanzaro (1995) conducted a survey on suicidal ideation and the quality of family contacts and found a strong relationship between suicidal ideation and perceived burdensomeness toward the family. Also consistent with de Catanzaro's theory, Brown, Dahlen, Mills, Rick, and Biblarz (1999) reported that feelings of being a burden on kin stood out as a unique and specific predictor of suicide-related symptoms even when other key variables were controlled.

Another theory emphasizing family dynamics was proposed by Richman (1986) and emphasizes hopelessness about social separation as a key factor in suicidal behavior. The theory places social separation and suicidal behavior within a dysfunctional family system marked by "unworkable transactions," the primary such transactions being role failure (i.e., decreased social competence), scapegoating (i.e., blaming family problems on one member, usually the suicidal individual), and double-bind relationships (i.e., any interpersonal response in a relationship leads to negative outcomes). The theory proposes that perceptions of separateness and hopelessness are created and maintained by a family system and that suicide prevention efforts must target the family system.

Moving to a more micro level emphasizing the intrapersonal consequences of interpersonal dynamics, attachment theory asserts that the fundamental driving desire of individuals is the need to maintain "felt security." Bowlby (1973) articulated a theory of suicide derived from attachment theory in which he asserts that the motivation that underlies suicidal behavior arises from a fear of losing a childhood attachment figures as a result of death or separation. This motivation, in Bowlby's view, operates differently for nonlethal attempts versus lethal suicides. When a person attempts suicide, according to this theory, the motivation is to attract the attention of an attachment figure with the goal of forcing the attachment figure to be more responsive. When a person dies by suicide, the goal is to exact revenge, make atonement, or reunite with a lost attachment figure. While Bowlby's theory differentiates between nonlethal and lethal suicidal behavior, the theory does not make precise predictions as to the conditions under which lethal suicidal behavior will occur.

The final theory we discuss is the Interpersonal Theory of Suicide (ITS), originally proposed by Joiner (2005) and elaborated by Van Orden et al. (2010). ITS builds upon many of the theoretical perspectives described here, including the perspectives of Durkheim, Richman, and Bowlby and similarly asserts that low belongingness is a key contributor to a desire for suicide. Durkheim described the problem as one of a lack of social integration, Richman as social separation, and Bowlby as the loss of an attachment figure. ITS proposes that when the need for belongingness is completely unmet (termed thwarted belongingness) and an individual perceives no hope for this changing, a desire to die will develop. Further, the theory proposes that various indices of disconnectedness that are associated with suicide, such as living alone, loss of a spouse, loneliness, and low social support, are associated with suicide because they are indicators that the need to belong has been thwarted.

The theoretical perspectives described above also indicate a role for discordant connections in suicidal behavior. Specifically, Sabbath proposed a role for feeling expendable or unwanted within a family system, and de Catanzaro proposed that feeling like a burden on others contributes to suicidal behavior. ITS integrates these perspectives with the hypothesis that when individuals believe that others in their life would be better-off if they were gone, termed perceived burdensomeness, a desire for death will result. Importantly, the theory also proposes that a passive desire for death will not elevate in severity to active thoughts of suicide unless an individual concurrently experiences both thwarted belongingness and perceived burdensomeness. Although not the focus of the current chapter, the theory proposes that in order to die by suicide, individuals must also acquire the capability for painful and frightening self-harm behaviors. Thus, thwarted belongingness and perceived burdensomeness are necessary, but not sufficient, for suicidal behavior to occur. Readers are referred to the section on Further Reading at the end of the chapter for additional information on acquired capability.

ITS proposes that risk factors are associated with suicide to the extent that they increase thwarted belongingness and/or perceived burdensomeness, while protective factors are protective to the extent that they prevent thwarted belongingness and/or perceived burdensomeness. Thus, known risk factors for suicide are more distal variables in the causal chain leading to suicidal ideations and behaviors, while the theory's constructs are proposed to be more proximal causes. Therefore, to extend the theory to the domain of prevention, if an intervention is to be effective in preventing suicide, it must reduce existing levels of (or prevent the incidence of) thwarted belongingness and perceived burdensomeness (Joiner, Van Orden, Witte, & Rudd, 2009). It need not target all of the known risk factors for suicide, nor must it tackle risk factors not easily amenable to change. Rather, an effective preventive intervention must create some degree of positive social connections so that a completely thwarted need to belong is avoided. According to the theory, even a small degree of belongingness can be lifesaving. An even more potent intervention, according to the theory, would be one that facilitates positive relationships (i.e., creating belongingness) in which individuals do not perceive themselves to be a burden. Even a minimal degree of positive contributions to others can similarly be lifesaving since perceptions of burdensomeness would not then be global. These examples serve to illustrate the potential benefits of using theory to guide scientific efforts in suicide prevention. Theory can generate testable hypotheses that could further our understanding of both etiological and health-promoting mechanisms. For further reading on ITS, readers are referred to Van Orden et al. (2010).

CONNECTED TO SOMEONE WHO IS SUICIDAL: CLINICIANS AND SURVIVORS

Although not relevant to all instances of suicidal behavior, given that many individuals who attempt or die by suicide are not in mental health treatment, an interpersonal context that is nonetheless germane to suicide prevention is that of the therapeutic relationship between the suicidal patient and his/her psychotherapist or psychiatrist. The possibility of a patient dying by suicide was the most frequently reported fear in a national sample of psychotherapists (Pope & Tabachnick, 1993). The fear felt by clinicians when working with suicidal patients may arise from beliefs about being unable to help patients and can in turn engender negative attitudes and feelings toward patients that can damage the therapeutic relationship (Jobes & Maltsberger, 1995).

A common misconception about suicidal behavior is that individuals who share suicidal thoughts with others, including with clinicians, do not intend to engage in suicidal behavior, but rather, are attempting to manipulate others. Another relevant descriptor is secondary gain. When applied to suicidal behavior, the term secondary gain implies that help seeking for suicidal thoughts is initiated or maintained (though not necessarily consciously) through gains other than those directly related to preventing suicidal behavior, such as sympathy from others, lessened responsibilities, or (temporary) cessation of relational turmoil. One of the most thoughtful and clinically useful discussions on this topic was put forth by Marsha Linehan (1993) who is a clinical psychologist and creator of Dialectical Behavior Therapy (DBT), a treatment for suicidal behavior that is supported by numerous scientific studies. Linehan proposed that using the term manipulative to describe the actions of suicidal patients is detrimental and inaccurate. Linehan proposed two key points in her argument. First, that individuals contemplating suicide are experiencing intolerable pain and, second, that the definition of manipulation involves engaging in a behavior with intention to influence another person either covertly or deviously. Linehan urged clinicians to consider the difference between behavior that influences others to respond (i.e., influential behavior) and behavior that manipulates others (i.e., manipulative behavior). The former does not require the presence of intention to cause resulting outcomes, while the latter does require this. Linehan further proposed that individuals in such a high degree of pain are rarely thinking clearly enough or are in enough behavioral control to engage in such an interpersonally skillful behavior as manipulation. Others may respond to suicidal threats by providing sympathy or admitting a patient to a hospital, but this does not mean these outcomes are what the suicidal patient intended. Rather, Linehan urged clinicians to consider that one of many possible functions of suicidal behavior may be communication of intense distress. She further urged clinicians to consider, however, that desiring to communicate one's distress does not equate to attempting to manipulate others. The latter interpretation of patient behavior is likely to engender anger and resentment and could preclude effective suicide prevention actions on the part of clinicians. She also proposed that a single behavior can serve numerous functions and that a patient's suicidal communications could function to communicate distress (i.e., communication behavior) and simultaneously be an indicator of potentially lethal suicidal intent.

Thus, as with much clinical lore, there is a grain of truth regarding this controversy, namely, that suicidal behaviors may function as "communication behaviors." However, it is absolutely essential that clinicians, family members, and friends of suicidal individuals not assume that all expressions of suicidal thoughts are solely expressions of distress, and thereby risk taking insufficient clinical actions to prevent suicide attempts. Family members, friends, and colleagues who are in contact with suicidal individuals are urged to call the National Suicide Prevention Hotline (1-800-273-TALK) for assistance in helping the suicidal person and managing his/her own distress.

It is also the case that some individuals who die by suicide will not express their intent to others. This appears to be particularly true among older adults, especially those older adults with a personality trait termed "low openness to experience" (Duberstein, 2001). This trait is part of the "Big Five" empirically derived taxonomy of personality and likely indicates behavioral and cognitive rigidity. It may indicate the presence of difficulties accessing and expressing emotions as well as difficulties creating meaning, all of which may account for lower levels of openness to experience among older adults who died by suicide. Duberstein (2001) reviewed findings that older adults who are low in openness to experience are less likely to report suicidal ideation but more likely to die by suicide. Duberstein hypothesized that those older adults low in openness may be less likely to endorse or acknowledge experiencing suicidal thoughts, thus precluding help-seeking behaviors and detection by others (e.g., primary care physicians). We return to this issue, and research needed, in the summary section.

Suicide survivors are family members, friends, and others closely connected to individuals who died by suicide. It is estimated that for each suicide death in the United States, six survivors are left behind (American Association of Suicidology, 2007). This estimate stands in apparent contrast to the fact highlighted above that one of the strongest risk factors for suicide is social disconnectedness. While some who die by suicide may indeed have few objective ties to others, many others who die by suicide may be well connected to others, but perceive themselves to be alone and cut off from others, and it may be that perceptions of connectedness are most important for mental and physical health. Data suggest that those who have lost family members to suicide may be at increased risk for traumatic grief (Mitchell, Kim, Prigerson, & Mortimer-Stephens, 2004). Effective cognitive-behavioral treatments for traumatic grief are available (Shear et al., 2001), and resources for survivors are also available through the American Association for Suicidology (www.suicidology.org).

PREVENTION

Only two randomized trials have yielded results indicating preventive effects on suicide deaths (Fleischmann et al., 2008; Motto & Bostrom, 2001). That there are only two studies for such a devastating public health problem is likely caused, in part, by the fact that suicide is incredibly difficult to study. This may result in fewer scientists choosing to specialize in this area, as well as difficulties designing sufficiently large and impactful designs to reduce a low base-rate phenomenon that is most certainly multifactorially caused. Thus, on the one hand, the state of the science for suicide prevention is rather grim. On the other hand, looking at the science as a whole yields clues as to the direction intervention scientists might take in order to reduce suicide. In particular, a common thread among those interventions that likely prevented suicide deaths (both randomized and nonrandomized) is the promotion of social connectedness to providers or peers.

Regarding the studies that examined suicide deaths, the "caring letters study" involved mailing postcards to individuals hospitalized for suicide attempts who refused further treatment (Motto & Bostrom, 2001). The World Health Organization's SUPRE-MISS study (Fleischmann et al., 2008) involved psycho-education and follow-up contacts. In addition, three interventions have been shown (in quasi-experimental studies) to reduce suicide rates among older adults, and all were multicomponent interventions that involved some element of increasing connectedness to providers or peers. First, DeLeo and colleagues' Telehelp/Telecheck intervention (De Leo, Carollo, & Dello Buono, 1995; De Leo, Dello Buono, & Dwyer, 2002) provided telephone-based outreach, evaluation, and support services. Second, Oyama and colleagues' intervention provided depression screening and referral for care, as well as engagement in health education, volunteer, and peer support activities (Oyama et al., 2008). Finally, Chan and colleagues' intervention provided connections with case managers, as well as supportive phone calls, psycho-education, and psychiatric care (Chan et al., 2011). The latter model of intervention is termed a collaborative care model (CCM) for depression management. CCMs for depression have been proposed as a means to addressing suicide risk. CCMs involve augmenting depression treatment in primary care with expert psychiatric consultation and medication recommendations, psycho-education for patients, and the option of brief psychotherapy that can be delivered by non-mental health specialists. CCMs that include Interpersonal Psychotherapy and Problem Solving Therapy have shown promise in the management and prevention of suicidal ideation among older adults (Alexopoulos et al., 2009; Unutzer et al., 2006).

In addition, Interpersonal Psychotherapy and Problem Solving Therapy, as well as Cognitive Therapy and Dialectical Behavior Therapy, show promise in the prevention of suicide attempts and the reduction of suicidal ideation when implemented without CCMs and for both younger and older age groups (Joiner et al., 2009). All of these psychotherapies include a substantial focus on interpersonal factors. Not surprisingly, Interpersonal Psychotherapy (IPT) places the greatest emphasis on interpersonal functioning. In fact, the stated goal of IPT is to improve interpersonal functioning and, thereby, reduce distress and symptoms of mental disorders. In IPT, the therapist and patient collaboratively choose a single interpersonal problem area to focus on during treatment. There are four problem areas to choose from: grief (e.g., loss of a loved one), interpersonal disputes (e.g., marital discord), role transitions (e.g., retirement), and interpersonal sensitivity/deficits (e.g., social isolation or social anxiety). To the extent that desire for death and suicide is caused by interpersonal factors, as is proposed by many theoretical models, including the ITS, it may be the case that IPT reduces suicide risk by ameliorating disconnectedness and discord.

A limitation of current research is that none of the intervention studies discussed above was designed in such a way to allow for inferences regarding the mechanism of effectiveness. Thus it is unclear how, or in what way, the interventions were effective. Without such information, it is difficult to disseminate these interventions, adapt them for use with other populations, or improve existing interventions. For example, suicide hotlines appear to be effective in reducing intent to die and hopelessness among callers (Gould, Kalafat, Harrismunfakh, & Kleinman, 2007), but it is not known whether this effect is due to the benefits of assessment, connection to local resources, instillation of hope, facilitation of motivation to use coping strategies, or the connection with the hotline worker.

SUMMARY AND FUTURE DIRECTIONS

In this chapter, we provided an overview of the interpersonal context of suicide. We reviewed findings demonstrating that interpersonal functioning has both interpersonal antecedents and consequences for suicidal individuals and those who interact with suicidal individuals. Social disconnectedness, manifested as low belonging (feeling that one has too few caring, meaningful connections) as well as social discord (feeling that one's interactions with others are marked by disagreement, tension, or negative emotions) are both associated with suicide ideation, attempts, and deaths across the lifespan and around the world. The extent to which discord impacts suicide by creating feelings of disconnectedness is not known, and thus represents an area for future research. Our review of the theoretical literature on the role of interpersonal factors in suicide revealed that many models did not include falsifiable hypotheses, thereby hampering efforts to empirically test the theories. Empirical tests have been conducted by Durkheim's (1897), Sabbath's (1969), de Catanzaro's (1995), and Joiner's (2005) theories of suicidal behavior, indicating potential etiological roles for societal changes in social and moral integration, feelings of expendability, perceiving oneself as a burden on family, and both thwarted belongingness and perceived burdensomeness, respectively. We proposed that these factors that are both theoretically and empirically linked to suicide, as well as the host of other indices of social disconnectedness, such as loneliness, social support and family discord, converge on the Interpersonal Theory's hypothesis that the proximal causes of desire for suicide are perceiving that one's need for belongingness is unmet (i.e., thwarted belongingness) and perceiving that others would be better-off if you were gone (i.e., perceived burdensomeness). Consistent with this theory's proposal for the centrality of interpersonal functioning in the etiology of suicide, we also described findings from intervention studies that yielded results consistent with a reduction of suicide risk or deaths and suggested that a common ingredient in all was the promotion of connection to peers or providers.

However, as we mentioned in the section on prevention, there are no studies examining mechanisms (social, psychological, or biological) that may have led to the prevention of suicide ideation, attempts, or suicide. This is particularly problematic because most of the interventions with some evidence of effectiveness for suicidal behavior are complex, multifaceted programs. Therefore, it is not clear how or why these interventions work for some individuals. For example, DBT is an intensive multimodal behavior therapy that involves individual therapy, group skills training, 24-hour phone coaching, and a consultation team for therapists. An awareness of 24-hour access to a therapist may create a form of connectedness for patients that prevents suicidal behaviors. However, to answer this question, belongingness would need to be measured throughout treatment to examine if changes in belongingness accounted for the effects on suicidal behaviors. Thus, creative research designs are needed to investigate how current suicide prevention interventions work to reduce suicide research.

Another important area for research will be translating findings on differences in interpersonal functioning across gender, age, race, and nationality to understand demographic differences in suicide ideation, attempts, and deaths. For example, in the United States, older white men have a dramatically elevated rate compared to black men. Might interpersonal factors contribute to this discrepancy? Results from a daily diary study compared affective responses to providing and receiving emotional responses for white and black adults and found that frequently receiving emotional support was associated with negative affect only for white adults, while frequently providing emotional support was more strongly associated with negative affect for black adults compared to white adults. Although speculative and in need of empirical testing, these results suggest that differences in the meaning attributed to the receipt of emotional social support may make older white men more prone to developing perceptions of burdensomeness.

Another example in need of empirical examination from an interpersonal perspective is the following. In most countries in the world, more men die by suicide than women, except in China, where in rural areas, more women die by suicide as men. In addition to the availability of lethal pesticides that might increase risk for women compared to men (since women are more likely to use the method of poisoning than men), it may be that the interplay between social structures and stigma about mental illness in rural China elevate risk.

Finally, a key area for researchers on interpersonal dynamics and suicide is connecting individuals at risk to resources, providers, and service systems. Resources might include crisis or suicide prevention hotlines. Research could investigate methods of disseminating information about this resource. For example, are radio ads, which feature a human voice, more successful than billboards at encouraging those at risk to call? Does online chat with a crisis worker address a suicidal crisis as effectively as talking to someone on the phone? Regarding providers, research is needed on the interpersonal processes occurring during suicide risk assessments, which involve sharing sensitive information and require some degree of trust between clinician and patient. This research is needed especially for older adults because research indicates that they may be less willing than younger adults to disclose suicidal ideation and depression. Further, a large number of older adults who die by suicide are seen by primary care physicians in the months and weeks before their deaths, but do not communicate their suicidal thoughts to providers (or these communications are not recognized and documented as suicide risk).

In sum, interpersonal factors are central to all aspects of prevention: risk assessment, crisis management, and intervention. Interpersonal factors also play a role in the etiology of suicide. Thus, consideration of individuals' degree of social connectedness (e.g., isolated or lonely), the quality of the connections (e.g., discordant or supportive), and their connections (or lack thereof) to providers, resources, family members, and peers, may promote the best suicide prevention strategies and science.

NOTES

1. Funding support: This work was supported in part by Grant No. T32MH20061 from the National Institute of Mental Health.
2. The term social connectedness is synonymous with interpersonal connectedness.

RECOMMENDED READING

Fleischmann, A., Bertolote, J. M., Wasserman, D., De Leo, D., Bolhari, J., Botega, N. J., & Thanh, H. T. (2008). Effectiveness of brief intervention and contact for suicide attempters: A randomized controlled trial in five countries. *Bulletin of the World Health Organization, 86,* 703–709.

Linehan, M. M. (1993). *Cognitive-behavioral treatment of borderline personality disorder.* New York: Guilford.

Motto, J. A., & Bostrom, A. G. (2001). A randomized controlled trial of postcrisis suicide prevention. *Psychiatric Services, 52,* 828–833.

Van Orden, K. A., Witte, T. K., Cukrowicz, K. C., Braithwaite, S. R., Selby, E. A., & Joiner, T. E., Jr. (2010). The interpersonal theory of suicide. *Psychological Review, 117,* 575–600.

REFERENCES

Alexopoulos, G. S., Reynolds, C. F., 3rd, Bruce, M. L., Katz, I. R., Raue, P. J., Mulsant, B. H., & Ten Have, T. (2009). Reducing suicidal ideation and depression in older primary care patients: 24-month outcomes of the PROSPECT study. *American Journal of Psychiatry, 166,* 882–890.

American Association of Suicidology. (2007). Suicide in the U.S.A. Based on Current (2007) Statistics. Retrieved December 1, 2011, from http://www.suicidology.org/web/guest/stats-and-tools/fact-sheets

Baumeister, R. F., & Leary, M. R. (1995). The need to belong: Desire for interpersonal attachments as a fundamental human motivation. *Psychological Bulletin, 117,* 497–529.

Bowlby, J. (1973). *Attachment and loss: Volume 2. Separation.* New York: Basic Books.

Brown, R. M., Dahlen, E., Mills, C., Rick, J., & Biblarz, A. (1999). Evaluation of an evolutionary model of self-preservation and self-destruction. *Suicide & Life-Threatening Behavior, 29,* 58–71.

Butzlaff, R. L., & Hooley, J. M. (1998). Expressed emotion and psychiatric relapse. *Archives of General Psychiatry, 55,* 547–552.

Cacioppo, J. T., & Patrick, W. (2008). *Loneliness: Human nature and the need for social connection.* New York: W.W. Norton & Company.

Chan, S. S., Leung, V. P., Tsoh, J., Li, S. W., Yu, C. S., Yu, G. K., & Chiu, H. F. (2011). Outcomes of a two-tiered multifaceted elderly suicide prevention program in a Hong Kong Chinese community. *American Journal of Geriatric Psychiatry, 19,* 185–196.

de Catanzaro, D. (1995). Reproductive status, family interactions, and suicidal ideation: Surveys of the general public and high-risk groups. *Ethology & Sociobiology, 16,* 385–394.

De Leo, D., Carollo, G., & Dello Buono, M. (1995). Lower suicide rates associated with a Tele-Help/Tele-Check service for the elderly at home. *American Journal of Psychiatry, 152,* 632–634.

De Leo, D., Dello Buono, M., & Dwyer, J. (2002). Suicide among the elderly: The long-term impact of a telephone support and assessment intervention in northern Italy. *British Journal of Psychiatry, 181,* 226–229.

Duberstein, P.R. (2001). Are closed-minded people more open to the idea of killing themselves? *Suicide & Life-Threatening Behavior, 31,* 9–14.

Duberstein, P.R., Conwell, Y., Conner, K., Eberly, S., Evinger, J., & Caine, E. (2004). Poor social integration and suicide: Fact or artifact? A case-control study. *Psychological Medicine, 34,* 1331–1337.

Durkheim, E. (1897). *Le Suicide: Etude de sociologie.* Paris, France: F. Alcan.

Fleischmann, A., Bertolote, J.M., Wasserman, D., De Leo, D., Bolhari, J., Botega, N.J., & Thanh, H.T. (2008). Effectiveness of brief intervention and contact for suicide attempters: A randomized controlled trial in five countries. *Bulletin of the World Health Organization, 86,* 703–709.

Fusé, T. (1980). Suicide and culture in Japan: A study of seppuku as an institutionalized form of suicide. *Social Psychiatry, 15,* 57–63.

Gould, M.S., Kalafat, J., Harrismunfakh, J.L., & Kleinman, M. (2007). An evaluation of crisis hotline outcomes: Part 2: Suicidal callers. *Suicide & Life-Threatening Behavior, 37,* 338–352.

Jobes, D.A., & Maltsberger, J.T. (1995). The hazards of treating suicidal patients. In M.B. Sussman (Ed.), *A perilous calling: The hazards of psychotherapy practice,* pp. 200–214. Oxford, UK: John Wiley & Sons.

Joiner, T. (2005). *Why people die by suicide.* Cambridge, MA: Harvard University Press.

Joiner, T.E., Van Orden, K.A., Witte, T.K., & Rudd, M.D. (2009). *The interpersonal theory of suicide: Guidance for working with suicidal clients.* Washington, DC: American Psychological Association.

Leighton, A.H., & Hughes, C.C. (1955). Notes on Eskimo patterns of suicide. *Southwestern Journal of Anthropology, 11,* 327–338.

Lifton, R.J., Reich, M.R., & Shuichi, K. (1979). *Six lives, six deaths: Portraits from modern Japan.* New Haven, CT: Yale University Press.

Linehan, M.M. (1993). *Cognitive-behavioral treatment of borderline personality disorder.* New York: Guilford.

McPherson, C.J., Wilson, K.G., & Murray, M.A. (2007). Feeling like a burden to others: A systematic review focusing on the end of life. *Palliative Medicine, 21,* 115–128.

Mitchell, A.M., Kim, Y., Prigerson, H.G., & Mortimer-Stephens, M. (2004). Complicated grief in survivors of suicide. *Crisis, 25,* 12–18.

Motto, J.A., & Bostrom, A.G. (2001). A randomized controlled trial of postcrisis suicide prevention. *Psychiatric Services, 52,* 828–833.

Nock, M. K., Borges, G., Bromet, E. J., Cha, C. B., Kessler, R. C., & Lee, S. (2008). Suicide and suicidal behavior. *Epidemiologic Reviews, 30,* 133–154.

Oyama, H., Sakashita, T., Ono, Y., Goto, M., Fujita, M., & Koida, J. (2008). Effect of community-based intervention using depression screening on elderly suicide risk: A meta-analysis of the evidence from Japan. *Community Mental Health Journal, 44,* 311–320.

Pope, K. S., & Tabachnick, B. G. (1993). Therapists' anger, hate, fear, and sexual feelings: National survey of therapist responses, client characteristics, critical events, formal complaints, and training. *Professional Psychology: Research & Practice, 24,* 142–152.

Richman, J. (1986). *Family therapy for suicidal people.* New York: Springer.

Rosenthal, P. A., & Rosenthal, S. (1984). Suicidal behavior by preschool children. *American Journal of Psychiatry, 141,* 520–525.

Sabbath, J. C. (1969). The suicidal adolescent: The expendable child. *Journal of the American Academy of Child Psychiatry, 8,* 272–285.

Shear, M. K., Frank, E., Foa, E., Cherry, C., Reynolds, C. F., 3rd, Vander Bilt, J., & Masters, S. (2001). Traumatic grief treatment: A pilot study. *American Journal of Psychiatry, 158,* 1506–1508.

Turvey, C. L., Conwell, Y., Jones, M. P., Phillips, C., Simonsick, E., Pearson, J. L., & Wallace, R. (2002). Risk factors for late-life suicide: A prospective community-based study. *American Journal of Geriatric Psychiatry, 10,* 398–406.

Unutzer, J., Tang, L., Oishi, S., Katon, W., Williams, J. W., Jr., Hunkeler, E., et al. (2006). Reducing suicidal ideation in depressed older primary care patients. *Journal of the American Geriatric Society, 54,* 1550–1556.

Van Orden, K. A., Witte, T. K., Cukrowicz, K. C., Braithwaite, S. R., Selby, E. A., & Joiner, T. E., Jr. (2010). The interpersonal theory of suicide. *Psychological Review, 117,* 575–600.

Wedig, M. M., & Nock, M. K. (2007). Parental expressed emotion and adolescent self-injury. *Journal of the American Academy of Child & Adolescent Psychiatry, 46,* 1171–1178.

Wilson, K. G., Chochinov, H. M., McPherson, C. J., Skirko, M. G., Allard, P., Chary, S., et al. (2007). Desire for euthanasia or physician-assisted suicide in palliative cancer care. *Health Psychology, 26,* 314–323.

Woznica, J. G., & Shapiro, J. R. (1990). An analysis of adolescent suicide attempts: The expendable child. *Journal of Pediatric Psychology, 15,* 789–796.

Young, J. (2002). Morals, suicide, and psychiatry: A view from Japan. *Bioethics, 16,* 412–424.

9
Self-Harm and Suicide

Amy M. Brausch and Jennifer J. Muehlenkamp

Behaviors in which a person deliberately tries to harm oneself or end his or her life often draw a certain level of interest among others because these behaviors are perplexing, and they go against deep-rooted beliefs about humans' innate desire to promote survival. Many people describe struggling to understand why a person would want to purposefully end his or her life, and a greater number report having significant difficulties with why people would intentionally cause a physical injury to themselves. Even among professionals who work with the topic of suicide and self-harm, there can be differences in reactions and attitudes toward individuals who engage in such self-damaging behaviors. It is because of this confusion and a strong desire to prevent unwanted injuries or losses of life that researchers are working hard to figure out why some people engage in these behaviors when others do not. Being able to answer aspects of the question *why* can help inform effective prevention and treatment programs.

The topic of self-harm is further complicated with mixed messages about what behaviors constitute a suicide attempt compared to those that would be considered nonsuicidal self-harm. Being able to accurately identify behaviors that are considered suicidal from nonsuicidal self-injuries is important because it helps researchers and mental health professionals figure out the relationship between, and the risks for, self-harm and suicide which can inform prevention and treatment. A number of experts have suggested that self-harmful behaviors be categorized according to some primary features of the behavior such as intent or motivation, lethality, and immediacy of harm (Nock & Favazza, 2009; Silverman, Berman, Sanddal, O'Carroll, & Joiner, 2007). Based on these recommendations, different terms are used to represent the behaviors being studied and treated. A *suicide attempt* is considered to be a self-inflicted act that could lead to injury in which there is some intent for the behavior to cause one's death. In contrast, *self-harm* is a behavior characterized by direct, intentional, and immediate destruction of bodily tissue that is engaged in without intent to die and for purposes not socially accepted by one's culture. This last part of the definition is important because it clarifies that behaviors such as tattoos, piercings, and other practices that may damage body tissue but are for aesthetic or culturally sanctioned practices are not considered to be self-harm.

However, self-harm is a broad term and researchers have tried to further clarify it by identifying examples of direct self-harm (e.g., cutting, burning, skin abrading) from indirect self-harm behaviors (e.g., self-starvation, binge drinking, self-poisoning). In an attempt to make the distinction from suicide explicit, researchers within the United States, Canada, and parts of Europe have begun using the term *nonsuicidal self-injury (NSSI)* instead of self-harm, whereas researchers throughout most of Europe, Australia, and Asian nations use the term *deliberate self-harm (DSH)* to represent similar behaviors. A recent study of the prevalence of DSH and NSSI in adolescents around the world found that rates were not significantly different from each other (Muehlenkamp, Claes, Havertape, & Plener, 2012), concluding that NSSI and DSH likely represent the same phenomenon. Thus, for this chapter we will use the term *self-harm* to represent self-inflicted injuries engaged in without intent to die and *suicide attempt/suicidal behavior* for self-inflicted injuries with intent to die. This chapter will (1) highlight the features that best differentiate suicide from self-harm which can inform assessments of these behaviors, (2) review psychosocial factors that can increase the risk for suicide behavior and/or self-harm, including current research on the effects of the Internet as both a risk and protective factor, (3) describe the relationship between self-harm and suicide, and (4) conclude with recommendations for prevention, treatment, and directions for future research.

PREVALENCE OF SUICIDE AND SELF-HARM

Both suicide attempts and self-harm behaviors show a pattern with increasing rates during adolescence and young adulthood. However, rates for suicide deaths are highest among elderly Caucasian males, and research around the world shows that the rate of suicide increases as age increases (CDC, 2011). In contrast, the highest rates for self-harm occur between the ages of 14 and 25, with rates of self-harm behavior significantly decreasing after middle age (Hawton & Harriss, 2008). Recent large-scale studies of adults in the United States estimate that 4 percent have a history of self-harm behavior, and approximately 1 percent currently self-harm (Klonsky, 2011; Klonsky, Oltmanns, & Turkheimer, 2003). This rate of current self-harm among adults is a little higher than the annual prevalence estimate for suicide attempts (0.5 percent), but comparable to the percent reporting having made a suicide plan (1.0 percent) (Crosby, Han, Ortega, Parks, & Gfroerer, 2011).

Within adolescent populations, there is a larger difference between the prevalence of suicide attempts and acts of self-harm. Current research estimates that around 18 percent of adolescents have engaged in self-harm in their life, often multiple times (Muehlenkamp et al., 2012). This same study found that rates of self-harm in the past year averaged 9.5 percent, which is consistent with large-scale epidemiological studies from select regions in the United States and internationally (Madge et al., 2008; Taliaferro et al., 2012). These rates are in sharp contrast to the concerning, but lower prevalence rates of suicide attempts among adolescents which are estimated to range between 2 percent and 6 percent of the population (CDC, 2009, 2011). The large number of individuals who engage in self-harm is particularly alarming because some studies and theories suggest that a history of self-harm is a strong risk factor for future suicide. Knowing the ways in which self-harm is different from suicide becomes important for identifying the unique experiences or factors that do increase the likelihood for suicide among those who engage in self-harm.

DIFFERENTIATING SUICIDE FROM SELF-HARM: INTENT AND FUNCTION

As mentioned earlier, the primary differentiation between self-harm and suicide attempts is whether or not the person expresses an intent to die as an outcome for the behavior. Using intent to die to discriminate self-harm from suicide attempts has reliability and validity (Nock & Kessler, 2006), with some research showing that people who self-harm, but have no history of suicide attempts, report less suicidal thinking and more attraction to life than those with histories of both self-harm and suicide (Muehlenkamp & Gutierrez, 2007). Individuals who self-harm report they do not expect, nor believe, that death would be a likely outcome, whereas, individuals who report intent to die often engage in more lethal behaviors (Harriss, Hawton, & Zahl, 2005). However, using lethal intent as the primary way to differentiate the behaviors can be problematic given that suicidal ideation can fluctuate and change in severity over time and in response to unpredictable events (Nock, Prinstein, & Sterba, 2009). It is also hard to be confident that people accurately report the intent of their self-harm behavior because they are reflecting back on a past behavior and trying to remember their state of mind during a very tumultuous moment. Despite the difficulties with assessing suicidal intent, recent research examining the functions reported for engaging in self-harm or suicide attempts can help differentiate the behaviors. When asked to identify various functions for their behavior, individuals who engage in self-harm and suicide attempts typically report multiple reasons for each episode. Self-harm incidents receive an average of 4.1 functions endorsed for one episode and range up to 12 (Whitlock, Muehlenkamp, & Eckenrode, 2008), while suicide attempts receive an average of three reasons, ranging up to 8 (Brown, Comtois, & Linehan, 2002). Research also shows that self-harm and suicide attempts tend to be motivated by very similar reasons that broadly involve the regulation of internal states and interpersonal environments (Baetens, Claes, Muehlenkamp, Grietens, & Onghena, 2011; Brown et al., 2002). However, the patterns of primary reasons endorsed for each behavior are significantly different for self-harm versus suicide.

The dominant function reported by individuals who engage in self-harm is to regulate an aversive internal state. Both adults and adolescents acknowledge that self-harm is used primarily to reduce the experience of intolerable negative emotional or cognitive states, to self-punish, or to generate some type of feeling (Baetens et al., 2011; Klonsky & Muehlenkamp, 2007). When asking individuals to report on their self-harming behavior, many note experiencing strong and increasing negative emotions prior to self-harming, followed by a large reduction in negative emotions and/or an increase in positive emotions, most often relief, after the self-harm (Nock, Prinstein, & Sterba, 2009). Recent studies that have focused on the physiological effects of engaging in self-harm have also found a significant decrease in physiological arousal after research subjects imagined acts of self-harm (Welch et al., 2008). Self-harm also seems to be motivated by interpersonal reasons (e.g., letting others see the severity of one's distress), but these intents tend to be secondary to managing negative internal emotions (Klonsky, 2007).

In contrast, suicide attempts appear to be dominated by strong desires to escape or to unburden others (Brown et al., 2002; Joiner, 2005). There have been very few studies directly comparing the reasons for engaging in suicide attempts versus self-harm. Among the studies that exist, suicide attempts are more likely to be motivated by reasons of wanting to die and making others better off, whereas self-harm is primarily motivated by desires to regulate emotions or self-punish (Baetens et al., 2011; Haas & Popp, 2006). Notably, there is evidence that some persons report using self-harm to prevent, or avert, an impulse to attempt suicide (e.g., Klonsky,

2007). This reason should alarm mental health professionals to possible increased risk for a suicide attempt, but nonetheless offers further evidence that these two behaviors are distinct. Therefore, there is evidence to suggest that the motivation, or reasons, underlying self-harm and suicide attempts offer a valid way to differentiate these behaviors.

Methods, Lethality, Frequency

Self-harm and suicide appear to be clearly differentiated by the methods used to inflict injury and the frequency of the behaviors. The methods used for suicide attempts tend to be highly lethal whereas most self-harm involves low-lethality methods that result in minimal damage (Berman, Jobes, & Silverman, 2006; Walsh, 2006). The most common methods of suicide attempts worldwide are hanging and ingestion of toxic substances (Berman et al., 2006). Within the United States, the three most frequent methods of suicide attempts in order are: firearms, suffocation, and poisoning/overdose. Cutting is among the *least* common methods of documented suicide attempts and accounts for less than 1.4 percent of all deaths in the United States (CDC, 2009). When cutting does result in death, it tends to be due to the location of the cuts, such as on the jugular vein or carotid artery (Berman et al., 2006). In contrast, cutting is the most commonly used method for self-harm and is usually performed on areas of the body associated with very low lethality such as the forearms and upper legs. Other common methods of self-harm, which are arguably less lethal than cutting, include skin abrading, interfering with wound healing, self-hitting/banging, and burning (Klonsky & Muehlenkamp, 2007; Whitlock et al., 2011). Among studies that examine self-injuries both with and without suicidal intent, significant differences are found between self-poisoners and self-cutters that are comparable to those found between suicide attempters and self-harm-only groups (Lilley et al., 2008), suggesting that methods reliably differentiate between these behaviors.

The number of methods used and frequency with which a person engages in self-harm or suicide attempts also significantly differ. Most people endorsing repeated acts of self-harm report using more than one method for their self-injury, an average of four different methods (Muehlenkamp & Gutierrez, 2004; Whitlock et al., 2009, 2011). In opposition, those endorsing repeated suicide attempts tend to use the same method. Among those engaging in self-harm who also attempt suicide, the suicide attempt method tends to be different from the methods used for self-harm and is most frequently an overdose (Walsh, 2006). For self-harm, the number of methods used is positively correlated with the frequency of the self-harm. While approximately one-quarter of community-based youth report engaging in only one or two acts of self-harm, a majority endorses a high frequency of repetitive self-harm that ranges over 100 separate episodes (Taliaferro, Muehlenkamp, Borowsky, McMorris, & Kugler, 2012; Whitlock et al., 2011). The frequency of suicide attempts across the lifetime tends to be comparatively low, with lifetime frequencies averaging around two attempts, and repeat episodes of self-harm are much more numerous than suicide attempt repetitions (Lilley et al., 2008). Despite this high frequency of self-harm, very few people report requiring medical help for the injuries (Nixon, Cloutier, & Aggarwal, 2002; Whitlock, Powers, & Eckenrode, 2006), highlighting the low lethality of self-harm. In contrast, more individuals who attempt suicide seek help or require medical attention than those who engage in nonsuicidal self-harm (Evans, Hawton, Rodham, & Deeks, 2005), even when controlling for the number of undocumented suicide attempts. Therefore, the existing data strongly support differentiating self-harm from suicide attempts on the basis of the method used, body locations injured, frequency of the behavior, and overall severity/lethality of the behavior.

Psychosocial Differences

One complication for differentiating self-harm from suicide attempts is that they appear to share many of the same risk factors. Although there are very few studies directly comparing self-harm and suicide attempts on such factors, a closer inspection of the research reveals that there are reliable, although small, differences. While suicide is generally associated with greater severity of psychosocial dysfunction than self-harm, it is important to remember that the global group differences described in the research may not always be applicable to an individual person.

Psychiatric Diagnoses. Suicide attempts and self-harm are associated with a variety of psychiatric diagnoses, and the presence of any diagnosis is associated with increased risk for self-harm and/or suicide. It has been documented that around the world, 94 percent–98 percent of persons who attempt or die from suicide meet criteria for at least one psychiatric disorder (Bertolote, Fleischmann, De Leo, & Wasserman, 2004). However, a more recent study reported that only 66 percent of those who attempted suicide across 21 different countries had a preexisting Axis-I disorder (Nock, Hwang et al., 2009). Many individuals who do not meet full criteria for a disorder still experience significant symptoms leading experts to conclude that it would be unusual for suicidal behavior to occur without some psychopathology being present (Hawton & van Heeringen, 2009).

Self-harm is associated with a wide variety of diagnoses, but to a lesser extent than suicide (Jacobson, Muehlenkamp, Miller, & Turner, 2008; Lofthouse, Muehlenkamp, & Adler, 2009). The research suggests that around 22 percent–40 percent of those in community samples and up to 87 percent of inpatient adolescents meet criteria for at least one disorder (Klonsky & Olino, 2008; Nock et al., 2006). The strength of the association between self-harm and psychiatric disorders appears weaker than for those who attempt suicide. For example, the presence of substance use or abuse has been found to be a critical factor in increasing suicide risk (Arsenault-Lapierre, Kim, & Turecki, 2004), yet substance use and abuse is much less common in those who self-harm and exhibits a weak relationship to self-harm (Whitlock et al., 2006). Other studies find differences in the severity of symptoms between those with self-harm versus suicide attempts (Jacobson et al., 2008). Yet, individuals endorsing even one act of self-harm in their lifetime tend to show greater levels of psychopathology compared to individuals with no self-harm history (Andover, Pepper, Ryabchenko, Orrico, & Gibb, 2005).

The research appears to support hypotheses that suicide is characterized to a greater degree by the presence and severity of psychiatric disorders than is self-harm. Due to the limited number of studies directly comparing self-harm to suicide on psychiatric diagnoses, using just the presence or severity of diagnoses is not sufficient to differentiate the behaviors.

Abuse/Family Environment. It is well established that childhood abuse, particularly sexual abuse, is a significant risk factor for suicide (Brodsky & Stanley, 2008), and similar ideas have been proposed for self-harm. Sexual abuse has been found to have a strong relationship to suicide even when other factors, such as the environment and co-occurring psychiatric symptoms, are taken into account (Joiner et al., 2007). A history of sexual abuse also appears to be related to a first suicide attempt occurring at an earlier age (Slama et al., 2009). In contrast, a recent review found the association between sexual abuse and self-harm to be somewhat small (Klonsky & Moyer, 2008). Studies have shown that the association between childhood sexual abuse and self-harm is often explained by other factors (Weierich & Nock, 2008). However, a strong connection remains between physical abuse and self-harm even when taking other factors into account, suggesting physical abuse may have a stronger relationship to engaging in self-harm than sexual abuse. The presence of sexual abuse seems to be associated with engaging in chronic and repetitive self-harm and so may play a role in the severity of self-harm behaviors (Klonsky & Moyer, 2008). Current research, then, indicates that physical abuse is strongly predictive of engaging in self-harm, while sexual abuse appears to be more strongly linked to suicide attempts (Hawton & van Heeringen, 2009; Nock & Kessler, 2006).

Along with abuse experiences, both self-harm and suicide have been associated with experiencing a conflictual and invalidating family environment that is characterized by high levels of parental criticism and low cohesiveness (Muehlenkamp & Gutierrez, 2007; Weierich & Nock, 2008). This research indicates that professionals who intervene with individuals engaging in either self-harm or suicidal behavior should at least assess for, and likely address, adverse family environments and experiences.

Impulsivity and Aggression. Both self-harm and suicide attempts have a relationship with impulsivity and aggression (Claes et al., 2010; Fazaa & Page, 2009), but these characteristics may have a stronger association with self-harm than with suicide. For example, aggression trait scores differentiated self-harm and suicide attempts among adult women with borderline personality disorder (Stanley, Gameroff, Michalsen, & Mann, 2001), with those reporting self-harm scoring higher on aggression. Similarly, Klonsky and Olino (2008) found that individuals who had engaged only in self-harm exhibited more traits of impulsivity than did those who had attempted suicide. Acts of self-harm are less likely to involve planning, with many individuals reporting that they engage in self-harm within an hour or less of experiencing an urge (Lloyd-Richardson, Perrine, Dierker, & Kelley, 2007). In contrast, many suicide attempts involve some planning, and those associated with planning and premeditation are often more lethal (Witte et al., 2008). Other research has found mixed results when trying to determine whether suicide attempts or self-harm are more strongly related to impulsivity (Baca-Garcia et al., 2005; Dougherty et al., 2009). Collectively, it appears that impulsivity and aggression are related to both self-harm and suicide, but impulsivity in particular may be more strongly related to self-harm than to suicide. This is consistent with Joiner's (2005) theory suggesting that impulsivity is a broad risk factor for suicide that is expressed via impulsive risk-taking, such as self-harm, resulting in an increased capacity for suicide. The inconsistent results across studies suggest there is no definitive answer at this point regarding the role of impulsivity or aggression, and additional research in this area is needed.

Bullying.   Recent reports in the media of adolescents and young adults who have died by suicide and were identified as being victims of bullying have sparked continued interest in the relationship between bullying and self-harm or suicide. Bullying has been defined as aggressive behavior toward others who are not able to defend themselves, or as a dominant person intending to cause mental or physical suffering in others (Kim & Leventhal, 2008). Researchers have recently made the distinction between traditional bullying, which occurs on a direct interpersonal level, and cyberbullying, which occurs through use of the Internet and/or cell phones. It is estimated that up to 30 percent of 11–16-year-olds are frequently involved in bullying behavior either as a bully, a victim, or both (Klomek, Marrocoo, Kleinman, Schonfeld, & Gould, 2007). Rates increase to 40 percent for cyberbulling among middle and high school students (Schneider, O'Donnell, Stueve, & Coulter, 2012).

A consistent link between bullying and suicidal behavior has been found for both adolescents and adults. In a large study of Korean middle school students, all students involved in bullying behavior (bully, victim, or bully-victim) reported more suicidal ideation and suicide attempts than students not involved in bullying (Kim, Koh, & Leventhal, 2005). Another large study of American high school students found very similar results and reported that, the greater the frequency of bullying behavior, the more likely a student was to endorse symptoms of depression, thoughts about suicide, and suicide attempts (Klomek et al., 2007). It is also important to note that the effects of bullying seem to be most harmful to those involved in bullying both as a bully and a victim, and appear to be more detrimental to girls than boys. This pattern holds for adults as well, with research finding that experiences of childhood bullying were predictive of adult suicide attempts even after accounting for other adverse life events such as childhood maltreatment and domestic violence (Meltzer, Vostanis, Ford, Bebbington, & Dennis, 2011). Bullying in childhood has also been found to be related to suicide death by the age of 25, and this relationship is stronger for females than for males (Klomek et al., 2009).

While there is less research available on the relationship between bullying and self-harm, the association for risk seems quite similar to that of suicide. One recent study of over 20,000 American high school students found that bullying significantly increased the chances that students experienced symptoms of depression, suicidal behavior, and self-harm. Students who experienced both cyberbullying and traditional bullying reported the most psychological distress and were four times more likely to report self-harm behavior (Schneider et al., 2012). Being both a bully and a victim also seems to increase the risk for self-harm, just as it does for suicidal ideation and attempts (Barker, Arseneault, Brendgen, Fontaine, & Maughan, 2008). When examining specific factors that may increase or decrease risk for self-harm among those who are bullied, it seems that experiencing negative emotions as a result of the bullying best explains engaging in self-harm. Bullying may have less of an impact on individuals and be less likely to lead to self-harm among those who are raised by more authoritative parents and exhibit higher levels of self-control (Hay & Meldrum, 2010). Continued research in this area will provide additional information about the effects of all types of bullying, as well as identifying the risk and protective factors for the negative effects resulting from bullying and whether aspects of bullying differentially affect engagement in self-harm versus suicide.

COGNITIVE FEATURES OF SELF-HARM AND SUICIDE

Problem-Solving

Overall, there is convincing evidence that suicidal persons experience limited abilities to generate and implement effective problem-solving strategies (Speckens & Hawton, 2005). Suicidal adults have been found to generate fewer and less effective problem-solving strategies and to be less flexible in their thinking when faced with tasks to be solved (Williams, Barnhofer, Crane, & Beck, 2005). Suicidal adolescents have also been found to be less adept at problem-solving than nonsuicidal adolescents, although these differences may be explained by the cognitive difficulties typically associated with depressive symptoms and hopelessness (Hawton & van Heeringen, 2009). The findings suggest that problem-solving difficulties may result from other factors that interfere with thinking, like hopelessness, which end up impairing the individual's ability for coping and problem-solving.

In contrast to suicidal individuals, adults and adolescents who engage in self-harm are able to generate a number of adaptive solutions to a problem that is presented to them. However, these individuals show difficulties choosing a solution to implement, as well as believing that they can effectively solve the problem (Nock & Mendes, 2008). One study found that self-harming individuals reported similar problem-solving methods for coping as nonharming individuals, but were more likely to use avoidance and less likely to use support from others as coping skills (Andover, Pepper, & Gibb, 2007). This indicates that while able to recognize effective solutions to problems, those who self-harm are not able to adequately use their solutions. Although there are no known studies directly comparing problem-solving skills between self-harm and suicide attempt groups, it seems that the primary difference in problem-solving difficulties between the two is in the ability to generate solutions, with suicidal persons being less able, and being able to utilize or implement a solution. This subtle difference between groups may be due to increased hopelessness among suicidal individuals which limits effective problem-solving.

Hopelessness. It has been noted that self-harm and suicidal behavior can be clearly differentiated in the level of hopelessness experienced (Walsh, 2006). Hopelessness is identified as a critical risk factor for suicidal behavior (Brown, Beck, Steer, & Grisham, 2000), but is less commonly found among individuals who self-harm. One explanation for the difference in level of hopelessness reported by these two groups may be the tendency for suicidal persons to use "all or nothing" thinking. Suicidal individuals may believe that their pain cannot be relieved, and suicide becomes the only and/or final answer. Consistent with this idea, a lack of positive thinking about the future has a strong relationship with suicide (O'Connor, Fraser, Whyte, MacHale, & Masterton, 2008). By comparison, individuals who self-harm may have less pessimistic thinking because they feel capable of changing their situation or modifying their pain via the self-harm and, therefore, are not hopeless about alleviating their distress. As expert clinicians have noted, self-harm can offer a sense of control over a distressing situation, and the perceived control is an opposite feeling to that of hopelessness (Walsh, 2006). Studies have also found that self-harming individuals report greater attraction to life, more reasons for living, more thinking about the future, and less hopelessness than those who had also attempted suicide (Brausch & Gutierrez, 2009; Muehlenkamp & Gutierrez, 2004, 2007). Thus, it appears as though hopelessness is a cognitive attitude that characterizes suicidal behavior rather than self-harm. If hopelessness begins to increase substantially for a person who is engaged in self-harm, one should be concerned about risk for suicidal behavior and use appropriate assessment and intervention methods to avert a potential suicide attempt.

INTERNET INFLUENCES: RISK OR PROTECTIVE?

As Internet use among youth has grown rapidly during the past decade, more attention is being paid to how the Internet may increase or decrease risk for suicide and self-harm. Because self-harm is typically performed in secret and tends to be misunderstood by those who do not engage in the behavior, use of the Internet to communicate about self-harm may be particularly appealing. Some researchers have conducted content analyses of online posts to either Facebook or YouTube in an effort to identify the possible risks and benefits to using such sites for sharing information about one's personal struggle with self-harm. The research suggests that a primary benefit to online communication about self-harm is that individuals receive social support from peers who share in the behavior (Lewis, Heath, Michal, & Duggan, 2012), with a substantial number of posts (28 percent) being categorized by outside observers as being positive and supportive (Whitlock et al., 2006). One study found that individuals who joined a self-harm "e-community" reported decreases in self-harm after becoming involved in the group (Johnson, Zastawny, & Kulpa, 2010), which may be explained by the experience of social acceptance and support gained from the online interactions.

Despite online social support being identified as a potential benefit, a substantial number of risks have also been observed. These risks include the potential for reinforcing self-harm behavior through sharing personal experiences and strategies, as well as triggering urges in vulnerable individuals for subsequent self-harm after viewing such information. An extensive review of Internet message boards for self-harm found that 19.5 percent of posts described motivation or triggers for self-harm, 9 percent described ideas for concealing the behavior, another 9 percent discussed self-harm as an addictive behavior, and about 6 percent focused on requesting or sharing self-harm techniques (Whitlock et al., 2006). Other content reviews of similar online sites note that discussion and posts frequently contain detailed descriptions of the self-harm behavior, emphasizing pain and suffering more than recovery. Themes of self-harm being an effective coping strategy and a glamorized behavior have also been observed (Lewis et al., 2012). Posts that fall under the theme of shared strategies tend to include tips on how to conceal the behavior, how to care for wounds and how to self-injure using techniques to minimize pain, and these are thought to possibly deter self-harming individuals from seeking treatment (Lewis et al., 2012).

A major concern for mental health professionals is that accessing images of self-harm on the Internet may serve as a trigger for vulnerable individuals to initiate or continue self-harm behavior. One extensive review of the top 100 self-harm themed videos posted to YouTube in 2009 noted that these videos had been viewed collectively over two million times. More than half of the videos did not contain a warning about the potential for content to trigger self-harm, and 80 percent of the videos were accessible to *all visitors* to the YouTube site. While many videos were categorized as neutral in their overall message about self-harm, many depicted images of moderate injuries (Lewis, Heath, St Denis, & Noble, 2011). A follow-up study that looked for themes among comments posted about the videos found that self-disclosure of one's own self-harm was the most frequent comment, followed by themes of feedback and encouragement for the maker of the video. Most of the comments did not mention recovery, and 34 percent of comments made reference to continued self-harm (Lewis, Heath, Sornberger, & Arbuthnott, 2012). While it appears there are some benefits and potentially substantial risks to online interactions around self-harm, more research is needed to study the actual effects of exposure to this type of media and whether such exposure triggers acts of self-harm or promotes help-seeking.

The themes and patterns of use identified for suicide and the Internet differ somewhat from those identified for self-harm. For example, Biddle, Donovan, Hawton, Kapur, and Gunnell (2008) identified three dominant types of suicide websites: pro-suicide websites, sites where individuals can make suicide pacts, and sites focusing on suicide prevention. An Internet search for "suicide" will yield a vast number ($n > 480$) of pro-suicide websites with almost 30 percent including content about specific suicide methods (Biddle et al., 2008), and roughly 25 percent of the content of these sites included information about suicide prevention. The potential negative impact of Internet sites focused on suicide appears to differ with age. McCarthy (2010) reported that, as general population search volumes for suicide increased, suicide rates actually decreased, suggesting individuals in crisis may be using the Internet for help-seeking. However, the opposite relationship was found for 15–24-year-olds, such that as the search volume for suicide-related terms increased, so did documented suicide deaths (McCarthy, 2010). Relatedly, when comparing suicide rates and the number of Internet users in 75 countries, Shah (2010) found that in both males and females, suicide rates tended to increase with the prevalence of Internet users. Another recent concern is the use of the Internet to create virtual "meeting places" for individuals who are experiencing suicidal thoughts and to provide the opportunity for strangers to make "suicide pacts" with one another. This phenomenon has been identified and studied mostly in Japan, where the overall suicide rates are relatively high when compared to countries such as the United States. There are a number of documented cases in Japan where groups of individuals, who found each other on Internet sites, were later discovered to have planned and then died by suicide together (Naito, 2007).

Conversely, there are websites that have been identified as focusing on suicide prevention and whose forum members post mostly positive and supportive comments. A survey of German-speaking individuals, some of whom reported past or current suicidal thoughts, examined their experiences of accessing a suicide-related forum (Eichenberg, 2008). Most participants in this survey reported accessing the forum because they were interested in meeting individuals with similar problems (81 percent) from whom to gain support and understanding, and most users indicated that they were not interested in finding a "suicide partner." This same study also found a significant reduction in suicidal thoughts from the time individuals began accessing the forum to the time of the survey, although one cannot determine that accessing the survey *caused* the decrease in thoughts (Eichenberg, 2008). Sites such as Facebook have also taken initiative and partnered with suicide prevention groups to establish mechanisms through which suicidal persons can be identified and linked to help via online channels. The public and various fields of study are recognizing the role online mechanisms play in both increasing and potentially decreasing risk for self-harm and suicide. This line of research is relatively new, and so a great deal of research is needed to fully understand the risk and protective benefits of online access and communication around these behaviors. To date, it appears that there is a better balance of protective versus risk-based websites for self-harm behavior than there are for suicidal behavior, but the limited amount of research suggests such conclusions may be premature. What the research appears to support is that monitoring Internet use and evaluating the content of Internet sites accessed could be important in reducing risk for engaging in, or relapsing back into, self-harm and suicidal behavior.

RELATIONSHIP BETWEEN SELF-HARM AND SUICIDE ATTEMPTS

While this chapter is mostly focused on describing how self-harm and suicide differ from each other, it is equally important to know how these two behaviors are related since they co-occur within some individuals. For example, one study found that thoughts of suicide overlap with thoughts of self-harm for approximately 40 percent of adolescents presenting to an Emergency Department's crisis service (Cloutier, Martin, Kennedy, Nixon, & Muehlenkamp, 2010). Another study of adolescents discharged from an inpatient treatment facility reported that increased frequency of self-harm was related to a weaker and slower cessation of suicidal ideation over time (Prinstein et al., 2008). Other studies find that many individuals who have attempted suicide also have a history of self-harm and that this history statistically predicts the suicide attempt behavior more strongly than many other known risk factors (Wichstrom et al., 2009). High rates of overlap between suicide attempts and histories of self-harm are found within clinical samples of adolescents with estimates ranging up toward 70 percent, whereas the co-occurrence of self-harm and suicide attempts within nontreatment settings, such as high school students, is estimated to be around 5 percent–10 percent (Asarnow et al., 2011; Muehlenkamp & Guttierez, 2007).

In an adult sample, Hawton and Harriss (2008) estimated self-harm to suicide ratios, finding that self-harm occurs approximately 36 times to every one suicide. The ratio between self-harm and suicide varied substantially across genders (lower ratio in males) and ages (lower as age increased), but remained high. Nock and colleagues (2006) found that using a greater number of self-harm methods and engaging in self-harm across multiple years were significantly associated with having a higher frequency of suicide attempts. In a large study of college students, Whitlock and her collaborators (2008) found that individuals who engaged in more frequent self-harm and who used more methods for their self-harm were significantly more likely to fall into a "severe" classification group. This "severe" group also had the highest rates of attempted suicide and a higher level of suicidal ideation. Others have also estimated that having a history of self-harm results in a 34-fold increased risk for death by suicide (Cooper et al., 2005). Collectively, this research indicates that self-harm and suicide are closely connected, with self-harm being a risk factor for suicide.

Cross-sectional studies have also offered evidence that self-harm may precede suicide attempts, providing further evidence of increasing risk for future suicide. Research consistently finds that individuals report first engaging in self-harm at earlier ages than the age they first attempt suicide (Cloutier et al., 2010; Klonsky & Olino, 2008), suggesting self-harm occurs first. Consistent with such findings, a three-year longitudinal study of college students (Whitlock et al., under review) reported that acts of self-harm occurred before a suicide attempt proportionally more often than the reverse. Other studies have focused on trying to predict, retrospectively, the occurrence of a suicide attempt while including history of self-harm as a risk factor. In a sample of adult psychiatric patients, Andover and Gibb

(2010) found those with a history of self-harm were more likely to have attempted suicide, and that the lethality of the suicide attempts was greater among those with a history of self-harm. Additionally, the frequency of self-harm predicted a history of suicide attempts as strongly as current suicidal ideation, and more so than scores for depression, hopelessness, and borderline personality disorder. This suggests that the presence and frequency of self-harm is important to understanding the potential likelihood of a future suicide attempt and that those who engage in self-harm are probably more vulnerable to attempting suicide than those who do not self-harm.

Studies of adolescents receiving treatment for depression have found similar results, with suicide attempts during follow-up periods being predicted by a history of self-harm, alongside factors such as poor family functioning and feelings of hopelessness (Asarnow et al., 2011; Wilkinson, Kelvin, Roberts, Dubicka, & Goodyer, 2011). In their longitudinal study of college students, Whitlock and colleagues (in review) reported that, among individuals with a history of self-harm, having engaged in 20 or more episodes of self-harm was predictive of a future suicidal action (creating a plan or attempting), even after a large number of known risk and protective factors were accounted for. Having engaged in a higher frequency of lifetime self-harm was associated with a 4-fold increased risk of suicidal action and represented the highest amount of risk compared to the other significant predictors. Some have found that the frequency of self-harm is not related to suicidal behavior, but that the severity of self-harm is (Nock et al., 2006; Wichstrom, 2009). However, the severity of self-harm tends to increase with frequency, and so the two are interrelated (Whitlock et al., 2008). These studies offer strong evidence in support of the idea that self-harm is a serious risk factor for future suicide attempts. It may be that the history and frequency of self-harm is a stronger predictor of suicidal behavior than many other commonly studied behaviors and is worthy of careful attention in efforts to prevent suicide.

INTERVENTIONS FOR SELF-HARM AND SUICIDE

Due to the strong relationship between self-harm and future suicidal behavior, one approach to prevention of suicide may be to focus on interventions for self-harm. Treatments that directly focus on reducing self-harm behavior first, before moving onto other problem areas, have shown some success in significantly reducing suicidal behavior and attempts (e.g., Linehan et al., 2006). In addition, a handful of studies have demonstrated that treatments that specifically address factors contributing to suicidal ideation and attempts can also significantly reduce suicidal behavior and prevent future attempts (Jobes, 2006). However, there remain very few empirically supported treatment options for addressing suicidal or self-harm behaviors.

In a review of treatment options for adults who engage in self-harm, Muehlenkamp (2006) identified cognitive-behavioral therapy (CBT) that emphasized a problem-solving approach and dialectical behavior therapy (DBT) as the treatments with the most promise for reducing self-harm. Both of these treatments tend to address some of the dominant deficits or areas of dysfunction common to self-harm. However, a recent review of empirical treatment studies for self-harm that examined these two treatment approaches showed limited support for their abilities to directly reduce self-harm. Problem-solving therapy was found to decrease suicidal ideation, hopelessness, depressive symptoms, and increase problem-solving ability, but was not found to directly reduce self-harm behavior. Similarly, studies evaluating the effectiveness of DBT show the treatment successfully decreasing depressive symptoms, suicidal ideation and attempts, and psychiatric hospitalizations, but no direct decrease in self-harm behavior could be identified (Brausch & Girresch, 2012). Some of the lack of success may be due to the fact the evaluations of the treatment effects did not focus specifically on self-harm. Given the known functions of self-harm and the focus of these types of treatments, both CBT and DBT approaches are considered acceptable and recommended frameworks from which to guide the treatment of self-harm (Klonsky, Muehlenkamp, Lewis, & Walsh, 2012) and suicide (McKeon, 2009).

CONCLUSIONS

Suicide and self-harm represent significant public health problems and devastating experiences for those individually affected. While these behaviors are conceptually different from each other, they do share a number of similarities and risk factors. Furthermore, suicide and self-harm are closely tied to one another with self-harm demonstrating a strong association with suicidal ideation and future suicidal behavior. Due to the close connections between these behaviors, it is essential that professionals and researchers closely attend to both behaviors in the work that is conducted. For example, Joiner (2005) offers a theory explaining suicide in which one of the key components is the acquired capability to engage in lethal self-inflicted injury. Participating in self-harm behaviors fits nicely within this theoretical model as a clear risk factor for suicide, and research supports this idea. Thus, professionals need to carefully assess both self-harm and suicidal behavior, paying careful attention to the differences and motives between the behaviors, so that appropriate interventions can occur. In addition, when working with someone who engages in self-harm, indicators of suicide risk need to be carefully monitored. Treatment focused on making changes for a person that reduce the frequency and severity of the self-harm is likely to be the first line of prevention against future suicide.

Despite the recent advances and growth of knowledge in this area, there are still many directions to pursue in order to gain a stronger understanding of the relationship between self-harm and suicide. Much of the current research has examined the link between these behaviors at one time point. To really understand the complex associations among the risk and protective factors for both behaviors as well as the true relationship between self-harm and suicide, longitudinal studies are required. Another area that has been largely neglected, but which is essential for enriching our knowledge and prevention efforts, is the study of the experiences of individuals who have overcome self-harm and those who have survived suicide attempts and are now functioning better in their lives. Creating and testing the impact of large-scale, global prevention messages or programs as well as more specifically targeted prevention initiatives will also help move the field forward. There has already been a substantial increase in the amount of research being conducted on the similarities and differences between self-harm and suicide in the past decade. The field is clearly moving in the right direction and, with more researchers and clinicians invested in this area, the hope is that effective prevention and intervention methods will soon be within reach.

REFERENCES

Andover, M. S., & Gibb, B. E. (2010). Non-suicidal self-injury, attempted suicide, and suicidal intent among psychiatric inpatients. *Psychiatry Research, 178,* 101–105.

Andover, M. S., Pepper, C. M., & Gibb, B. E. (2007). Self-mutilation and coping strategies in a college sample. *Suicide & Life-Threatening Behavior, 37,* 238–243.

Andover, M. S., Pepper, C. M., Ryabchenko, K. A., Orrico, E. G., & Gibb, B. E. (2005). Self-mutilation and symptoms of depression, anxiety, and borderline personality disorder. *Suicide & Life-Threatening Behavior, 35,* 581–591.

Arsenault-Lapierre, G., Kim, C., & Turecki, G. (2004). Psychiatric diagnoses in 3275 suicides: A meta-analysis. *BMC Psychiatry, 4,* 37.

Asarnow, J. R., Porta, G., Spirito, A., Emslie, G., Clarke, G., Wagner, K. D., . . . Brent, D. A. (2011). Suicide attempts and nonsuicidal selfinjury in the treatment of resistant depression in adolescents: Findings from the TORDIA study. *Journal of the American Academy of Child & Adolescent Psychiatry, 50,* 772–781.

Baca-Garcia, E., Diaz-Sastre, C., Resa, E. G., Blasco, H., Conesa, D. B., Oquendo, M. A., . . . de Leon, J. (2005). Suicide attempts and impulsivity. *European Archives of Psychiatry & Clinical Neuroscience, 255,* 152–156.

Baetens, I., Claes, L., Muehlenkamp, J. J., Grietens, H., & Onghena, P. (2011). Non-suicidal and suicidal self-injurious behavior among Flemish adolescents: A web-survey. *Archives of Suicide Research, 15,* 56–67.

Barker, E. D., Arseneault, L., Brendgen, M., Fontaine, N., & Maughan, B. (2008). Joint development of bullying and victimization in adolescence: Relations to delinquency and self-harm. *Journal of the American Academy of Child & Adolescent Psychiatry, 47,* 1030–1038.

Berman, A. L., Jobes, D. A., & Silverman, M. M. (2006). *Adolescent suicide: Assessment and intervention* (2nd ed.). Washington, DC: American Psychological Association.

Bertolote, J. M., Fleischmann, A., De Leo, D., & Wasserman, D. (2004). Psychiatric diagnoses and suicide: Revisiting the evidence. *Crisis, 25,* 147–155.

Biddle, L., Donovan, J., Hawton, K., Kapur, N., & Gunnell, D. (2008). Suicide and the Internet. *British Medical Journal, 336,* 800–802.

Brausch, A. M., & Girresch, S. K. (2012). A review of empirical treatment studies for adolescent nonsuicidal self-injury. *Journal of Cognitive Psychotherapy, 26,* 3–16.

Brausch, A. M., & Gutierrez, P. M. (2009). The role of body image and disordered eating as risk factors for depression and suicidal ideation in adolescents. *Suicide & Life-Threatening Behavior, 39,* 58–71.

Brodsky, B., & Stanley, B. (2008). Adverse childhood experiences and suicidal behavior. *Psychiatric Clinics of North America, 31,* 223–235.

Brown, G., Beck, A. T., Steer, R., & Grisham, J. (2000). Risk factors for suicide in psychiatric outpatients: A 20-year prospective study. *Journal of Consulting & Clinical Psychology, 68,* 371–377.

Brown, M. Z., Comtois, K. A., & Linehan, M. M. (2002). Reasons for suicide attempts and nonsuicidal self-injury in women with borderline personality disorder. *Journal of Abnormal Psychology, 111,* 198–202.

Centers for Disease Control and Prevention. (2009). Youth risk behavior surveillance—United States, 2009. *MMWR, 59* (SS-5), 1–142.

Centers for Disease Control and Prevention. (2011). Web-based Injury Statistics Query and Reporting System (WISQARS). Available from www.cdc.gov/ncipc/wisqars/default.htm

Claes, L., Muehlenkamp, J. J., Vandereycken, W., Hamelinck, L., Martens, H., & Claes, S. (2010). Comparison of non-suicidal self-injurious behavior and suicide attempts in patients admitted to a psychiatric crisis unit. *Personality & Individual Differences, 48,* 83–87.

Cloutier, P., Martin, J., Kennedy, A., Nixon, M. K., & Muehlenkamp, J. J. (2010). Characteristics and co-occurrence of adolescent non-suicidal self-injury and suicidal behaviours in pediatric emergency crisis services. *Journal of Youth & Adolescence, 39,* 259–269.

Cooper, J., Kapur, N., Webb, R. Lawlor, M., Guthrie, E., Mackway-Jones, K., & Appleby, L. (2005). Suicide after deliberate self-harm: A 4-year cohort study. *American Journal of Psychiatry, 162,* 297–303.

Crosby, A. E., Han, B., Ortega, L.A.G., Parks, S. E., & Gfroerer, J. (2011). Suicidal thoughts and behaviors among adults aged ≥18 years—United States, 2008–2009. *Surveillance Summaries MMWR, 60,* 1–22.

Dougherty, D. M., Mathias, C. W., Marsh-Richard, D. M., Prevette, K. N., Dawes, M. A., Hatzis, E. S., . . . Nouvion, S. O. (2009). Impulsivity and clinical symptoms among adolescents with non-suicidal self-injury with or without attempted suicide. *Psychiatry Research, 169,* 22–27.

Eichenberg, C. (2008). Internet message boards for suicidal people: A typology of users. *CyberPsychology & Behavior, 11,* 107–113.

Evans, E., Hawton, K., Rodham, K., & Deeks, J. (2005). The prevalence of suicidal phenomena in adolescents: A systematic review of population based studies. *Suicide & Life-Threatening Behavior, 35,* 239–250.

Fazaa, N., & Page, S. (2009). Personality style and impulsivity as determinants of suicidal subgroups. *Archives of Suicide Research, 13,* 31–45.

Haas, B., & Popp, F. (2006). Why do people injure themselves? *Psychopathology, 39,* 10–18.

Harriss, L., Hawton, K., & Zahl, D. (2005). Value of measuring suicidal intent in the assessment of people attending hospital following self-poisoning or self-injury. *British Journal of Psychiatry, 186,* 60–66.

Hawton, K., & Harriss, L. (2008). How often does deliberate self-harm occur relative to each suicide? A study of variations by gender and age. *Suicide & Life-Threatening Behavior, 38,* 650–660.

Hawton, K., & van Heeringen, K. (2009). Suicide. *Lancet, 373,* 1372–1381.

Hay, C., & Meldrum, R. (2010). Bullying victimization and adolescent self-harm: Testing hypotheses from general strain theory. *Journal of Youth & Adolescence, 39,* 446–459.

Jacobson, C. M., Muehlenkamp, J. J., Miller, A. L., & Turner, J. B. (2008). Psychiatric impairment among adolescents engaging in different types of deliberate self-harm. *Journal of Clinical Child & Adolescent Psychology, 37,* 363–375.

Jobes, D. (2006). *Managing suicidal risk: A collaborative approach.* New York: Guilford.

Johnson, G. M., Zastawny, S., & Kulpa, A. (2010). E-message boards for those who self-injure: Implications for e-health. *International Journal of Mental Health Addiction, 8,* 566–569.

Joiner, T. E. (2005). *Why people die by suicide.* Cambridge, MA: Harvard University Press.

Joiner, T. E., Sachs-Ericsson, N. J., Wingate, L. R., Brown, J. S., Anestis, M. D., & Selby, E. A. (2007). Childhood physical and sexual abuse and lifetime number of suicide attempts: A persistent and theoretically important relationship. *Behaviour Research & Therapy, 45,* 539–547.

Kim, Y. S., Koh, Y., & Leventhal, B. (2005). School bullying and suicidal risk in Korean middle school students. *Pediatrics, 115,* 357–363.

Kim, Y. S., & Leventhal, B. (2008). Bullying and suicide: A review. *International Journal of Adolescent Mental Health, 20,* 133–154.

Klomek, A. B., Marrocoo, F., Kleinman, M., Schonfeld, I. S., & Gould, M. S. (2007). Bullying, depression, and suicidality in adolescents. *Journal of the American Academy of Child & Adolescent Psychiatry, 46,* 40–49.

Klomek, A. B., Sourander, A., Niemela, S., Kumpulainen, K., Piha, J, Tamminen, T., . . . Gould, M. S. (2009). Childhood bullying behaviors as a risk for suicide attempts and completed suicides: a population-based birth cohort study. *Journal of the American Academy of Child & Adolescent Psychiatry, 48,* 254–261.

Klonsky, E. D. (2007). The functions of deliberate self-injury: A review of the evidence. *Clinical Psychology Review, 27,* 226–239.

Klonsky, E. D. (2011). Non-suicidal self-injury in United States adults: Prevalence, sociodemographics, topography, and functions. *Psychological Medicine, 41,* 1981–1986.

Klonsky, E. D., & Moyer, A. (2008). Childhood sexual abuse and non-suicidal self-injury: Meta-analysis. *British Journal of Psychiatry, 192,* 166–170.

Klonsky, E. D., & Muehlenkamp, J. J. (2007). Non-suicidal self-injury: A research review for the practitioner. *Journal of Clinical Psychology/In Session, 63,* 1045–1056.

Klonsky, E. D., Muehlenkamp, J. J., Lewis, S., & Walsh, B. W. (2011). *Nonsuicidal self-injury: Advances in psychotherapy: Evidence-based practice.* Cambridge, MA: Hogrefe.

Klonsky, E. D., & Olino, T. M. (2008). Identifying clinically distinct subgroups of self-injurers among young adults: A latent class analysis. *Journal of Consulting & Clinical Psychology, 76,* 22–27.

Klonsky, E. D., Oltmanns, T. F., & Turkheimer, E. (2003). Deliberate self-harm in a non-clinical population: Prevalence and psychological correlates. *American Journal of Psychiatry, 160,* 1501–1508.

Lewis, S. P., Heath, N. L., Michal, N. J., & Duggan, J. M. (2012). Non-suicidal self-injury, youth, and the Internet: What mental health professionals need to know. *Child & Adolescents Psychiatry & Mental Health, 6(1),* 13.

Lewis, S. P., Heath, N. L., St Denis, J. M., & Noble, R. (2011). The scope of non-suicidal self-injury on YouTube. *Pediatrics, 127,* 552–557.

Lewis, S. P., Heath, N. L., Sornberger, M. J., & Arbuthnott, A. E. (2012). Helpful or harmful? An examination of viewers' responses to nonsuicidal self-injury videos on YouTube. *Journal of Adolescent Health, 51,* 380–385.

Lilley, R., Owens, D., Horrocks, J., House, A., Noble, R., Bergen, H., . . . Kapur, N. (2008). Hospital care and repetition following self-harm: Multicentre comparison of self-poisoning and self-injury. *British Journal of Psychiatry, 192,* 440–445.

Linehan, M. M., Comtois, K., Murray, A., Brown, M., Gallup, R., Heard, H., . . . Lindenboim, N. (2006). Two year randomized control trial and follow up of dialectical behavior therapy vs. therapy by experts for suicidal behaviors and borderline personality disorder. *Archives of General Psychiatry, 63,* 757–766.

Lloyd-Richardson, E. E., Perrine, N., Dierker, L., & Kelley, M. L. (2007). Characteristics and functions of non-suicidal self-injury in a community sample of adolescents. *Psychological Medicine, 37,* 1183–1192.

Lofthouse, N., Muehlenkamp, J. J., & Adler, R. (2009). Nonsuicidal self-injury and co-occurrence. In M. K. Nixon & N. L. Heath (Eds.), *Self-Injury in youth: The essential guide to assessment and intervention,* pp. 59–78. New York: Routledge.

Madge, N., Hewitt, A., Hawton, K., Jan de Wilde, E., Corcoran, P., Fekete, S., . . . Ystgaard, M. (2008). Deliberate self-harm within an international community sample of young people: Comparative findings from the Child & Adolescent Self-harm in Europe (CASE) study. *Journal of Child Psychology & Psychiatry, 49,* 667–677.

McCarthy, M. J. (2010). Internet monitoring of suicide risk in the population. *Journal of Affective Disorders, 122,* 277–279.

McKeon, R. (2009). *Suicidal behavior: Advances in psychotherapy: Evidence-based practice.* Cambridge, MA: Hogrefe & Huber.

Meltzer, H., Vostanis, P., Ford, T., Bebbington, P., & Dennis, M. S. (2011). Victims of bullying in childhood and suicide attempts in adulthood. *European Psychiatry, 26,* 498–503.

Muehlenkamp, J. J. (2006). Empirically supported treatments and general therapy guidelines for non-suicidal self-injury. *Journal of Mental Health Counseling, 28,* 166–185.

Muehlenkamp, J. J., Claes, L., Havertape, L., & Plener, P. L. (2012). International prevalence of adolescent non-suicidal self-injury and deliberate self-harm. *Child & Adolescent Psychiatry & Mental Health, 6:10.*

Muehlenkamp, J. J., & Gutierrez, P. M. (2004). An investigation of differences between self-injurious behavior and suicide attempts in a sample of adolescents. *Suicide & Life Threatening Behavior, 34,* 12–23.

Muehlenkamp, J.J., & Gutierrez, P.M. (2007). Risk for suicide attempts among adolescents who engage in non-suicidal self-injury. *Archives of Suicide Research, 11,* 69–82.

Naito, A. (2007). Internet suicide in Japan: Implications for child and adolescent mental health. *Clinical Child Psychology & Psychiatry, 12,* 583–597.

Nixon, M.K., Cloutier, P.F., & Aggarwal, S. (2002). Affect regulation and addictive aspects of repetitive self-injury in hospitalized adolescents. *Journal of the American Academy of Child & Adolescent Psychiatry, 41,* 1333–1341.

Nock, M.K., & Favazza, A.R. (2009). Nonsuicidal self-injury: Definition and classification. In M.K. Nock (Ed.), *Understanding nonsuicidal self-injury: Origins, assessment, and treatment,* pp. 9–18. Washington, DC: American Psychological Association.

Nock, M.K., Hwang, I., Sampson, N., Kessler, R.C., Angermeyer, M., Beautrais, A., . . . Williams, D. R. (2009). Cross-national analysis of the associations among mental disorders and suicidal behavior: Findings from the WHO World Mental Health Surveys. *PLOS Medicine, 6(8),* e1000123.

Nock, M.K., Joiner, T.E., Gordon, K.H., Lloyd-Richardson, E., & Prinstein, M.J. (2006). Non-suicidal self-injury among adolescents: Diagnostic correlates and relation to suicide attempts. *Psychiatry Research, 144,* 65–72.

Nock, M.K., & Kessler, R.C. (2006). Prevalence of and risk factors for suicide attempts vs. suicide gestures: Analysis of the national comorbidity survey. *Journal of Abnormal Psychology, 115,* 616–623.

Nock, M.K., & Mendes, W.B. (2008). Physiological arousal, distress tolerance, and social problem-solving deficits among adolescent self-injurers. *Journal of Consulting & Clinical Psychology, 76,* 28–38.

Nock, M.K., Prinstein, M.J., & Sterba, S. (2009). Revealing the form and function of self-injurious thoughts and behaviors: A real-time ecological assessment study among adolescents and young adults. *Journal of Abnormal Psychology, 118,* 816–827.

O'Connor, R.C., Fraser, L., Whyte, M.-C., MacHale, S., & Masterton, G. (2008). A comparison of specific positive future expectancies and global hopelessness as predictors of suicidal ideation in a prospective study of repeat self-harmers. *Journal of Affective Disorders, 110,* 207–214.

Prinstein, M.J., Nock, M.K., Simon, V., Aikins, J.W., Cheah, C.S.L., & Spirito, A. (2008). Longitudinal trajectories and predictors of adolescent suicidal ideation and attempts following inpatient hospitalization. *Journal of Consulting & Clinical Psychology, 76,* 92–103.

Schneider, S.K., O'Donnell, L., Stueve, A., & Coulter, R.W.S. (2012). Cyberbullying, school bullying, and psychological distress: A regional census of high school students. *American Journal of Public Health, 102,* 171–177.

Shah, A. (2010). The relationship between general population suicide rates and the Internet: A cross-national study. *Suicide & Life-Threatening Behavior, 40,* 146–150.

Silverman, M. M., Berman, A. L., Sanddal, N. D., O'Carroll, P. W., & Joiner, T. E., Jr. (2007). Rebuilding the tower of Babel: A revised nomenclature for the study of suicide and suicide behaviors Part 2: Suicide-related ideations, communications, and behaviors. *Suicide & Life-Threatening Behavior, 37,* 264–277.

Slama, F., Courtet, P., Golmard, J., Mathieu, F., Guillaume, S., Yon, L., . . . Bellivier, F. (2009). Admixture analysis of age at first suicide attempt. *Journal of Psychiatric Research, 43,* 895–900.

Speckens, A. E., & Hawton, K. (2005). Social problem solving in adolescents with suicidal behavior: A systematic review. *Suicide & Life-Threatening Behavior, 35,* 365–387.

Stanley, B., Gameroff, M. J., Michalsen, V., & Mann, J. J. (2001). Are suicide attempters who self-mutilate a unique population? *American Journal of Psychiatry, 158,* 427–432.

Taliaferro, L. A., Muehlenkamp, J. J., Borowsky, I. W., McMorris, B. J., & Kugler, K. C. (2012).Factors distinguishing youth who report self-injurious behavior: A population-based sample. *Academic Pediatrics, 12 (3),* 205–213.

Walsh, B. W. (2006). *Treating self-injury: A practical guide.* New York: Guilford.

Weierich, M. R., & Nock, M. K. (2008). Posttraumatic stress symptoms mediate the relation between childhood sexual abuse and non-suicidal self-injury. *Journal of Consulting & Clinical Psychology, 76,* 39–44.

Welch, S. S., Linehan, M. M., Sylvers, P., Chittams, J., & Rizvi, S. L. (2008). Emotional responses to self-injury imagery in borderline personality disorder. *Journal of Consulting & Clinical Psychology, 76,* 45–51.

Whitlock, J., Muehlenkamp, J. J., & Eckenrode, J. (2008). Variation in non-suicidal self-injury: Identification and features of latent classes in a college population of emerging adults. *Journal of Clinical Child & Adolescent Psychology, 37,* 725–735.

Whitlock, J., Muehlenkamp, J. J., Purington, A., Eckenrode, J., Barreira, J., Abrams, G. B., . . . Knox, K. (2011). Non-suicidal self-injury in a college population: General trends and sex differences. *Journal of American College Health, 59,* 691–698.

Whitlock, J., Muehlenkamp, J. J., Eckenrode, J., Purington, A., Baral-Abrams, G., Barreira, P., & Kress, V. (2012). Nonsuicidal self-injury as a gateway to suicide in young adults. *Journal of Adolescent Health, 52 (4),* 486–492.

Whitlock, J. L., Powers, J. L., & Eckenrode, J. (2006). The virtual cutting edge: The Internet and adolescent self-injury. *Developmental Psychology, 42,* 407–417.

Wichstrom, L. (2009). Predictors of non-suicidal self-injury versus attempted suicide: Similar or different? *Archives of Suicide Research, 13,* 105–122.

Wilkinson, P., Kelvin, R., Roberts, C., Dubicka, B., & Goodyer, I. (2011). Clinical and psychosocial predictors of suicide attempts and nonsuicidal self-injury in the Adolescent Depression Antidepressants and Psychotherapy Trial (ADAPT). *American Journal of Psychiatry, 168,* 495–501.

Williams, J.M., Barnhofer, T., Crane, C., & Beck, A.T. (2005). Problem solving deteriorates following mood challenge in formerly depressed patients with a history of suicidal ideation. *Journal of Abnormal Psychology, 114,* 421–431.

Witte, T.K., Merrill, K.A., Stellrecht, N.E., Bernieert, R.A., Hollar, D.L., Schatschneider, C., & Joiner, T. (2008). "Impulsive" youth suicide attempters are not necessarily all that impulsive. *Journal of Affective Disorders, 107,* 107–116.

10
Explaining National Suicide Rates

David Lester and Bijou Yang

There is a tremendous variation in the suicide rates of the nations of the world. The official data, which are compiled by the World Health Organization, are always a few years delayed, but Table 10.1 lists suicide rates for the latest year (after the year 1998) as reported on their website (www.who.int). It can be seen that the rates for men varied from 1.1 per 100,000 per year in Peru to 63.3 in Belarus, and for women from 0.3 in Azerbaijan to 14.1 in the Republic of Korea (South Korea). It is noticeable that, unfortunately, many nations in Africa and Asia do not report suicide rates to the World Health Organization.

Suicide rates vary by sex, as can be seen in Table 10.1, and by age. In Asian nations, female suicide rates are much closer in magnitude to the suicide rates of males than in other nations. Suicide rates for men typically increase with age, whereas the peak for women varies with the economic level of development (Girard, 1993). Suicide rates for women peak in middle age in the wealthiest nations, in old age in nations of moderate wealth, and in younger women in the poorest nations. A few examples are given in Table 10.2.

The methods used for suicide vary considerably from nation to nation. For example, the use of firearms is very common in the United States, whereas jumping is very common in Singapore. There are also "fads" in suicide methods. Car exhaust became more popular in England, especially after domestic gas was detoxified when the utility companies switched from using coal gas (with a high carbon monoxide content) to using natural gas. Charcoal burning in an enclosed space recently became very popular in Hong Kong.

Suicide rates also vary over time, and occasionally a nation experiences a large increase or decrease in the suicide rate. For example, from 1975 to 2000, the suicide rate in Ireland rose from 4.7 to 12.2 while in Denmark the rate declined from 24.1 to 13.6 (Table 10.3). However, overall, there is also some stability in suicide rates. For example, suicide rates in

Table 10.1. National Suicide Rates

	Year	Male	Female
Albania	2003	4.7	3.3
Argentina	2005	12.7	3.4
Armenia	2006	3.9	1.0
Australia	2004	16.7	4.4
Austria	2007	23.8	7.4
Azerbaijan	2007	1.0	0.3
Belarus	2003	63.3	10.3
Belgium	1999	27.2	9.5
Belize	2001	13.4	1.6
Brazil	2005	7.3	1.9
Bulgaria	2004	19.7	6.7
Canada	2004	17.3	5.4
Chile	2005	17.4	3.4
China: Hong Kong	2006	19.3	11.5
Colombia	2005	7.8	2.1
Costa Rica	2006	13.2	2.5
Croatia	2006	26.9	9.7
Cuba	2006	19.6	4.9
Cyprus	2006	3.2	1.8
Czech Republic	2007	22.7	4.3
Denmark	2006	17.5	6.4
Dominican Republic	2004	2.6	0.6
Ecuador	2006	9.1	4.5
El Salvador	2006	10.2	3.7
Estonia	2005	35.5	7.3
Finland	2007	28.9	9.0
France	2006	25.5	9.0
Georgia	2001	3.4	1.1
Germany	2006	17.9	6.0
Greece	2006	5.9	1.2
Guatemala	2006	3.6	1.1
Guyana	2005	33.8	11.6
Hungary	2005	42.3	11.2
Iceland	2007	18.9	4.6
Ireland	2007	17.4	3.8
Israel	2005	8.7	3.3
Italy	2006	9.9	2.8

(*Continued*)

Table 10.1. (*Continued*)

	Year	Male	Female
Japan	2007	35.8	13.7
Kazakhstan	2007	46.2	9.0
Kuwait	2002	2.5	1.4
Kyrgystan	2006	14.4	3.7
Latvia	2007	34.1	7.7
Lithuania	2007	53.9	9.8
Luxembourg	2005	17.7	4.3
Malta	2007	12.3	0.5
Mauritius	2007	16.0	4.8
Mexico	2006	6.8	1.3
Netherlands	2007	11.6	5.0
New Zealand	2005	18.9	6.3
Nicaragua	2005	11.1	3.3
Norway	2006	16.8	6.0
Panama	2006	10.4	0.8
Paraguay	2004	5.5	2.7
Peru	2000	1.1	0.6
Poland	2006	26.8	4.4
Portugal	2004	17.9	5.5
Puerto Rico	2005	13.2	2.0
Republic of Korea	2006	29.6	14.1
Republic of Moldova	2007	28.0	4.3
Romania	2007	18.9	4.0
Russian Federation	2006	53.9	9.5
Serbia	2006	28.4	11.1
Singapore	2006	12.9	7.7
Slovakia	2005	22.3	3.4
Slovenia	2007	33.7	9.7
Spain	2005	12.0	3.8
Suriname	2005	23.9	4.8
Sweden	2006	18.1	8.3
Switzerland	2006	23.5	11.7
Tajikistan	2001	2.9	2.3
Thailand	2002	12.0	3.8
TFYR Macedonia	2003	9.5	4.0
Trinidad & Tobago	2002	20.4	4.0
Turkmenistan	1998	40.9	7.0

(*Continued*)

Table 10.1.   (*Continued*)

	Year	Male	Female
United Kingdom	2007	10.1	2.8
USA	2005	17.7	4.5
Uruguay	2004	26.0	6.3
Uzbekistan	2005	7.0	2.3
Venezuela	2005	6.1	1.4

Latest available data from www.who.int/mental_health/prevention/suicide_rates/en/, accessed May 12, 2011.

Table 10.2.   Suicide Rates by Age

	15–24	25–34	35–44	45–54	55–64	65–74	75+
Women							
United States (2005)	3.5	4.7	6.8	8.0	6.1	4.0	4.0
Canada (2004)	4.8	5.3	7.7	9.5	5.8	5.5	3.7
United Kingdom (2006)	1.9	3.5	3.7	5.6	4.6	2.7	3.0
Germany (2006)	2.3	3.3	5.2	7.7	7.9	9.3	13.4
Hong Kong (2006)	5.2	13.6	12.8	10.9	14.5	23.2	22.1
Singapore (2006)	1.3	8.2	5.9	12.3	14.0	14.7	28.1
Venezuela (2005)	3.1	1.5	1.3	1.9	1.5	1.6	0.7
Argentina (2005)	4.5	3.5	3.5	4.2	5.4	5.6	5.4
Men							
United States (2005)	16.1	19.9	23.0	25.2	22.2	22.7	37.8
Canada (2004)	17.0	21.5	23.2	25.5	19.9	15.7	20.7
United Kingdom (2006)	7.5	14.3	18.3	15.9	12.5	9.1	11.1
Germany (2006)	9.1	12.9	17.4	22.6	23.6	28.5	52.0
Hong Kong (2006)	11.6	17.7	19.9	21.6	22.8	29.5	70.1
Singapore (2006)	6.2	9.4	17.3	21.1	23.1	21.1	30.0
Venezuela (2005)	8.0	9.6	6.9	8.5	8.8	14.5	15.1
Argentina (2005)	19.1	15.0	11.0	14.3	18.6	21.3	37.5

Latest available data from ww.who.int, accessed May 12, 2011.

16 European nations in 1875 and 1975 are shown in Table 10.3. Although the rate in some countries rose, in Finland for example from 3.1 per 100,000 per year in 1875 to 25.0 in 1975, the correlation between the two sets of rates was 0.42, a moderately strong association.[1] Over shorter periods of time, the correlation is stronger. The correlation between the suicide rates in 1975 and 2000 was 0.86.

It is noteworthy that, on the whole, suicide rates have declined in recent years. Thirteen nations experienced a decrease in their suicide rate from 2000 to the latest year available. It has been argued that this decline is possibly a result of the increasing recognition of depression by general practitioners and mental health professionals and the increasing prescription of antidepressants, especially the SSRIs (Selective Serotonin Reuptake Inhibitors, such as Prozac and Zoloft). We will explore this further later in this chapter.

Table 10.3. Suicide Rates in Selected European Nations, 1875, 1975, 2000, and Latest Available Year

	1875	1975	2000	Recent Rate	Year
Austria*	21.2	24.1	19.8	15.2	2009
Belgium	6.8	16.2	21.1	19.4	2005
Denmark	25.8	24.1	13.6	11.9	2006
England (UK)	8.6	7.5	6.6	6.9	2009
Finland	3.1	25.0	22.5	19.3	2009
France	15.0	15.8	18.4	16.3	2007
Germany*	16.7	20.9	13.5	11.9	2006
Hungary	5.2	38.4	32.0	24.6	2009
Ireland	1.8	4.7	12.2	11.8	2009
Italy	3.5	5.6	7.2	6.3	2007
Netherlands	3.5	8.9	9.4	9.3	2009
Norway	7.3	9.9	12.1	11.9	2009
Portugal	1.3	8.5	5.1	9.6	2009
Spain	1.7	3.9	8.4	7.6	2008
Sweden	8.1	19.4	12.7	12.7	2008
Switzerland	19.6	22.5	19.1	18.0	2007
Average	9.3	16.0	14.6		

*The boundaries of Austria and Germany changed from 1875 to 1975.

From www.who.int/mental_health/prevention/suicide/country_reports/en/index.html, accessed October 11, 2011.

There are also changes over time in particular age groups, and some of these have received a great deal of media attention. For example, during some eras, youth suicide rates increased in some countries, but a closer examination of this increase showed that it was not found in every nation and that the increase was more common in young men than in young women. Sometimes the rise in youth suicide rates was accompanied by an increase in the suicide rates of the elderly, but this latter increase is not usually considered as newsworthy. For example, Table 10.4 shows some changes in national suicide rates by age and sex in the 1980s, and it can be seen that New Zealand witnessed a tremendous increase in the suicide rate of young men (+95%), but only in young men. In contrast, in Israel, the largest increase was in young women. Finland experienced an increase in the suicide rates of young and old men and women, whereas Canada experienced small decreases in all of the suicide rates. Explaining these differences is difficult, if not impossible at the present time.

Table 10.4. Changes in Youth Suicide Rates from 1980 to 1990 in Selected Nations (Percentage Increase from 1980 to 1990)

	Men			Women		
	Total	**15–24**	**65+**	**Total**	**15–24**	**65+**
Australia	+26	+51	−2	−7	+4	−13
Austria	−8	−13	+26	−10	−18	+5
Bulgaria	+8	+25	−11	+7	−43	+22
Canada	−4	−1	−15	−24	−7	−29
Czechoslovakia	−10	−38	−5	−10	−4	−10
Denmark	−12	−13	−6	−27	−87	+2
England/Wales	+10	+83	−10	−45	−33	−44
Finland	+19	+36	+50	+16	+21	+5
France	+6	−10	+6	0	−19	+5
Greece	+17	+73	+5	−21	+83	−61
Hong Kong	−12	−10	+6	−14	−12	−29
Hungary	−7	−36	−3	−19	+2	−17
Ireland	+73	+154	+289	+9	+21	−47
Israel	+17	−38	−1	−5	+175	−47
Italy	+13	+11	+34	−11	−17	−8
Japan	−8	−45	−14	−5	−43	−19
Netherlands	−4	−1	−17	−3	−3	+24

(Continued)

Table 10.4. *(Continued)*

	Men			Women		
	Total	15–24	65+	Total	15–24	65+
New Zealand	+51	+95	+8	−24	−17	−65
Norway	+27	+8	+29	+21	+91	+68
Portugal	+21	+42	+8	+15	−24	+45
Scotland	+30	+72	−7	−37	−42	−60
Singapore	+19	+48	−26	+15	−34	+14
Spain	+67	+65	+81	+86	+53	+102
Sweden	−13	−13	+13	−8	−9	+31
Switzerland	−14	−27	+8	−16	−49	+1
United States	+10	+9	+33	−11	−9	+11
USSR	−24	−24	+6	−16	+5	+6
West Germany	−21	−21	−1	−32	−20	−8
Yugoslavia	+4	−5	+22	+6	−36	+28

From Lester and Yang (2005).

THE RELIABILITY OF NATIONAL SUICIDE RATES

It is often argued that national suicide rates are not valid since nations differ in the procedures to certify deaths and vary in who does the certification (a lawyer, a physician, or a qualified pathologist). Certainly, it has been documented that many deaths from suicide are classified as accidental or of undetermined cause. In England, studies by teams of researchers of all deaths in a region have typically found an undercount by the government of 40 percent in the number of suicides. Nevertheless, when the suicide rates in samples of nations (each of which has its own certification procedure) are compared with the suicide rates of immigrants from those nations, say, in the United States or Australia, the rank ordering of nations is roughly the same. An example of one such data set is shown in Table 10.5. The correlation between the two sets of suicide rates is 0.87, indicating a great degree of similarity. Ireland and Mexico had the lowest national suicide rates, and their immigrants to the United States also had the lowest suicide rates of the immigrant groups, even though the suicide rates of immigrants as a whole was higher than the rate in the home nations. This association has been found in more than 20 studies (Voracek & Loibl, 2008).

Table 10.5. **Suicides Rates in Immigrants and in the Home Nations**

Nation	Suicide rate in USA in 1959*	Suicide rate in home nation in 1959
Austria	32.5	24.8
Canada	17.5	7.4
Czechoslovakia	31.5	21.6
England & Wales	19.2	11.4
Germany	25.7	18.7
Ireland	9.8	2.5
Italy	18.2	6.3
Mexico	7.0	1.6
Norway	23.7	7.9
Poland	25.2	6.8
Sweden	34.2	18.1
Average	22.2	11.6

*These rates come from Dublin, L. I. (1963). *Suicide*. New York: Ronald.

EXPLAINING THE NATIONAL DIFFERENCES: METHODOLOGICAL PROBLEMS

What are possible explanations for these differences between national suicide rates and for the variations over time? There are three main methods that have been used to answer these questions. First, a sample of nations is taken and their suicide rates correlated with a set of characteristics of those nations. These studies are called cross-sectional or ecological studies. As will be seen below, these characteristics can include social indicators such as divorce rates or caffeine consumption, physiological characteristics such as the distribution of blood types, and environmental characteristics such as latitude and average temperature.

The results of ecological studies vary depending on the sample of nations chosen—for example, all nations with available data, only the most industrialized nations, or only those in one region (such as Europe). The sample chosen is limited by the fact that many nations do not report suicide rates, especially those in Africa and the Middle East. To illustrate this problem, Lester and Stack (1989) explored the finding that nations with the higher quality of life tend to have higher suicide rates. Lester and

Stack examined this association for the 18 most industrialized nations, for European nations, for all nations for which there were available data, and for a sample of nations from 12 regions of the world such that each region contributed a number of nations roughly proportional to the number of nations in that region. They found that a measure of the quality of life in the nations was significantly associated with the suicide rates *only* in the total sample of nations with available data and for the representative sample. The association was not statistically significant for the sample of industrialized nations or for the set of European nations, although there was still a positive (but weak) association.

Other investigators look at changes in national suicide rates over time, correlating the nations' suicide rates with various social indicators. The results here depend on the time period chosen, which is especially important if economic or social crises have occurred,[2] and also on the particular statistical techniques used. There are many ways of analyzing time-series data, and there is often the suspicion that researchers manipulate the data until the analysis provides interesting results. For example, rather than using the actual divorce rate, marriage rate, and so forth, some investigators transform the data by using the logarithm of every score, or they look at difference scores (the change from year to year). There are also many competing statistical techniques for analyzing time-series data, many more than for the ecological studies discussed above, and this introduces possible bias in the research. Finally, some researchers combine both time-series and ecological data, that is, data from many nations measured each year for several years. For example, if we were to take 20 nations and a 20-year period, we would have 20×20 ($= 400$) data points. These data are often called panel data.

Two final points before moving on. All of the methodologies use correlational techniques. Correlational studies do not provide evidence for cause and effect. If two characteristics, let us call them A and B, are associated, then A could cause B, B could cause A, or some third characteristic (C) could cause both A and B which end up associated because of the influence of this third factor.

Second, associations at the aggregate level (i.e., over nations or over time within a nation) do not necessarily imply associations at the individual level.[3] They may, but not necessarily. For example, we will see that national suicide rates are associated with national divorce rates and, in this case, individuals who are divorced do have higher suicide rates than those who are married. However, whereas research on individuals suggests that suicide rates are lower in those with higher intelligence test scores (Andersson, Allebeck, Gustafson, & Gunnell, 2008), nations whose citizens have higher intelligence test scores tend to have higher suicide rates (Voracek, 2008). It is, therefore, necessary to check the association at the individual level rather than assume that an association over nations automatically applies to individuals.

Let us first examine what national characteristics are associated with national suicide rates.

EXPLAINING THE VARIATION IN NATIONAL SUICIDE RATES

Physiological Differences

One possible explanation for differences in national suicide rates is that different nationalities differ in their physiology. For example, there are clear differences in the frequency of genes in the people from the different nations of Europe (Menozzi, Piazza, & Cavalli-Sforza, 1978). Thus, nations and cultures may differ in their genetic structure. Current research on identical twins and adopted children has shown that psychiatric disorders have a strong genetic basis. These differences in inherited psychiatric disorders, particularly affective disorders (major depressive disorder and bipolar disorder, commonly known as manic-depressive disorder), or in brain concentrations of serotonin, the neurotransmitter believed to be responsible for depression, may be responsible for the differences in the suicide rates of nations and cultures. Gonda, Vazquz, Akiskal, and Akiskal (2011) have argued that genes affect people's development of temperaments,[4] such as the depressive and cyclothymic temperaments which have been found to predict suicidal behavior, and that the prevalence of these temperaments differs considerably by nation. For example, the cyclothymic temperament was more dominant in Koreans and least dominant in Argentinians in the sample that they studied.

One study has attempted to demonstrate an association between physiological factors and suicide rates at the cross-national level. Lester (1987) found that the suicide rates of nations were associated with the proportion of people with Types O, A, B, and AB blood—the higher the proportion of people in the nation with Type O blood, the lower the suicide rate. Voracek (2004) has confirmed the existence of this association. However, few studies have explored the role of physiological differences in accounting for national differences in suicide rates.

Some researchers have noted that people of Finnish and Hungarian ancestry (known as Finno-Ugrians) seem to have higher suicide rates, and research has shown that regions and nations with a higher proportion of Finno-Ugrians have higher suicide rates (e.g., Voracek & Marusic, 2008). This association may be a result of cultural variables, but it may be also a result of genetic predispositions. Voracek and Formann (2004), however, have shown that latitude and longitude account for the variation of suicide rates in Europe better than the proportion of blood types and the distribution of the Finno-Ugrian gene. This raises the question of what the alternative mediating factors in this association of geographic position and suicide rates might be, and Voracek and Formann did not propose alternative mediators.

Recently, Ling, Lester, Mortensen, Langenberg, and Postolache (2011) found that the prevalence of a brain parasite, *Toxoplasma gondii,* in the residents of European nations was strongly associated with the suicide rates. This parasite is thought to exacerbate risk factors for suicide, such as depression, by affecting levels of important neurochemicals in the brain.

Research on the impact of these physiological variables on national suicide rates is at an early stage, and much more research is needed before we can identify reliable and meaningful associations.

Psychological and Psychiatric Differences

The major psychological factors found to be associated with suicidal behavior are depression, especially hopelessness, and psychological disturbance (often labeled as neuroticism, anxiety, or emotional instability). Psychiatric disorder appears to increase the risk of suicide, with affective disorders and alcohol and drug abuse leading the list. Nations may differ in the prevalence of these conditions, and such differences could account for the differences in suicide rates. For example, nations certainly do differ in their consumption of alcohol (Adrian, 1984), as well as the incidence of depression (Weissman & Klerman, 1977).

Social Composition

Moksony (1990) noted that one simple explanation of national differences in suicide rates is that the national populations differ in the proportion of those at risk for suicide. For example, typically in developed nations, suicide rates are highest among the elderly, especially elderly males. Therefore, nations with a higher proportion of elderly males will have a higher suicide rate.

Societal Differences

The most popular explanation of the variation in national suicide rates focuses on social variables. These social variables may be viewed in two ways: (1) as direct causal agents of the suicidal behavior, or (2) as indices of broad social characteristics which differ between nations.

Durkheim (1897) hypothesized that the suicide rate is related to the level of social integration (the degree to which the people are bound together in social networks) and the level of social regulation (the degree to which people's desires and emotions are regulated by societal norms and customs). According to Durkheim, *egoistic* and *anomic* suicides result from too little social integration and social regulation, respectively, while *altruistic* and *fatalistic* suicides result from too much social integration and social regulation, respectively. Later sociologists have argued that altruistic and fatalistic suicides are rare in modern societies. Therefore, suicide rarely results from excessive social integration or regulation. As a result, suicide in modern societies seems to increase as social integration and regulation *decrease* (e.g., Johnson, 1965).

Studies of samples of nations have found that suicide rates are associated with such variables as low rates of church attendance, the amount of immigration and interregional migration, and divorce. Some investigators view these associations as suggesting a positive relationship between broken relationships and suicidal behavior. For example, divorce may be associated with suicide at the societal level because divorced people have a higher suicide rate than those with other marital statuses.

In contrast, Moksony (1990) and Taylor (1990) suggested that these *specific* social variables may not be directly related to social suicide rates, but rather these specific social variables are measures of more basic, abstract and broad social characteristics which determine social suicide rates. Lester (2004) proposed that the strong association between social variables argues for the importance of basic broad social characteristics. For example, in the United States, interstate migration, divorce, church non-attendance and alcohol consumption are all strongly correlated with one another, supporting the importance of a social characteristic, perhaps best labeled *social disorganization,* as a determinant of societal suicide rates. In this case, regions of the world with high rates of divorce would have high rates of suicide for those in all marital statuses. This is found for the United States where states with higher divorce rates have higher suicide rates among the single, the married, and the widowed as well as for the divorced (Lester, 1995).

Combining Predictors of National Suicide Rates

Lester (2005) entered the percentage Type O blood type, alcohol consumption, the percentage of elderly, the divorce rate, and the birth rate into a multiple regression for 17 industrialized nations.[5] The multiple correlation (R) was 0.85. He then used the regression equation to successfully predict the relative suicide rates of seven other European nations (Bulgaria, Czechoslovakia, Greece, Hungary, Poland, Portugal, and Yugoslavia)—the correlation between the actual suicide rate and the predicted suicide rate was 0.89. However, using the regression equation to predict the suicide rates in seven non-European nations (Egypt, El Salvador, Mexico, Sri Lanka, Thailand, Trinidad, and Venezuela) resulted in a correlation of zero! Thus, the predictors (and, therefore, possibly the causes) of suicide rates in non-Western nations may be quite different from those for European nations. There is clearly much more research needed to compare and contrast these competing explanations for differences in national suicide rates.

Multivariate Studies

The association of sociodemographic and economic variables with national suicides has been best analyzed using factor analysis, a statistical technique that identifies clusters of related variables. Conklin and Simpson (1987) identified two clusters of variables that appear to be associated with national suicide rates: one cluster had the highest loading from the Islam religion and the second cluster assessed economic development. Lower suicide rates were found for nations with less economic development and where Islam was the dominant religion.

The role of religion, in particular Islam, is illustrated by the suicide rates in the nations that had been controlled by the Soviet Union. Those nations began to report their suicide rates in 1990, and the association between the proportion of Muslims in the nations and their suicide rates are shown in Table 10.6, where the correlation between the two rates is -0.60, that is, the greater the proportion of Muslims in the nation, the lower the suicide rate.

In a cross-national study of suicide rates in 72 countries, Lester (1996) identified 13 independent factors for the social variables, only one of which was associated with suicide rates. This factor was economic development, with high loadings from such social variables as low population growth and high gross domestic product per capita.

Table 10.6. Suicide Rates in Nations and the Percentage of Muslim Residents

	Suicide rate in 1990	Muslim (%)
Armenia	2.8	0
Azerbaijan	1.6	87
Belarus	20.4	0
Estonia	27.1	0
Georgia	3.6	11
Kazakhstan	19.1	47
Kyrgyzstan	12.5	70
Latvia	26.0	0
Lithuania	26.1	0
Moldova	14.8	0
Tajikistan	4.4	85
Turkmenistan	8.1	87
Ukraine	20.7	0
Uzbekistan	7.2	88

From Lester (2006).

TIME SERIES STUDIES

One of the most extensive time series studies of suicide was reported by Lester and Yang (1998) who looked at correlates of suicide rates from 1950 to 1985 for 29 different nations (see Table 10.7). They found, for example, that marriage rates were negatively correlated with suicide rates for 20 of these 29 nations (the higher the marriage rate, the lower the suicide rates), divorce rates were positively correlated with suicide rates for 22 of the 29 nations (the higher the divorce rate, the higher the suicide rate), while, for birth rates, 12 of correlations were positive and 17 negative, indicating much more inconsistency. Lester and Yang could not find any characteristics of the nations that accounted for these variations between nations. For example, the divorce rate was a risk factor for suicide in Austria, Canada, and the United States (at the aggregate level), but a protective factor in Yugoslavia.

For recent years, Lester and Yang found that suicide rates were higher in nations when the nation's unemployment rate was higher and when the nation's consumption of alcohol was higher. For marriage and birth rates, Lester and Yang also studied these associations for the period 1901 to 1988 for 12 nations and for as far back as 1751 for three nations with

Table 10.7. **Results of the Multiple Time-Series Regressions of the Suicide Rate for 29 Nations, 1950–1985 (Correcting for Serial Autocorrelation)**

	Constant	Marriage rate	Birth rate	Divorce rate	R^2
Australia	8.928	0.004	0.189	−0.181	0.69
Austria	11.787**	−0.150	0.219	6.967***	0.81
Belgium	19.050	−0.869	−0.076	5.476*	0.95
Canada	10.796***	0.130	−0.192**	1.961***	0.98
Costa Rica	4.312**	0.050	−0.047*	1.495*	0.63
Czechoslovakia	28.449***	0.382	−0.327	−2.649	0.79
Denmark	23.383	−0.251	−0.363	3.410	0.84
England/Wales	8.434**	−0.653*	0.390**	−0.043	0.95
Finland	19.639**	−0.137	−0.075	3.487*	0.86
France	12.078**	−1.068**	0.437*	4.872***	0.95
Hungary	49.455**	−0.550	−0.213	3.204	0.96
Iceland	27.981	−0.355	−0.469	−2.904	0.20
Japan	3.126	0.590	−0.249	10.292*	0.86
Luxembourg	21.666**	−1.113	−0.284	3.651	0.69
Mauritius	1.060	0.033	−0.014	16.033*	0.45
Mexico	1.418	−0.084	0.018	−0.121	0.27
Netherlands	5.286	0.036	−0.021	2.712***	0.96
New Zealand	11.322***	−0.282	−0.010	0.632	0.49
N. Ireland	−1.602	−0.352	0.373*	4.721***	0.65
Norway	0.242	−0.738**	0.462	6.323***	0.96
Portugal	8.424***	−0.217	0.100	1.134	0.34
Puerto Rico	2.104	−0.078	0.273*	0.407	0.65
Scotland	6.653	−0.051	0.083	1.008	0.83
Sweden	12.078*	−1.076	0.968*	0.337	0.58
Switzerland	15.412	0.924	−0.488	5.357	0.90
Taiwan	2.040	0.205	0.266*	2.649	0.80
United States	16.310***	−0.368**	−0.151***	0.430***	0.92
West Germany	26.757***	−0.754*	−0.038	−0.359	0.80
Yugoslavia	32.110***	−1.175***	−0.242***	−3.701***	0.93
Positive		9	12	22	
Negative		20	17	7	
Significant and positive		0	6	12	
Significant and negative		6	4	1	

*$p < .05$. **$p < .01$. ***$p < .001$.

available data (Finland, Sweden, and Switzerland), confirming the protective nature of marriage and births.

Alcohol consumption may play an important role in affecting suicide rates. At the individual level, individuals who use alcohol and abuse alcohol do have a high rate of suicidal behavior, and alcohol is often used during the actual suicidal act, both to amplify the effect of the medications utilized for suicide and to help the individual carry out the act. Alcohol consumption also appears to be associated with the suicide rate at the aggregate level. For example, Ramstedt (2001) studied the time-series association of alcohol consumption and suicide rates and found a positive association in northern European nations (where alcohol consumption per capita is relatively low) but no association in high alcohol-consumption countries (such as Italy, Portugal, and Spain). Ramstedt concluded that cultural factors must play a role in this association.

Economic Booms and Busts

One of the most interesting issues, especially in light of the financial crises of 2008–2011, is the relationship between the economy and suicide rates. Durkheim (1897) argued that, as the economy expands or contracts, it leads to a decline in social integration and social regulation, both of which are stabilizing forces for preventing suicide. Therefore, according to Durkheim, the suicide rate should rise when the economy experiences contractions or expansions.

Ginsberg (see Lester & Yang, 1998) argued that the anomie experienced by people was determined by the discrepancy between the actual reward they received and their aspirations. When the economy is expanding, the level of rewards in the society also grows, as does the level of aspiration, but the level of aspiration grows at a faster rate than will the level of rewards. (People get greedy!) This leads to a higher suicide rate as a result of the increasing level of anomic dissatisfaction from the disparity between aspirations and rewards. By the same token, when the economy is in a recession, the level of aspiration is decreasing because the level of rewards is decreasing. As the economy approaches the trough, the rate of decline of the economy slows down, the level of aspiration decreases at faster rate than the level of rewards, and the discrepancy between the levels of reward and aspiration shrinks. This leads to a lower level of societal dissatisfaction and ultimately a lower suicide rate. For Ginsberg, therefore, the suicide rate as a function of the business cycle should be an upward-sloping curve.

Henry and Short (1954) based their theory on an old frustration-aggression hypothesis, namely that frustration leads to aggression. When the economy is booming, high status people, whom Henry and Short thought had the highest suicide rate, gain status relative to low status people. As a result, their suicide rates declines. During recessions, high status persons lose status relative to low status persons, and so their suicide rate should increase. Therefore, according to Henry and Short, suicide rates tend to fall during times of business prosperity and rise during times of business depression.

If we draw a diagram using the vertical axis to indicate the suicide rate and the horizontal axis to indicate the business cycle index (see Figure 10.1), then Durkheim's theory of suicide and the business cycle will be a pointed V-shaped curve intersecting the vertical axis at a level indicating a minimum possible suicide rate. The minimum level of suicide is called the *natural suicide rate* because this rate occurs when the economy is growing normally with a long-term level trend. Ginsberg's theory results in an upward-sloping curve, while Henry and Shorts' theory results in a downward-sloping curve. Both curves should cross at the natural suicide rate joining Durkheim's on the vertical axes.

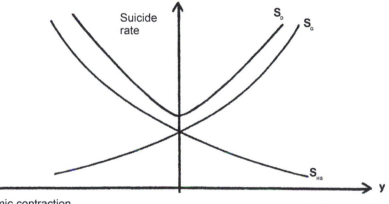

S_D the suicide rate as a function of the business cycle for Durkheim
S_G the suicide rate as a function of the business cycle for Ginsburg
S_{HS} the suicide rate as a function of the business cycle for Henry and Short
Y   the business cycle index

Figure 10.1.   The Three Models of Suicide and the Business Cycle

Which of these theories is correct? There are several criteria that could be used to measure the business cycle, such as growth in the gross national product and the unemployment rate. Lester and Yang (1998) found that, for the period 1950–1985, the unemployment rate was positively associated with the suicide rate for 10 of the 14 nations they examined, and the 4 significant associations were all positive. This result lends general support for Henry and Short's theory. Lester and Yang also looked for curvilinear associations, and found U-shaped trends in seven nations and inverted U-shaped trends in seven nations. The only significant U-shaped trend was for the Netherlands.

The *hypothesis of a natural rate of suicide* was tested by Yang and Lester (2009). They used divorce and unemployment rates to predict the suicide rate of nations over time. They then set the divorce and unemployment rates to zero (i.e., a utopian society!) and investigated what the suicide rate would be. The suicide rates were always greater than zero. For example, the natural suicide rate for in the United States was estimated to be 8.8, England and Wales 11.5, and Norway, 2.9 (see Table 10.8).

A recent research study explored the impact of globalization on national suicide rates. Milner, McClure, Sun, and De Leo (2011) derived a globalization index based on the nation's integration into the world market economy, the movement of people between nations, and social factors

Table 10.8.   Estimates of the Natural Suicide Rate of Nations from Time-Series Analyses

	Estimated natural suicide rate
Australia	12.5
Austria	15.9
Belgium	10.3
Canada	7.0
Denmark	11.2
England & Wales	11.5
Japan	25.0
Netherlands	5.0
Norway	2.9
Sweden	19.3
Taiwan	10.3
United States	8.8
West Germany	18.0

From Yang and Lester (2009).

associated with globalization such as computer ownership, expenditures on information and technology, and telephone coverage. They found that the higher the globalization index of the nation, the higher the suicide rate for both men and women. This association was much weaker once they introduced controls for a dozen other social and economic variables, but was still present for the suicide rates of men.

In older research, Lester and Yang (1997) found that the suicide rate was high in nations with a higher quality of life. Milner and her colleagues found that globalization is associated with a higher suicide rate. Thus, the future looks grim from this perspective. As the world becomes more globalized and as the quality of life improves in all nations, then the prospect is that suicide rates will increase.

THE EFFECT OF TREATMENT

One of the complicating factors in study the changes over time of national suicide rates in more recent years is the impact of treatment. The increasing prescribing of antidepressants, especially the serotonin reuptake inhibitors (SSRIs), which reduce the levels of depression and anxiety in individuals, may be having a beneficial impact and reducing the incidence of suicide, in addition to social and economic changes.

Studies in Finland from 1994 to 2001 (Korkella, Salminen, Hiekkanen, & Salokangas, 2007), Sweden from 1977 to 1997 (Carlsten, Waern, Ekedahl, & Ranstam, 2001), and the United States from 1960 to 2002 (Milane, Suchard, Wong, & Licinio, 2006) have shown that, as more fluoxetine (an SSRI) was prescribed, the suicide rate declined. Not all nations show this effect, but the majority does show the association. This research suggests that the detection and treatment of depression is a more potent determinant of national suicide rates than social and economic variables. However, social and economic changes were occurring in the nations during the time periods studied, and the research studies noted above did not control for these possible social and economic changes.

There is some evidence too that regional variations in prophylactic medications, some of which occur naturally, may have an impact on suicide rates. For example, lithium is a popular and effective medication for treating patients with bipolar affective disorder, and lithium occurs in natural water supplies. Ohgami, Terao, Shiotsuki, and Ishii (2009) found that prefectures in Japan with more lithium in the drinking water had lower suicide rates, and the same association has been found in Texas counties. Again, this research has not controlled for regional variations in social and economic variables, but it would be of interest to extend this research to international comparisons.

DISCUSSION

It is clear from the research reviewed in this chapter that national differences in suicide rates are substantial. Nations also differ in the pattern of suicide rates by sex and by age, and the methods used for suicide differ considerably by nation. Although the results of research differ depending on the methodology used (over nations versus over time), it is also evident that social and economic factors play a major role in determining national suicide rates. These factors may also interact with psychological, cultural, and biological differences between the nations.

Several studies reported above should serve as warnings for the future. Lester and Stack (1989) found that the suicide rates were higher in nations with a higher quality of life, and Milner et al. (2011) found that nations with higher levels of globalization had higher suicide rates. In the future, therefore, suicide rates may increase. On the other hand, if the impact of detecting and treating depression on suicide continues to be beneficial, these improvements may counteract the possibility of rising suicide rates worldwide in the future.

NOTES

1. The absolute size of correlations ranges from 0 to 1.
2. Prior to 1990, the two nations with the highest reported suicide rates were Hungary and Sri Lanka but, after the break-up of the Soviet Union and its satellite countries, the highest suicide rates were in the newly liberated nations of Estonia, Latvia, and Lithuania.
3. This is called the *ecological fallacy.*
4. *Temperament* is the terms psychologists use for those personality traits determined by our genes and our physiology.
5. Australia, Austria, Belgium, Canada, Denmark, Finland, France, Germany, Ireland, Italy, Japan, the Netherlands, Norway, New Zealand, Sweden, the United Kingdom, and the United States.

REFERENCES

Adrian, M. (1984). International trends in alcohol production, trade and consumption, and their relationship to alcohol-related problems, 1970 to 1977. *Journal of Public Health Policy, 5,* 344–367.

Andersson, L., Allebeck, P., Gustafson, J. E., & Gunnell, D. (2008). Association of IQ scores and school achievement with suicide in a 40-year follow-up of a Swedish cohort. *Acta Psychiatrica Scandinavica, 118,* 99–105.

Carlsten, A., Waern, M., Ekedahl, A., & Ranstam, J. (2001). Antidepressant medication and suicide in Sweden. *Pharmacoepidemiology & Drug Safety, 10,* 525–530.

Conklin, G. H., & Simpson, M. E. (1987). The family, socioeconomic development and suicide. *Journal of Comparative Family Studies, 18,* 99–111.

Durkheim, E. (1897). *Le suicide.* Paris, France: Felix Alcan.

Girard, C. 1993). Age, gender, and suicide. *American Sociological Review, 58,* 553–574.

Gonda, X., Vazquz, G. H., Akiskal, K. K., & Akiskal, H. S. (2011). From putative genes to temperament and culture. *Journal of Affective Disorders, 131,* 45–51.

Henry, A. F., & Short, J. F. (1954). *Suicide and homicide.* New York: Free Press.

Johnson, B. D. (1965). Durkheim's one cause of suicide. *American Sociological Review, 30,* 875–886.

Korkella, J., Salminen, J. K., Hiekkanen, H., & Salokangas, R.K.R. (2007). Use of antidepressants and suicide rate in Finland. *Journal of Clinical Psychiatry, 68,* 505–511.

Lester, D. (1987). National distribution of blood groups, personal violence (suicide and homicide), and national character. *Personality & Individual Differences, 8,* 575–576.

Lester, D. (1995). Explaining the regional variation of suicide and homicide. *Archives of Suicide Research, 1,* 159–174.

Lester, D. (1996). *Patterns of suicide and homicide in the world.* Commack, NY: Nova Science.

Lester, D. (2006). Suicide and Islam. *Archives of Suicide Research, 10,* 77–97.

Lester, D., & Stack, S. (1989). Bias resulting from the choice of sample and results of cross-national analyses of suicide rates. *Quality & Quantity, 23,* 221–223.

Lester, D., & Yang, B. (1997). *The economy and suicide.* Commack, NY: Nova Science.

Lester, D., & Yang, B. (1998). *Suicide and homicide in the 20th century.* Hauppauge, NY: Nova Science.

Lester, D., & Yang, B. (2005). Regional and time-series studies of suicide in nations of the world. *Archives of Suicide Research, 9,* 123–133.

Ling, V. J., Lester, D., Mortensen, P. B., Langenberg, P. W., & Postolache, T. T. (2011). *Toxoplasma gondii* seropositivity and suicide rates in women. *Journal of Nervous & Mental Disease, 199,* 440–444.

Menozzi, P., Piazza, A., & Cavalli-Sforza, L. (1978). Synthetic maps of human gene frequencies in Europeans. *Science, 201,* 786–792.

Milane, M. S., Suchard, M. A., Wong, M. L., & Licinio, J. (2006). Modeling of the temporal patterns of fluoxetine prescriptions and suicide rates in the United States. *PLOS Medicine, 3(6),* 1–9, e190.

Milner, A., McClure, R., Sun, J., & De Leo, D. (2011). Globalisation and suicide. *Health & Place, 17,* 996–1003.

Moksony, F. (1990). Ecological analysis of suicide. In D. Lester (Ed.), *Current concepts of suicide,* pp. 121–138. Philadelphia, PA: Charles Press.

Ohgami, H., Terao, T., Shiotsuki, I., & Ishii, N. (2009). Lithium levels in drinking water and risk of suicide. *British Journal of Psychiatry, 194,* 464–465.

Ramstedt, M. (2001). Alcohol and suicide in 14 European countries. *Addiction, 96 (Supplement 1),* S59–S75.

Taylor, S. (1990). Suicide, Durkheim, and sociology. In D. Lester (Ed.), *Current concepts of suicide,* pp. 225–236. Philadelphia, PA: Charles Press.

Voracek, M. (2004). Suicide rate and blood groups. *Perceptual & Motor Skills, 99,* 896–898.

Voracek, M. (2008). Cross-national social ecology of intelligence and suicide prevalence. *Perceptual & Motor Skills, 106,* 550–556.

Voracek, M., & Formann, A. K. (2004). Variation in suicide rates is better accounted for latitude and longitude than by national percentages of Finno-Ugrians and Type O blood. *Perceptual & Motor Skills, 99,* 1243–1250.

Voracek, M., & Loibl, L. M. (2008). Consistency of immigrant and country-of-birth suicide rates. *Acta Psychiatrica Scandinavica, 118,* 259–271.

Voracek, M., & Marusic, A. (2008). Testing the Finno-Ugrian suicide hypothesis. *Nordic Journal of Psychiatry, 62,* 302–308.

Weissman, M. M., & Klerman, G. L. (1977). Sex differences and the epidemiology of depression. *Archives of General Psychiatry, 34,* 98–111.

Yang, B., & Lester, D. (2009). Is there a natural suicide rate? *Applied Economics Letters, 16,* 137–140.

11
Suicide and Culture

David Lester

C ulture provides a set of rules and standards that are shared by members of a society. These rules and standards shape and determine the range of appropriate behavior. The aim of this chapter is to present an overview of some of the topics and issues which are important in the interaction of suicide and culture. One area of interest is to compare the suicidal behavior of different cultures, and another is to examine the impact of culture on the individual. But it is first necessary to discuss some of the problems that face those who study the interaction between culture and suicidal behavior.

SOCIAL AND POLITICAL ISSUES IN STUDYING CULTURES

Nations versus Cultures

Many of the studies of the impact of culture on suicide use samples of nations. The obvious reason for this is that the suicide rates of nations are of interest and concern. Government policies and funding for suicide research operate on nations as a whole. But more importantly, governments of nations collect statistics on suicidal behavior in their nations and fund research on suicide in their nations. However, a nation is not the same as a culture.

Nations do differ in culture. Although national stereotypes are often criticized (all Englishmen do not have "stiff upper lips"), there is some validity to these stereotypes.[1] For example, Americans are perceived by members of other nations as very extraverted, and research confirms this. Using national social indicators (such as divorce rates and tobacco use) and scores from samples of residents in nations on standardized psychological tests, Americans typically score higher on extraversion (Lynn, 1971).

However, not all the residents of the nation consider themselves identical. They identify themselves by region (e.g., Welsh, Scots, or English in Great Britain), by language or dialect (e.g., Cantonese or Mandarin in China), by religion, by their parents' ethnic background (e.g., Italian American or Irish American), and so forth. In some nations, this diversity is celebrated. The United States holds parades and other events on many days of the year in cities across the nation, celebrating, for example, St. Patrick's Day (when everyone is Irish), Polish American Day, and Black American History Month.

The ease of conducting research on suicidal behavior in nations versus the difficulty in even identifying homogenous cultures to study has resulted in many "cultural" studies of suicide being conducted on nations rather than cultures. This is perhaps more reasonable in countries that are relatively homogenous (such as Ireland, at least in the past) than in countries that are less homogeneous (such as the United States), but it is never ideal.

Political Concerns

In many countries, these cultural differences, especially if based on ethnicity or religion, threaten to divide the nation. In some Muslim nations, the Sunni/Shiite distinction can be divisive. Not surprisingly, many nations seek to thwart divisive movements. Sometimes the government engages in a civil war to prevent division as, for example, when Nigeria acted to stop a movement by the Ibo ethnic group to carve off Biafra as an independent nation (1967–1970).

In other cases, these is a long "liberation" movement until the region gets partial or total independence, as in the current devolution of Wales and Scotland from the United Kingdom or the conflict between French-speaking Quebec and English-speaking Canada. Nations such as Australia and the United States have escaped much of this divisiveness, partly because the many ethnic groups are rarely concentrated in one state, but rather scattered across the country. In view of the problems that multiethnic nations face, the split of Czechoslovakia into the Czech Republic and Slovakia on January 1, 1993, is remarkable, even unique, in the way that this was accomplished without any armed conflict, let alone the genocidal actions that the world observed during the breakup of Yugoslavia in 1991–2008.

In countries facing divisiveness and liberation movements, recognition of ethnic minorities (and, even more so, the recognition of ethnic majorities in countries in which an ethnic minority is in command, as in some Middle Eastern nations such as Bahrain where Sunni Muslims rule a population the majority of whom are Shiite), there is a fear that studies of cultural subgroups might lead to further divisiveness, even to the point of civil war.

This fear can be found even in countries such as the United Kingdom where Lester (1994d) had a paper on suicide in Wales rejected by the *British Journal of Psychiatry* as being "of no interest."[2] For a country such as Zimbabwe, where the Shona dominate the Ndebele, reporting suicide rates by ethnic group is opposed by the government which suppresses any liberation movement by the oppressed Ndebele. Lester and Wilson (1988) were able to report suicides rates in Zimbabwe only for blacks, coloreds, and whites, but not by ethnic group.

Recently, Lester, Saito, and Park (2011) were able to calculate and report suicide rates for foreigners in Japan, including Koreans living in Japan who form a large, but stigmatized, ethnic group, even if they have been born in Japan (rather than being immigrants to Japan), but data for the suicide rates of aboriginal groups (such as the Ainu) were unavailable.

Cultural anthropologists have occasionally been able to report on suicidal behavior in ethnic groups, but epidemiologists and suicidologists rarely conduct studies of these groups. There is no research on suicide in the Basque people in Spain (members of which have, in the past, waged war in order to gain independence) and very little on suicide in Gypsies in Europe (who are the target of prejudice and efforts to expel them, for example, recently from France).

There is perhaps no other area of research in suicidology that is subject to such strong political considerations, and this has hampered research into the impact of culture of suicide.

A RARE CULTURAL STUDY: GYPSIES AND TRAVELLERS

Gypsies (more appropriately known as Roma) number several million scattered across Europe, and most authorities trace their ancestry to the Indian subcontinent. They are unwelcome in many of the nations through which they travel, and they are less educated than the native residents and have poorer health status. In England, Goward, Repper, Appleton, and Hagan (2006) found that they had much higher levels of depression and anxiety than the general population.

In the only study of suicide in gypsies, Zonda and Lester (1990) studied three districts in northern Hungary and calculated a suicide rate for gypsies of only 7.1 per 1,000,000 per year as compared to a suicide rate of non-gypsies of 22.4. In contrast, the rates of nonfatal suicide attempts were 143 for gypsies versus only 54 for non-gypsies. Some of the gypsies had assimilated and lived among other Hungarians, but even those who had assimilated felt as if they were outsiders and experienced stigma from being a gypsy. Gypsy youths also experienced cultural conflict. One young girl said, "My parents did not attend school. That I understand. But now they forbid me to go out with Hungarian boys." These adolescents face the pull from the larger culture, combined with resistance from their parents.

Walker (2008) recently studied suicide among the Traveller community in Ireland. Travellers are an indigenous minority group making up about 1 percent of the total Irish population. They have their own language, customs, and traditions, and they prefer to be nomadic. Between 2000 and 2006, Walker calculated a suicide rate of 37 per 100,000 per year for the Travellers, three times the Irish suicide rate. Suicide was more common in men than in women. Half (52%) of the suicides had never married, while 65 percent of the suicides were under the age of 30, much higher proportions than among suicides in the general population in Ireland. The most common method for suicide was hanging (80%). Suicide was more common in those who dwell at roadsides compared to those living in houses.

Walker suggested that hostility from non-Travellers (the majority of the Irish population), cultural conflict, especially for the youth (and young men in particular), and loss of the cultural traditions (travelling and keeping horses has become difficult because of legal restrictions and the economy) result in boredom in the young men. To alleviate this boredom, they drink, take drugs, and engage in risky and illegal activities. The loss of self-esteem and hope for a better future increases the risk of suicide in these young men.

It is not surprising that only two studies have ever been published on these two ethnic minorities who are the focus of hostility and discrimination in the countries in which they live.

CULTURAL INFLUENCES ON THE MOTIVES FOR SUICIDAL BEHAVIOR

Suicidal behavior is differently determined and has different meanings in different cultures. Hendin's (1964) study of suicide in Scandinavian countries illustrates this. In Denmark, Hendin suggested that strong dependency needs were the root of depression and suicidal behavior after adult experiences of loss or separation. Reunion fantasies with lost loved ones were common in those committing suicide. In Sweden, suicide typically followed failure in performance and the resulting damage to the men's self-esteem. Hendin attributed this difference to the child-rearing practices in Denmark and Sweden, but this study was on nations rather than cultures.

In her account of suicide among females in Papua New Guinea, Counts (1988) has illustrated the ways in which a culture can determine the meaning of the suicidal act. In Papua New Guinea, female suicide is a culturally recognized way of imposing social sanctions. Suicide also holds political implications for the surviving kin and for those held responsible for the events leading women to commit suicide. In one such instance, in Kaliai, a political district in West New Britain Province, the suicide of a rejected fiancée led to sanctions being imposed on the family which had rejected her. Counts described this woman's suicide as a political act which symbolically transformed her from a position of powerlessness to one of power. The Joshua Project (www.joshiaproject.net) list 879 people groups in Papua New Guinea, of which the Lusi-speaking people in Kaliai are one. It is important, therefore, that anthropologists identify precisely the cultural group from where their examples come.

Cultures also differ in the degree in which suicide is condemned. It has been argued that one explanation for the low suicide rate in African-Americans is that suicide is a less acceptable behavior for African-Americans (Early, 1992). Murder rates are much higher in African-Americans, both as murderers and as victims, and a larger proportion of the murders involving African-Americans are victim-precipitated, that is, the victim played some role, conscious or unconscious, in precipitating their own demise (Wolfgang, 1957). African-American culture appears to view a victim-precipitated murder as a more acceptable method of dying than suicide (Gibbs, 1988).

CHOICE OF METHOD FOR SUICIDE

The methods chosen for suicide differ between cultures. De Catanzaro (1981) documented culturally unique methods for suicide, such as hanging by tying a noose around one's neck and running to another part of the house in Tikopia. Sati, which is suicide by burning on the husband's funeral pyre, is found in India, while seppuku, which is ritual disembowelment, is found in Japan. These well-known examples of cultural influences on suicide methods also have culturally determined motives (grief and shame, respectively, for sati and seppuku).

For nations, firearms are the most common method for suicide in the United States and Canada, while in Switzerland, whose residents typically own firearms as part of their participation in the civilian militia, hanging is the most common method for suicide. A method may come to symbolize the act of suicide, as in England in the early 20th century when "to take the pipe" meant to commit suicide since domestic gas was brought into houses by means of pipes and this was the most common method for suicide. (After the 1960s, domestic gas became less toxic as a result of the switch from coal gas to natural gas.) Burvill, McCall, Woodings, and Stenhouse (1983) found that immigrants to Australia shifted over time from using the most common methods of suicide in their home nations to those most common in Australia.

Research indicates that increased availability of a method for suicide is associated with an increase in its use for suicide (Clarke & Lester, 1989). For example, Killias, Kesteren, and Rindlisbacher (2001) found that, in nations where a larger proportion of the population owned guns, higher numbers of suicide were committed with guns. However, ownership of guns had no association with the total suicide rate. This suggests that, if guns are not freely available, people use guns less often for committing suicide but switch instead to other methods for suicide, such as poisons, hanging, stabbing, jumping, and drowning.

SUICIDE IN ONE CULTURE: THE CHINESE

Studies by Lester (1994a, 1994b) on suicidal behavior in Chinese individuals illustrates the role of culture, a culture of particular interest because the Chinese are native to many nations (such as mainland China and Hong Kong) and have emigrated in large numbers to nations such as America.[3]

The suicide rates of Asian-Americans are relatively low compared to European Americans in the United States. For example, in 1980, the suicide rates were 13.3 per 100,000 per year for Native Americans, 13.2 for European Americans, 9.1 for Japanese Americans, 8.3 for Chinese Americans, 6.1 for African-Americans, and 3.5 for Filipino Americans (Lester, 1994b).

Lester noted that the patterns of suicide also differed for these ethnic groups. The ratio of the male to female suicide rates was much larger for European Americans and African-Americans than for Asian-Americans for whom the suicide rates of men and women were more similar. In addition, suicide rates increased with age for Asian-Americans, whereas the suicide rates peaked in young adulthood for African-Americans and Native Americans. Asian-Americans used hanging for suicide much more often than European Americans and African-Americans, and they used firearms relatively less often. Lester concluded that the epidemiology of suicide in Asian-Americans in America showed similarities to the results of epidemiological studies of suicide in their home nations, indicating that cultural factors have an important influence on the circumstances of suicidal behavior.

Lester (1994a) then examined the epidemiology of suicide in Chinese individuals in Hong Kong, Singapore, Taiwan, mainland China, Hawaii, and the United States as a whole. A couple of examples here will illustrate the results. The ratio of the male to female suicide rates in 1980 were 1.2 for Chinese Americans, 1.2 for Hong Kong residents, 1.2 for Taiwanese residents, and 1.2 for Singapore Chinese, identical gender ratios. Suicide rates peaked in the elderly in all the nations: for those 65 and older in Chinese Americans, 75 and older in Hong Kong and Taiwan, and 70 and older in Singapore Chinese.[4]

However, the methods used for suicide did differ for the different groups of Chinese: jumping was more common in the Chinese in Singapore and Hong Kong, hanging in Chinese Americans and poisons in Taiwan, probably a result of the difference between the nations in the availability of methods for suicide.[5] Furthermore, the suicide rates differed: in 1980 the suicide rates were 13.5 in Singapore and Hong Kong Chinese, 10.0 in Taiwan, and 8.3 for Chinese Americans. Thus, the gender and age patterns in Chinese suicide seem to be affected strongly by culture, while the absolute suicide rates and methods used are affected by the nation in which the Chinese dwell.

CULTURE, LINGUISTICS, AND SUICIDE

As Douglas (1967) pointed out, a shared linguistic terminology for suicidal behavior is associated with shared meanings of the behavior, and there are also shared associated terms and phrases, such as despair, hopelessness, and "life isn't worth living." Douglas emphasized that these terms are not the phenomenon itself but rather are adopted by members of the culture (or subculture) to construct meanings for suicidal behavior. However, since the terms are rarely clearly defined or detailed and since there is often disagreement among commentators on their meaning, it follows that the meaning of suicide is ambiguous. Furthermore, since the terms are used to construct meanings for suicidal behavior, then estimates of the incidence and circumstances of suicidal behavior are in part a social construction.

For example, according to the Mohave, a Native American tribe in the southwest of the United States, a fetus which presents itself in the transverse position for birth, leading to its own death and that of its mother, is viewed as having intended to commit suicide and to murder its mother so that they can be together in the spirit world (Devereux, 1961). Medical examiners and coroners in the rest of the United States would not view such a still-born infant as a suicide.

Counts (1980), who has studied the suicidal behavior of women in the Kaliai district of Papua New Guinea, noted that in the past elderly widows sometimes immolated themselves on their husband's funeral pyre. The German and Australian colonial governors considered this behavior to be a form of ritual murder rather than suicide, and they outlawed it. Counts, however, saw neither term (suicide or murder) as appropriate for this custom since it differed so much from what North Americans and Europeans regard as either suicide or murder. Neither term describes the behavior, the interpersonal relationships involved, or the attitudes toward the widow and those assisting in her death, nor do they predict how the community will respond to her death.

THE STUDY OF CULTURE CAN CHALLENGE MYTHS

Many theories of human behavior, including suicidal behavior, are based on physiological factors. Cultural anthropology helps challenge such theories by showing, for example, that behaviors which we consider gender-specific are not found in every culture. In the United States and in European nations, nonfatal suicidal behavior appears to occur at a higher rate in women than in men, and as a result it is has come to be viewed as a "feminine" behavior by the general public (Linehan, 1973) and by suicidologists as well. Other cultures, however, provide examples where nonfatal suicidal behavior, often carried out in front of others, is more common in men rather than women.

Among the Washo, located in Nevada and California, nonfatal suicidal behavior seems to be equally common in men and women.

> In one case, a man had been having difficulty with his wife; she was interested in another man. The husband ate wild parsnip, but was saved. As a result his sons brought pressure on the wife and made her behave. The couple stayed together until the husband died. . . . Pete also says that men attempt suicide more than women, who just leave home when interpersonal difficulties arise. The destruction of the self is an ultimate, and the fact that men are more likely to invoke it than women indicates a lack of male authority in Washo culture. (D'Azevedo et al., 1963, pp. 50–51)

The Washo man is described as lacking authority and lacking in self-confidence, perhaps because the Washo man has had more difficulty adapting to the changing culture in this century than has the Washo woman. Interestingly, the explanation provided by these Western anthropologists for the occurrence of nonfatal suicidal behavior among Washo men may be generalizable to societies where nonfatal suicidal behavior is more common in women. It may be that nonfatal suicidal behavior is not simply a "feminine" behavior, but rather a behavior found more commonly in those who are oppressed in a society, perhaps because the oppressed have fewer options for expressing their discontent.

THE IMPACT OF CULTURE CONFLICT

An issue that has become important in recent years is the impact of the pervasive Western culture on the suicidal behavior of those living in less modern cultures. The high suicide rates in some Native American groups and First Peoples in Canada and in some Micronesian islands has made this an issue of grave concern rather than mere academic debate.

Cultures often come into conflict. For example, the conflict between the traditional Native American culture and the dominant American culture has often been viewed as providing a major role in precipitating Native American suicide. May and Dizmang (1974) noted that there were three major sociological theories which have been proposed for explaining the Native American suicide rate. One theory focuses on *social disorganization*. The dominance of the Anglo-American culture has forced Native American culture to change and has eroded traditional cultural systems and values. This changes the level of social regulation and social integration, important causal factors for suicide in Durkheim's (1897) theory of suicide. A second theory focuses on *cultural conflict* itself. The pressure from the educational system and mass media on Native Americans, especially the youth, to acculturate, a pressure which is opposed by their elders, leads to great stress for the youths. A third theory focuses on the *breakdown of the family* in Native American tribes. Parents are often unemployed, substance abusers, and in trouble with the law. Divorce and desertion of the family by one or more parents is common.

Acculturation occurs when a culture encounters a dominant alternative culture. The resulting pressure from the dominant culture leads to a variety of changes in the nondominant culture (Berry, 1990): physical changes (such as type of housing, urbanization, and increasing population density), biological changes (resulting from changing diet and exposure to new diseases), political changes (such as loss of autonomy for the non-dominant culture), economic changes (such as changes in type of employment), cultural changes (in language, religion, education, and the arts), social relationships (both within the culture and between the two cultures), and psychological changes at the individual level (in behavior, values, attitudes, and motives).

Berry noted that four possibilities are open to the nondominant culture: *integration*—maintaining relations with the dominant culture while maintaining cultural identity; *assimilation*—maintaining relations with the dominant culture but not maintaining cultural identity; *separation*—not maintaining relations with the dominant culture but maintaining cultural identity; and *marginalization*—not maintaining relations with the dominant culture and not maintaining cultural identity. It would be of great interest to categorize minority cultural groups as to which strategy appears to have been chosen and to examine the different consequences for the society and for the individuals in the society.

RESEARCH ON ACCULTURATION

Supportive results for the influence of acculturation on suicide in Native Americans comes from Van Winkle and May (1986) who examined suicide rates in three groups of Native Americans in New Mexico (the Apache, Navajo, and Pueblo) and attempted to account for the differences in terms of the degree of acculturation. Overall, the crude suicide rates were 43.3 per 100,000 for the Apache, 27.8 for the Pueblo, and 12.0 for the Navajo.

The Jicarilla and Mescalero Apache of New Mexico were originally nomadic hunters and gatherers, organized into self-sufficient bands whose leaders held limited power. Their religion had no organized priesthood and was not a cohesive force in their lives. Individualism was a highly valued characteristic. Today they live in homes scattered about the reservation or in border towns. They raise livestock, cut timber, or work in tribally owned businesses. Formal tribal governments have been established, but religion remains unimportant. Individualism is still valued. However, the raiding parties which formerly provided some degree of social integration have been eliminated. The Apache appear, therefore, to have few integrating forces in their culture, and Van Winkle and May saw their high suicide rate as a direct result of this lack of integration. The Apache have been in close contact with whites. Their reservations are small and surrounded by white communities. Indeed many Apache live in mixed communities. Thus, the Apache have high acculturation in addition to their low social integration.

The Pueblo traditionally lived in compact towns and engaged in agriculture. Religion permeated their lives and was a strong integrating force. There was an organized priesthood and religious societies which took care of religious and civil matters. Individualism was discouraged and conformity valued. Thus, the Pueblo were the most integrated group, and Van Winkle and May found their intermediate suicide rate a puzzle. They tried to explain the Pueblo suicide rate using the role of acculturation. The Pueblo have had increasing contact with whites since 1959. Many of the Pueblos are near large cities such as Albuquerque and Santa Fe. Thus, they have high social integration and moderate but increasing acculturation. For the larger Pueblo tribes, Van Winkle and May compared the suicide rates of those tribes which had acculturated and those which had remained traditional and found a clear tendency for the acculturated and transitional tribes to have the higher suicide rates.

The Navajo, who have the lowest suicide rate, were nomadic hunters and gatherers who later settled down and turned to agriculture. They are organized into bands, but matrilineal clans exert a strong influence. Although religion is important in their lives, they have no organized priesthood. Individualism is valued but not as strongly as among the Apache. Thus, their social integration appears to be intermediate between that of the Apache and that of the Pueblo. However, the Navajo were the most geographically and socially isolated from whites of the three groups until the 1970s when mineral exploration increased on their reservations and some Navajo began to take wage-earning jobs.

Table 11.1 summarizes Van Winkle and May's explanation of the suicide rates in the three groups. It can be seen that acculturation performed better than social integration and as explanation of the differing suicide rates.

In contrast, however, Bagley (1991) found in Alberta that it was those native Canadian reservations which were more isolated (and, incidentally, poorer) which had the higher suicide rates. In Taiwan also, Lee, Chang,

Table 11.1.   Suicide Rates and Acculturation in Three Native American Groups

	Social integration	Acculturation	Suicide rate
Apache	Low	High	High
Pueblo	High	Moderate	Moderate
Navajo	Moderate	Low	Low

and Cheng (2002) found that the less assimilated aboriginal groups had higher suicides rates than those groups which were more assimilated into the mainstream culture.

These studies indicate that when different cultures encounter each other, the problems of acculturation can result in stress and its consequences, including increased rates of suicidal behavior, especially in the less dominant cultural group. But acculturation may not always lead to an increased incidence of suicide (and other disturbed behaviors). In the future, anthropologists may be able to identify which cultural characteristics enable some cultures to acculturate with few social and personal problems while other cultures develop many problems.

OTHER ISSUES

The Assumption of Cultural Invariability

Investigators often assume that a research finding found in one culture will apply to other cultures. It is, therefore, important to replicate research findings in cultures other than the one in which the results were first obtained to check on this assumption. For example, in a comparison of depression and suicide in mainland China and the United States, Chiles et al. (1989) found that suicidal intent was predicted better by the level of depression for Chinese psychiatric patients and better by the level of hopelessness for American psychiatric patients. It is important, therefore, for researchers to identify which findings have cross-cultural generality (and to which cultures) and which are specific to one culture.

Subcultures

Wolfgang and Ferracuti (1967) examined the role that a subculture of violence plays in producing high murder and assault rates. For example, Gastil (1971) argued that such a subculture of violence pervaded the southern portion of the United States, and Marks and Stokes (1976) used this to account for the greater use of firearms for suicide in southern states as compared to the rest of America.

Suicide among Indigenous Peoples

In some nations there has been a good deal of research on and speculation about suicidal behavior in indigenous peoples, sometimes called aborigines. A great deal of research has been conducted on Native Americans in the United States, and some on aborigines in Australia and Taiwan and on the Inuit in Canada and Greenland.

What is noteworthy, however, is that many nations have indigenous peoples, yet we hear little about their suicidal behavior and other self-destructive behaviors. For example, in Central and South America, almost every nation has an indigenous population: 71 percent in Bolivia, 66 percent in Guatemala, 47 percent in Peru, 38 percent in Ecuador, 14 percent in Mexico, 8 percent in Chile, 2 percent in Colombia, 1.5 percent in Paraguay, 1 percent in Venezuela, and 0.4 percent in Brazil (Anon, 2004). In recent years, these indigenous peoples have become organized politically. They have begun to protest against the governments of their nations, often toppling governments (as in Bolivia and Ecuador) and in some cases assuming power.

In Africa, the situation is odd in a different way. Setting aside the remnants of the European colonialists, all of the peoples there can be considered indigenous. Yet, when data on suicide are reported, they are reported for the artificial nations that the colonial rulers established with no regard for the tribal groups in each country. For example, suicide rates have been reported for Zimbabwe (Lester & Wilson, 1988; Rittey & Castle, 1972), yet Zimbabwe has two major ethic groups, the Shona (the dominant ethnic group) and the Ndebele. It would make much more sense to explore and compare suicide in these two ethnic groups.

Some nations are only now beginning to organize their mortality-reporting procedures and structures. In many of these, it will be important to take into account the various indigenous groups in the country, such as China which has a multitude of ethnicities within its borders.

Comparisons of Indigenous Peoples within a Nation

In a couple of nations, it has been possible to compare different ethnic groups within a nation. Lester (1997) reviewed all of the studies on Native American suicide and summarized the suicide rates by tribe and by era (see Table 11.2). It can be seen that there was a slight tendency for the suicide rates to rise during the 20th century and for the tribes to differ greatly in their suicide rate, ranging in the 1970s from 149 per 100,000 per year in the Kwakiutl and 73 in the Sioux to 7 in the Pima and 9 in the Lumbee.

Cheng (1995, 1997) compared suicide in Taiwan in two aboriginal groups (the Atayal and the Ami) with suicide in the dominant Han Chinese. The Atayal had a suicide rate of 68.2 per 100,000 per year, the Ami 15.6, and the Han Chinese 18.0. The suicides in all three groups had a

Table 11.2. **Tribal Suicide Rates in America**

Tribe	1910s	1920s	1930s	1940s	1950s	1960s	1970s	1980s
Aleut							16	
Apache					26	18	40	
Blackfoot						125		
Cherokee							23	
Cheyenne	22	21	13	6	40	48		
Eskimo							42	
Kwakiutl						40	149	
Lumbee							9	
Navajo					8	13		
Ojibway					6		56	
Papago							100	
Pima						40	7	
Pueblo					10	55		
Pueblo (Hopi)					8	13	30	17
Shoshoni							38	
Shoshoni-Bannock						98		
Shoshoni-Paiute					113			
Sioux							73	31
Tlingit							30	
Yaqui						30		

From Lester (1997).

similarly high incidence of psychiatric disorder, and the high suicide rate in the Atayal was attributed to their high rate of alcoholism and earlier onset of major depressive disorders.

We need many more studies comparing the different groups of indigenous peoples within a nation, not simply the crude suicide rates, but also the circumstances, motives, and meanings of suicide in these different groups.

COMPARING DIFFERENT PRIMITIVE SOCIETIES

Anthropologists have typically studied historical societies or societies which have been relatively less influenced by modernization, often called preliterate, nonliterate, or primitive societies, societies composed of whom we would now call indigenous peoples. The Human Relations Area Files (HRAF) has collected and coded historical data on indigenous peoples, including suicide (www.yale.edu/hraf).

Masumura (1977) had two judges rate 35 of these societies for the frequency of suicide by having them read the suicide entries in the HRAF, and his ratings are shown in Table 11.3.[6] From this group of cultures, it would appear that, among Native American groups, the Kwakiutl have a relatively high suicide rate and the Pomo a relatively low suicide rate. In a research study on this sample, Masumura found that the estimated suicide rate was *positively* associated with a measure of social integration in opposition to a prediction from Durkheim's (1897) classic sociological theory of suicide.[7]

Table 11.3. **Estimates of Relative Suicide Rates for 35 Nonliterate Societies**

Group	Suicide score (range 2–8)
Ainu	6
Andamanese	2
Araucanians	5
Ashanti	6
Bakongo	6
Banks Islanders	7
Bushmen	6
Chippewa	7
Chukchee	8
Creek	6
Crow	6
Dahomeans	6
Fang	6
Hottentot	6
Iban	7
Iroquois	5
Jivaro	7
Kazak	6
Kutenai	4
Kwakiutl	8
Lango	8

(*Continued*)

Table 11.3. *(Continued)*

Group	Suicide score (range 2–8)
Maori	8
Navajo	2
Norsemen	5
Omaha	4
Pomo	2
Rwala	7
Samoans	8
Sema Naga	6
Semang	2
Toda	6
Trobrianders	8
Tuareg	4
Vedda	4
Yahgan	2

From Masumura (1977).

CASE STUDIES

On occasions, anthropologists who have studied particular cultures write specifically on suicide. For example, Bohannan (1967) edited a book on suicide in Africa in which the contributors looked at suicidal behavior in several tribes from Uganda and Kenya. Bohannan was not so much interested in the individual motives that people had for killing themselves in a society (he viewed what was in the mind of the suicide as unknowable), but rather he was interested in the causes ascribed to the suicide by members of the society. These popular ideas about suicide tell us something about the culture.

For example, Fallers and Fallers (1967) examined suicide among the Busoga of southeastern Uganda. The Busoga view suicide as an irresponsible and foolish act, probably impulsive. Thus, suicide, like homicide, is an act which must be punished. The body of a suicide is burnt, along with the tree or hut from which the person hung himself, and buried in waste land or at a crossroads. For the period from 1952 to 1954, the official suicide rate for the society was 7.0 per 100,000 per year, which the Fallers thought was a slight underestimate.

Taking 100 cases of suicide, the Fallers found that 86 percent hung themselves, in most cases impulsively. Sixty-nine percent were men. The most common motive was disease (31%) followed by quarrels with spouse, lover or kinsman (23%). Quarrels with a spouse was present in

48 percent of the homicides and 21 percent of the suicides, suggesting that marriage was full of conflict. The patrilineal nature of the society means that spouses have divided loyalties. The wife, in particular, feels drawn back to her family, and wives who feel oppressed by their husbands (which is not uncommon) often flee back to their father. The Fallers noted that the breaking down of the cultural traditions in recent times had decreased the incidence of suicide and homicide, probably as a result of the weakening of intergenerational family ties, which in turn has reduced marital conflicts.

In commenting on this and other reports, Bohannan (1967) noted that domestic institutions are responsible for the greatest number of the suicides. Women committed suicide as wives—they were unable to play the role of wife or mother because of husbands or fathers, co-wives, or fate. Men, to a lesser extent, committed suicide as husbands, but impotence and loss of status played roles too. Suicide is consistently viewed as irresponsible and evil, and rituals involve destruction of the suicide's possessions and ritual cleaning. Bohannan felt that the suicide rates were moderate to low, though accurate estimates were mostly absent.

It should be noted that historical studies of indigenous peoples may become more important as indigenous peoples cross-marry with the dominant cultures. For example, at the present time in New Zealand, there are no "pure" Maoris. All surviving Maoris have at least one white ancestor.

Psychotherapeutic Implications

All of this scholarly discourse is important at the theoretical level, but it may be asked whether there are implications for counseling and psychotherapy. It is sometimes argued that only "like" can counsel "like," that is, that only homosexuals can counsel homosexuals, women counsel women, ex-addicts counsel addicts, and so on. Is the same true also for different cultures? The majority of counselors and psychotherapists deny this, claiming that a good counselor or psychotherapist can counsel any kind of patient. However, to counsel someone very different in background from oneself may require that the counselor learn about the background and culture from which the individual comes. Sue and Sue (1990) have addressed the issues that psychotherapists of one culture must confront when counseling clients from different cultures, such as racism and cultural differences in verbal and nonverbal communication styles.

Zimmerman and Zayas (1995) have illustrated this point in their discussion of treating the suicidal adolescent Hispanic female. They noted that, in New York City, the values of the adolescent Latina often clash with those of her more traditional mother. Both mother and daughter experience problems in communication and a rupture in their relationship. Thus, the problem of acculturation exacerbates the normal adolescent turmoil. The Latina's mother wants her daughter to succeed in this new culture, yet she also wants her daughter to maintain traditional cultural attitudes and roles. The adolescent Latina feels overwhelmed by this conflict and, in extreme cases, makes a suicide attempt in an effort to reduce the tension felt in this conflict. After a suicide attempt, the psychotherapist must explain the conflict to the mother and daughter and help them find ways to reestablish mutual understanding and empathy. It is possible, of course, that psychotherapists could identify the nature of the problems confronting suicidal people and their families each time they encounter such a family, but the psychotherapeutic process is facilitated if psychotherapists have some notion of the cultural issues which they are likely to encounter.

Sue and Sue (1990) presented the case of Janet, a Chinese-American female college senior majoring in sociology, who came to the college counseling center complaining of depression, feelings of worthlessness, and suicidal thoughts. She had difficulty identifying the causes of her depression, but she seemed quite hostile to the psychotherapist who was also Chinese-American. Discussion of this revealed that Janet resented being seen by a Chinese psychotherapist, feeling that she had been assigned to one because of her own race. Janet disliked everything Chinese, including Chinese men whom she found sexually unattractive. She dated only white men, which had upset her parents. However, her last romance had broken up partly because her boyfriend's parents objected to him dating a Chinese woman.

Janet clearly had difficulties stemming from her continuing denial of her Chinese heritage. She was being forced to realize that she was Chinese for she was not fully accepted by white America. Initially she blamed the Chinese for her dilemma, but then she turned her hostility toward herself. Feeling alienated from her own culture and rejected by the white culture, she was experiencing an identity crisis with a resulting depression. The psychotherapist in such a case must deal with cultural racism and its effects on minorities. Positive acculturation must be distinguished from rejection of one's own cultural values, as well as typical adolescent rebellion from one's parents. Psychotherapists can work with such a client more effectively if they are conversant with the cultural history and experiences of Asian-Americans.

Does Cultural Conflict Cause Suicide?

Although the problem of acculturation has been proposed as one of the major causes of depression and suicidal behavior among Native Americans, the majority of research reports on Native American individuals who attempt or complete suicide mention precipitating causes such as grief over loss and quarrels with relatives and friends. Rarely is cultural conflict listed among the precipitating causes. Of course, it may be that the problems of acculturation raise the stress level of individuals so much that stressors, which under ordinary circumstances would not precipitate suicide, now do so.

A few brief case histories have been published which do illustrate the problems of acculturation and culture conflict. For example, Berlin (1986) described the case of a bright young Native American woman who completed undergraduate school and qualified as a teacher and who was admitted to graduate school. Her clan, however, told her that she was required to teach on the reservation. Her desire to go to graduate school was seen as striving to be better than her peers, and this was unacceptable and forbidden. The young woman had a psychiatric breakdown and was hospitalized. In a similar situation, the tribe and another family could not decide whether to let a young woman go to graduate school for an MBA after she obtained her undergraduate degree and, during the long wait for a decision, she attempted suicide.

In this latter case, the young woman, whom Berlin called Josie, had alcoholic parents who frequently sent her and her brothers and sisters to live with relatives while they went on drinking sprees. A teacher realized Josie's potential and received permission for Josie to live with her. With this teacher's help, her academic performance improved, and she went to college. Josie now resented that her parents, who had neglected her, were involved in decisions about her life. The clan leadership and tribal council were relatively enlightened about the issues and eventually gave permission for Josie to attend graduate school. While at graduate school, Josie underwent psychotherapy to deal with her depression and anger and other personal problems. After graduation, she returned to the tribe to manage their business office, marrying a young man who had fought a similar battle in order to obtain an MSW degree.

Westermeyer (1979) provided cases of Native Americans seen at the University of Minnesota Hospitals for whom trying to live in the mainstream American culture had presented problems. Westermeyer felt that identity problems were perhaps no more common in Native Americans than in whites, but that Native Americans did show a unique type of identity problem, namely, ambivalent or negative feelings about their ethnic identity. Westermeyer presented cases of urban Native Americans who illustrate this problem.

Five of the patients, ranging in age from 12 to 23, had identity crises— they experienced conflict about their Native American identity and about what being "Indian" meant. All were students and economically dependent upon others. For example, one young girl, who was seen after a suicide attempt, had her Indian mother die two years earlier. She then lived with her white father and six siblings for a year. The father had trouble supporting them and sent the children to live with their Indian maternal grandmother. The patient began to use drugs and had problems with her white teachers at school. Eventually a white welfare worker sent her to a white foster home, at which point she attempted suicide. In the hospital, she said, "I'm the only Indian here and I hate everybody like they hate me." She had a recurrent dream in which she gave birth to baby girl with blue eyes which she loved but which she also wanted to injure.

Five of the cases were judged to have a negative identity. These were older than the patients with identity crises, and all were male. They were estranged from their Indian family members, and they lived as lower class individuals on the periphery of the white society. One patient was admitted with hallucinations and paranoid delusions after a drinking binge. He had a record of multiple psychiatric admissions. Although he supported the idea of Indian activism, he felt estranged from Indians, had little respect for them, and avoided them. He had joined a Jewish student activist group which he admired, and he wondered whether his Indian tribe might be a lost tribe of Israel. He identified himself as a Zionist.

CONCLUSIONS

There are large cultural differences in the incidence of suicidal behavior, and culture influences also the methods used for committing suicide and the reasons for doing so. Although these cultural differences may be a result of physiological differences between the members of the different cultures, the more plausible explanations involve psychological and social variables, such as the abuse of alcohol, the level of social integration and regulation, and the acceptability (versus condemnation) of suicide. When competing cultures interact, there may be increased stress in the less dominant culture (and, as a result, an increase in suicidal behavior). It should be noted also that, in societies which are culturally heterogeneous, such as the United States, Canada, and Australia, it cannot be assumed that suicides from the different cultural groups are similar in rate, method, motive, and precipitating factors. Those working to prevent suicide in such societies must take these cultural influences into account.

This chapter has attempted to raise and briefly discuss several of the issues involved in the interaction of culture and suicide. These issues should not be viewed as problems, but rather as opportunities to plan and execute innovative and exciting research and to work more effectively with suicidal clients from diverse cultures.

NOTES

1. There is a well-known joke about a conference on elephants to which each nation could send a team to present one paper. The Italians spoke on the love life of elephants, the French on cuisine involving elephants, the British on "Elephants I have shot," the Americans on how to build a better elephant, and the Finns on how to preserve an elephant in alcohol (there are more nations represented), while the Germans brought a 24-volume encyclopedia containing current knowledge about elephants.
2. Great Britain has ethnic groups in Wales and the county of Cornwall who predate the Roman, Danish, and French invaders and who have their own languages and ethnic identity. Yet their suicidal behavior has received no attention.
3. Bear in mind that the Chinese in any country may not be a homogenous cultural group.
4. The nations used different classifications by age.
5. For example, Lester (1994c) showed that the frequency of jumping as a method for suicide in Singapore was strongly associated with the development of high rise apartments.
6. Each judge rated the suicide rate of each society on a scale of 0–4, and their ratings were summed.
7. Ember and Ember (1992) drew attention to the fact that the materials on suicides in the HRAF come from very different time periods. Therefore, they urged that it was important to specify the year from which the data were derived. For example, they rated the Creek suicide rate as 1.74 (on a scale of 0–8) *in 1800* and the Omaha as 1 *in 1860.*

REFERENCES

Anon. (2004). A political awakening. *The Economist, 370(8363),* 35–37.

Bagley, C. (1991). Poverty and suicide among native Canadians. *Psychological Reports, 69,* 149–150.

Berlin, I.N. (1986). Psychopathology and its antecedents among American Indian adolescents. *Advances in Clinical Child Psychology, 9,* 125–152.

Berry, J.W. (1990). Acculturation and adaptation. *Arctic Medical Research, 49,* 142–150.

Bohannan, P. (Ed.) (1967). *African homicide and suicide.* New York: Atheneum.

Burvill, P., McCall, M., Woodings, T., & Stenhouse, N. (1983). Comparison of suicide rates and methods in English, Scots and Irish immigrants in Australia. *Social Science & Medicine, 17,* 705–708.

Cheng, A.T.A. (1995). Mental illness and suicide. *Archives of General Psychiatry, 52,* 594–603.

Cheng, A.T.A. (1997). Personality disorder and suicide. *British Journal of Psychiatry, 170,* 441–446.

Chiles, J.A., Strosahl, K., Ping, Z.Y., Clark, M., Hall, K., Jemelka, R., Senn, B., & Reto, C. (1989). Depression, hopelessness and suicidal behavior in Chinese and American psychiatric patients. *American Journal of Psychiatry, 146,* 339–344.

Clarke, R.V., & Lester, D. (1989). *Suicide: Closing the exits.* New York: Springer-Verlag.

Counts, D.A. (1980). Fighting back is not the way: Suicide and the women on Kaliai. *American Ethnologist, 7,* 332–351.

Counts, D.A. (1988). Ambiguity in the interpretation of suicide. In D. Lester (Ed.), *Why women kill themselves,* pp. 87–109. Springfield, IL: Charles Thomas.

D'Azevedo, W.L., Freed, S.A., Freed, R.S., Leis, P.E., Scotch, N.A., Scotch, F.L., Price, J.A., & Downs, J.F. (1963). *The Washo Indians of California and Nevada.* Salt Lake City, UT: University of Utah.

De Catanzaro, D. (1981). *Suicide and self-damaging behavior.* New York: Academic Press.

Devereux, G. (1961). *Mohave ethnopsychiatry.* Washington, DC: Smithsonian Institution.

Douglas, J.D. (1967). *The social meanings of suicide.* Princeton, NJ: Princeton University.

Durkheim, E. (1897). *Le suicide.* Paris, France: Felix Alcan.

Early, K.E. (1992). *Religion and suicide in the African-American community.* Westport, CT: Greenwood.

Ember, C.R., & Ember, R. (1992). Warfare, aggression, and resource problems. *Behavior Science Research, 26,* 169–226.

Fallers, L.A., & Fallers, M.C. (1967). Homicide and suicide in Busoga. In P. Bohannan (Ed.), *African homicide and suicide,* pp. 65–93. New York: Atheneum.

Gastil, R. (1971). Homicide and a regional culture of violence. *American Sociological Review, 36,* 412–427.

Gibbs, J. (1988). Conceptual, methodological, and sociocultural issues in black youth suicide. *Suicide & Life-Threatening Behavior, 18,* 73–89.

Goward, P., Repper, J., Appleton, L., & Hagan, T. (2006). Crossing boundaries. *Journal of Mental Health, 15,* 315–327.

Hendin, H. (1964). *Suicide and Scandinavia.* New York: Grune & Stratton.

Killias, M., Kesteren, J. van, & Rindlisbacher, M. (2001). Guns, violent crime, and suicide in 21 countries. *Canadian Journal of Criminology, 43,* 429–448.

Lee, C. S., Chang, J. C., & Cheng, A.T.A. (2002). Acculturation and suicide. *Psychological Medicine, 32,* 133–141.

Lester, D. (1994a). The epidemiology of suicide in Chinese populations in six regions of the world. *Chinese Journal of Mental Health, 7,* 21–24.

Lester, D. (1994b). Differences in the epidemiology of suicide in Asian Americans by nation of origin. *Omega, 29,* 89–93.

Lester, D. (1994c). Suicide by jumping in Singapore as a function of high-rise apartment availability. *Perceptual & Motor Skills, 79,* 74.

Lester, D. (1994d). Predicting the suicide rate in Wales. *Psychological Reports, 75,* 1054.

Lester, D. (1997). *Suicide in American Indians.* Commack, NY: Nova Science.

Lester, D., Saito, Y., & Park, B.C.B. (2011). Suicide among foreign residents of Japan. *Psychological Reports, 108,* 139–140.

Lester, D., & Wilson, C. (1988). Suicide in Zimbabwe. *Central African Journal of Medicine, 34,* 147–149.

Linehan, M. (1973). Suicide and attempted suicide. *Perceptual and Motor Skills, 37,* 31–34.

Lynn, R. (1971). *Personality and national character.* New York: Pergamon.

Marks, A., & Stokes, C. S. (1976). Socialization, firearms and suicide. *Social Problems, 23,* 622–629.

Masumura, W.T. (1977). Social integration and suicide. *Behavior Science Research, 12,* 251–269.

May, P. A., & Dizmang, L. H. (1974). Suicide and the American Indian. *Psychiatric Annals, 4(11),* 22–28.

Rittey, D.A.W., & Castle, W. M. (1972). Suicides in Rhodesia. *Central African Journal of Medicine, 18,* 97–100.

Sue, D. W., & Sue, D. (1990). *Counseling the culturally different.* New York: Wiley.

Van Winkle, N. W., & May, P. A. (1986). Native American suicide in New Mexico, 1959–1979. *Human Organization, 45,* 296–309.

Walker, M. R. (2008). *Suicide among the Irish Traveller community.* Wicklow, Ireland: Wicklow County Council.

Westermeyer, J. (1979). Ethnic identity problems among ten Indian psychiatric patients. *International Journal of Social Psychiatry, 25,* 188–197.

Wolfgang, M. E. (1957). Victim-precipitated criminal homicide. *Journal of Criminal Law, Criminology & Police Science, 48,* 1–11.

Wolfgang, M. E., & Ferracuti, F. (1967). *The subculture of violence.* London, UK: Tavistock.

Zimmerman, J. K., & Zayas, L. (1995). Suicidal adolescent Latinas. In S. Canetto & D. Lester (Eds.), *Women and suicide,* pp. 120–132. New York: Springer.

Zonda, T., & Lester, D. (1990). Suicide among Hungarian gypsies. *Acta Psychiatrica Scandinavica, 82,* 381–382.

12

A Case Study: Seeking to Understand a Suicide[1]

Thomas E. Ellis

HAS IT REALLY COME TO THIS?

He was only a few years out from an exemplary medical education, an award-winning surgical residency, and a lucrative start on a career as a cosmetic surgeon in a southeastern city. His divorce, following an ill-advised fling with an assistant, merciless publicity, and subsequent estrangement from his two young daughters, had rocked his world. Largely a stranger to loss and adversity, he had been unable to accept emotional support from friends or disclose the depth of his suffering to a therapist, and had turned first to alcohol and then to self-prescribed (and abused) anxiety medications to find relief. Missed meetings and complaints from patients about suspected intoxication had led to an investigation by the hospital Chief of Staff, resulting in a mandated leave of absence and remedial treatment. Notice of a malpractice complaint was the last straw.

Even as he took the pills, he wasn't sure what he was after. Relief, yes, but what sort?

MAYBE IF I CAN JUST GO TO SLEEP FOR A WHILE

Yet he took much more of the alprazolam than he knew would induce sleep. He also knew the alcohol in his system would serve as a potentiator, greatly enhancing the effect of the benzodiazepine.

IF I DIE, WELL, THAT WOULDN'T BE SO BAD

It did not occur to him to write a suicide note.

Suicide is well understood in some respects but quite mysterious in others. Men kill themselves four times as often as women, white people constitute more than 90 percent of suicides, and psychiatric disorders such as depression and alcoholism put people at risk for suicide that is many times greater than the general population. These are well-established facts. Yet most men, most white people, and most people with psychiatric disorders (the vast majority, in fact) do not die by suicide. While many authors report that up to 15 percent of people with major depression die by suicide, more recent analyses have shown that the actual figure is closer to 3 percent–4 percent (Bostwick & Pancratz, 2000; Inskip, Harris, & Barraclough, 1998). Suicide rates for other at-risk diagnoses, such as alcohol addiction and schizophrenia, are in this range as well. Of course, a 4 percent mortality rate for any illness is alarming, but we must ask what it is about these individuals that sets them apart from the other 96 percent. In other words, it is crucial to pay attention to the fact that suicide is not the rule for depression (or alcoholism, schizophrenia, etc.), but actually the exception to the rule.

Despite thousands of studies, journal articles, books, and conference presentations on the problem of suicide, overall rates of suicide in the United States and worldwide have shown little movement. Suicide rates in the United States have ranged between 10 and 12 per 100,000 population for more than 50 years (Maris, Berman, & Silverman, 2000). In an age characterized by an exponential increase in the use of antidepressant, antipsychotic, and anxiolytic medications (e.g., Mojtabai & Olfson, 2010), researchers have been hard-pressed to find indications of impact on population suicide rates (e.g., Montgomery, 1997).

Surprisingly, given this context, rigorous outcome studies on the effects of psychotherapeutic interventions with suicidal individuals are quite scarce. One review identified only 40 randomized controlled trials (Linehan, 2006), as compared to the thousands of studies examining treatments for other conditions such as depression and anxiety disorders. One of a number of factors accounting for this is lack of funding. For example, federal funding for suicide research in 2010 totaled $37 million; by comparison, in the same year, NIH funding for HIV/AIDS research, which kills one-third as many Americans annually, was more than $3 billion.

The field is not without its bright spots. The past two decades have seen the beginnings of a general shift in treatment strategies, based on a foundation of research evidence. This shift essentially moves suicidal behavior from the status of symptom to a problem in its own right. Conventional thought has viewed suicidal behavior as a manifestation of psychiatric illness, with the assumption that treating the illness would eliminate the suicidal behavior much like treatment of an infection eliminates fever. It is a surprise to many that studies have not supported this prediction (Linehan, 2006).

An alternate model holds that suicidal thinking and behavior is fundamentally a *coping response* to emotional distress in absence of an apparent other means of reducing that distress. An accumulating body of evidence (Ellis & Rutherford, 2008) shows that many suicidal individuals have distinctly different thinking patterns (such as impaired problem-solving and overgeneral memory) that interfere with finding solutions to problems and reducing emotional arousal. On the other hand, the suicide option, in the mind of a suffering individual, carries with it the expectation of relief, making it a seductive prospect.

The view of suicidal behavior as a coping response points naturally toward a treatment approach that emphasizes the cultivation of cognitive and behavioral skills that many people acquire naturally to reduce emotional suffering, such as self-soothing, connecting with caring others for support, or pursuing activities that bring a sense of meaning and fulfillment. Initial research, including randomized studies published in the *Journal of the American Medical Association* and the *Archives of General Psychiatry* have indicated that interventions that target suicidal thinking and associated cognitive vulnerabilities can reduce the risk of future suicidal behavior by as much as 50 percent (Brown et al., 2005; Linehan et al., 2006).

When Suicide Happens

So how are we to make sense of it when a particular individual decides, freely or not, that all hope is lost and it is time to end it all? Indeed, how are we to learn to recognize this in advance, to anticipate when an individual is approaching the precipice, so we might supply him or her with the resources needed to step back from the edge?

Following three days in the ICU and another two days in hospital for stabilization, Mark arrived at the prestigious psychiatric facility with little more than a suitcase and a gnawing sense of shame that had shut down his usually keen insight and sense of humor. He was chagrined that his landlord had stumbled into his apartment and called paramedics, yet glad (mostly) that he was still around. During his psychiatric interview, he disclosed for the first time ever that his mother had struggled for years with symptoms of bipolar disorder, and his strong suspicion that a paternal uncle's death in a single car accident had actually been a suicide.

During his initial workup, it was learned that Mark had been taking a subtherapeutic dose of Zoloft, intended to relieve both depressive symptoms and his anxiety. Because of his lack of response, as well as sexual side-effects, Mark was switched to a new antidepressant with both serotonergic and adrenergic mechanisms of action. He was also prescribed Ativan as needed for anxiety and continued on his bedtime dose of Ambien. In addition, because of the role of alcohol in his deterioration and suicide attempt, the treatment team recommended that he begin participating in community Alcoholics Anonymous (AA) meetings. Mark protested briefly, but then reluctantly agreed to "give it a try."

In the treatment milieu, fellow patients sometimes wondered why he was in a psychiatric hospital, and were mystified when they learned of his suicide attempt. He participated actively in therapy groups, although it was noted that he was more inclined to provide support for others than to explore his own vulnerabilities. Before long, he was elected unit president, ferrying information between patients and staff regarding issues in the treatment milieu.

His individual therapy took an unremarkable course. Generally dismissive of the importance of his suicidal "gesture," when his therapist asked him how he felt about surviving, he managed only to respond, "I guess it just wasn't my time." He consistently denied any future intent or plans to harm himself, although he allowed that the thought of suicide "occasionally crosses my mind—doesn't it everybody's?"

If they think I'm going to tell them I fantasize about being dead, they're the ones who need their heads examined. If I tell them, they'll just freak out, over-react, probably ship me off to a locked facility. I'll probably be fine; but at least I have a way out if I don't get better.

He quickly absorbed psychotherapy theory and jargon, accurately commenting on his need to "take better care of myself," but lacking in concrete plans to do so. During one session, he dissolved into tears as he told of his daughter's departure following a recent visit to the hospital. Other than this, the therapist consistently noted, "no acute distress." He continued to require sleep medication throughout his hospital stay.

One of the greatest pitfalls for those seeking to help suicidal patients is failing to grasp the vexing nature of conversations about suicide. At the root of this difficulty is the questionable assumption on the part of helpers that the helper's agenda of keeping the patient safe is actually shared by the patient. For the patient, the situation is not nearly so straightforward.

While voicing a (generally sincere) desire to live and pursue a happier life, the patient rarely has this wish without an opposing (sometimes unconscious) wish, if not to be dead, then at least to retain the suicide option "just in case." Countless patients have said this to helpers, directly or indirectly: *"Don't take this away from me (you can't, anyway); It's all I have to comfort me these days."*

Motivation to discuss suicide openly is seriously compromised by a wide array of issues, including shame about having a death wish in the first place, not wanting to disappoint the therapist, being afraid of opening up a frightening can of worms, not wanting to endure the loss of hospital privileges that often follows disclosure of active suicidal ideation, and fears (often realistic) of involuntary hospitalization, to name just a few. Moreover, the anxiety that the discussion of suicide brings to both patient and helper makes it more likely that the progress notes afterward will state, simply, "patient denies suicidal ideation or intent." Both parties are relieved to move on to other topics. Whether the conclusion that suicide risk is low is a valid assessment is a different matter altogether.

As the days passed, Mark's appearance improved. He was observed to be interacting more in the milieu, signs of humor began to return, appetite improved, and he began to show more willingness to address the numerous problems in his work and private lives. Indeed, the social worker on his treatment team expressed concern that he looked *too* upbeat, that he was perhaps failing to grasp the complexity and depth of problems he would face as he attempted to resume his medical practice and face life as an unmarried, middle-age man. Fellow patients marveled at his resilience and "positive attitude." His individual therapist noted that he had made a significant cognitive shift from negativity and pessimism to a "one day at time" outlook. As discharge approached, the team noticed increased anxiety, irritability, and difficulty sleeping. Faithful to his style, he attributed this to what anyone would be feeling, wondering what the future might hold, and worrying that he might not remember enough from his time in the hospital. He continued to request anxiety medications up until the day before discharge.

After discharge, Mark busied himself with addressing the requirements of the office of the medical chief of staff at the hospital where he sought to get his privileges restored. He reluctantly adhered to his discharge plan by attending three AA meetings per week, although these declined steadily as he became more convinced that he was "not an alcoholic like those other people," but had merely encountered "a rough patch." He resumed seeing his individual therapist, and after a couple of catch-up sessions, the conversation resumed a familiar tone and cadence.

His prior reputation for excellence, together with his participation in treatment, resulted in quick action by the hospital administration, and he was back working in the operating room barely more than two weeks after discharge. This was conditional upon close supervision by the surgery chairman, a process which Mark found humiliating. Moreover, although he was glad to be back at work, he was disappointed that "getting back on track" did not provide more of a lift to his mood. Returning to an empty apartment every day and seeing his children only on Saturdays left him feeling hollow and bored. He tried online dating, but after one outing with a fellow physician who spent the entire dinner talking derisively about her ex and laughing about the large quantities of alcohol she had consumed "after dumping the bastard," he resolved to focus his energies even more on his work, perhaps pursuing sub-specialty training.

It was soon thereafter that his attorney notified him that the judge assigned to his malpractice case had refused a motion to dismiss and that the plaintiff had declined a generous offer to settle out of court. He would now need to review the reams of medical records and other documents that had been produced by the discovery process and prepare for what promised to be a difficult deposition process. As he combed through the reams of paper, Mark began to doubt himself and wonder if his confidence in his medical skills and professional integrity was overblown. He found his mood rapidly descending back into the depths of melancholy and despair. His insomnia returned with a vengeance, untouched by the increasing doses of Ambien and the narcotics that he used to treat it. His grogginess at work began to be noticed by his team in the operating room. It was soon thereafter that he was discovered injecting himself with the stimulant Dexedrine in the hospital pharmacy. His mug shot appeared prominently in the next day's newspaper, with a caption reading in part, "Released on personal recognizance."

The transition from psychiatric hospital back to one's normal environment is difficult in any case, often downright hazardous in the case of a suicidal patient. The shift can amount to a form of culture shock, from a supportive, healing setting to the same environment that contributed to one's decline in the first place. Studies on this are clear. Whereas it seems logical to expect that the first few weeks and months postdischarge would be low risk thanks to carryover effects from treatment, this period is actually one of *heightened* risk (Kan, Ho, Dong, & Dunn, 2007). For this reason, it is essential that treatment providers make airtight plans for support and rapid follow-up after discharge, as well as educate the patient about "taking it slow" and anticipating stressors and setbacks.

Aaron Beck's cognitive model of psychiatric illness (Beck, 1998) sheds light on this vulnerability via the construct of "latent schemas." A schema is a constellation of beliefs, attitudes, rules, feelings, and action tendencies that give organization to the personality and account for stylistic differences from one person to another. This helps explain why one person may hardly notice someone cutting in line at a box office, while another may take this as a personal affront and a challenge to his manhood. Latent schemas may lie dormant for long periods of time, activated only when an event relevant to schema content occurs. For example (and relevant to this case), one whose sense of worth is invested heavily or entirely in his accomplishments may flourish while these accomplishments are flowing, but crash when circumstances obstruct this supply of "life blood." Such latent schemas may again go underground when circumstances improve, but the vulnerability remains unless it is modified in therapy.

His ex-wife and children receded into the background of his awareness.

They don't need me. They'll be better off, in the long run.

The only thing—*only* thing—occupying his mind, indeed virtually hijacking his thought processes, was the need for relief. Relief from this unending and unbearable grind of anxiety, fear, despair, and self-loathing. A desperate longing for peace. As he climbed the stairs of the parking garage, he felt as if it had been years since he had enjoyed a good night's sleep, a fog of exhaustion shrouding him every waking hour. A day in the future when he could enjoy life again was beyond his imagination. He felt a mixture of terror and an unfamiliar lightness as he plunged toward the street six stories below.

Suicide is sometimes characterized as a "selfish" act, in which the subject disregards the impact on loved ones. By the same token, clinicians often try to help the suicidal individual by urging him or her to consider how devastated loved ones would be, were he or she to die. Although the patient may respond by promising to stay safe, the promise is often without substance; for the very nature of the exchange suggests a failure to grasp the true nature of the suicidal mind. Much as a "survival mode" would cause us to cease being polite when fleeing a burning building, the "suicide mode" narrows the attention to a veritable one-track obsession with obtaining relief from suffering through death. Prior buffers to suicide, including religious beliefs, future aspirations and concern for loved ones, fall away, essentially inaccessible, drowned out by the drumbeat of death.

This state has been variously referred to as "cognitive constriction" (Shneidman, 1993), "desperation" (Hendin et al., 2004), and "attentional fixation" (Wenzel, Brown, & Beck, 2009), in which the individual is unable to think of anything other than his or her suffering and how to end it. Appreciating the nature of this state helps us to understand, not only the apparent disregard for the feelings of others, but also the uselessness of the no-suicide contract. The patient may be perfectly sincere in signing it, but it becomes irrelevant in the context of the suicidal mode.

This time he left a note, evidence that the act was not impulsive. The ambivalence so clear in his prior attempt was now practically absent. Like most real-world suicide notes (Elkind, 1997), any hopes that the reader would discover satisfying insights into this self-inflicted death were quickly dashed. The tone was matter-of-fact, though not without a poignant subtext: *"Sorry to let everybody down (again). Just can't keep doing this. Instructions in my will. No funeral please."*

In the Aftermath

The Morbidity and Mortality meeting began without the typical banter that preceded this normally routine meeting whose purpose is to review causes of "negative outcomes" in the hospital. Because the suicide occurred within one month of discharge, hospital policy required a formal review. Mark had died on a Saturday, allowing enough time for members of the group to get word that today's duties would include reviewing a colleague's work in a situation—suicide—in which answers are always in short supply. An outside consultant, known for her research and forensics work in suicidology, had been invited in.

How might this tragedy be understood? Why had the treatment failed? Had everything been done that should have been done?

An initial foray into the records revealed what had started as a routine hospitalization: a medical review of systems, a mental status exam revealing "passing thoughts of suicide but without intent or plan," a standard request for a "no-suicide contract" to which the patient had readily agreed.

The "no-suicide contract" comprises one of the most striking disconnects between science and practice in the mental health field. Its use is ubiquitous. One study found that 83 percent of therapists from a variety of mental health disciplines use it (Page & King, 2008). Remarkably, there is no research evidence to speak of that the practice is safe or effective, or that it protects providers in the event of a lawsuit. To the contrary, one study revealed that, of 100 patients who had made life-endangering suicide attempts, 83 percent had a no-suicide contract in place at the time (Hall, Platt, & Hall, 1999). Further, liability experts warn that such a document is of no use in court (Bennett et al., 2006). An increasing chorus of authors is urging the elimination of the practice, citing concerns such as patient alienation and the likelihood of a false sense of security on the part of those providing treatment. Preferable alternatives such as a safety plan (Wenzel et al., 2006) and a commitment to treatment statement (Rudd, Mandrusiak, & Joiner, 2006) have been proposed.

The medical record indicated that Mark had shown a fairly typical hospital course, at first submitting to his shame by remaining quiet in therapy groups and withdrawing to his room during unstructured hours. With time, however, and with pharmacological intervention, he had appeared to rally. Reviewers observed that nursing notes consistently indicated "No SI/HI," for no suicidal or homicidal ideation. On his Beck Depression Inventory, administered on three occasions, he reported, "I have thoughts of killing myself but would not carry them out."

The psychiatrist's discharge summary reflected a hospitalization without the drama of major emotional dysregulation or interpersonal conflict sometimes found in psychiatric inpatients. He noted that the patient's premorbid history was unremarkable, with the exception of an episode of binge drinking and possible depression after he failed to gain entry into his top-choice medical school. The psychiatrist also made note of one and possibly two suicides in Mark's family history. He described an unremarkable hospital course, during which Mark showed steady, although not dramatic, progress. After noting that Mark's work in therapy and in the treatment milieu had remained "somewhat superficial," and that he continued to show signs of sleep disturbance, he concluded that Mark's prognosis should be considered "fair." He noted that Mark had continued to report anxiety ("near-panic attacks"), but he attributed this to his approaching discharge.

The external reviewer expressed concerns that had not been raised by others. She noted that clinicians were quick to accept Mark's dismissal of his suicide "gesture," even after establishing a trusting therapeutic alliance that might have allowed fuller exploration of the meaning of this act. His individual therapist had not brought the matter up again, choosing instead to pursue Mark's feelings about his father's inability to express affection to him. She also noted that Mark had been quick to agree to abstain from alcohol, given its role in his difficulties at work, but coping skills that might have given him alternate means of addressing his stress and insomnia were not pursued. Finally, she noted that, despite a number of suicide risk assessments over the course of hospitalization, no one had inquired about the presence of a firearm or other means of suicide in Mark's home. (Because Mark had killed himself by jumping, this turned out not to have been a crucial oversight.) In general, while the consultant found several causes for concern, she concluded that the hospital had provided solid, conventional services to Mark and, as such, had not fallen short of the community standard of care. The committee concluded that further pursuit of the case was "not indicated at this time."

What Postmortem Studies Tell Us about Death by Suicide

One of the most popular research strategies in suicidology is to analyze records from samples of people who have died by suicide, in a search for strategies that might be useful in identifying and intervening with at-risk patients going forward. Such studies have produced useful, though predictable, findings, such as the fact that 90 percent–95 percent of people who die by suicide were suffering from a treatable psychiatric disorder (Robins, 1981). However, one of the most eye-opening findings, replicated several times since it was published, is that of Fawcett and associates in 1990. In a study looking for factors that discriminated which patients had died in the near term (12 months) versus long term (up to 10 years), it was shown that it was not depression but activating processes such as anxiety, panic attacks, and insomnia that placed patients at more imminent risk (Fawcett et al., 1990).

The relevance of this line of research to Mark's case, and countless others like him, is clear. While the burden of depression and despair certainly set the stage for the wish to die, the engine driving the urgency to carry it out, the "desperation" so eloquently described by Hendin and associates (2004), is the intolerable distress comprised of unremitting agitation and anxiety within a fog of chronic sleep deprivation. Such a state not only produces an urgent need for relief, but also impairs the individual's executive functioning, the aspect of cognition that includes judgment, reflection, problem-solving, and anticipation of the consequences of one's actions.

Another recent area of work that is helping to demystify suicidal behavior has to do with the vital connection between one human being and another. In his recent contribution, *Why People Die by Suicide,* Thomas Joiner (2007) presents evidence for his view that suicide occurs in the context of three factors: an acquired ability to self-harm, a failure in one's sense of belongingness, and a sense of being a burden to others. In other words, Joiner's theory essentially maintains that a human being *cannot* kill himself or herself as long as he or she feels connected to others.

My colleague Jon Allen reaches essentially the same conclusion, although from a different perspective. Trauma, he notes, is distinguished from other forms of suffering by its unique association of intolerable pain with the experience of aloneness (Allen, 2005). The absence of interpersonal connection (attachment) deprives the sufferer of an essential source of comfort, an understanding and supportive connection with a caring other. Attachment theory and research have long viewed connectedness as essential to mental health, not only during child development, but throughout life, and certainly in the context of psychotherapy. Intriguing findings in the closely related area of mentalization-based psychotherapy have provided robust evidence of the relevance of interpersonal connection to the effective treatment of people at risk of suicide (Bateman & Fonagy, 2009).

Mark's sense of disconnection was not obvious, given his persona as the successful and charming professional; but it was palpable in the context of failure. His infidelity to his wife, focus on his career to the exclusion of close relationships with his friends and colleagues, and difficulty expressing vulnerability with therapists all pointed to an inclination toward desperate measures when beset with major losses in his personal and professional lives.

While it is tempting to blame Mark's treatment providers for not detecting his suicide risk and intervening with him, it is important not to lose sight of the challenges facing clinicians in anticipating what the future holds for an at-risk patient. Despite numerous attempts with a variety of scientific strategies, researchers long ago acknowledged that it was unlikely that a statistical algorithm would ever be discovered that would accurately predict suicide on an individual level (Pokorny, 1983). The realities of a low probability event such as suicide (around 12 occurrences per 100,000 population per year) are such that any effort at prediction is doomed to an unacceptably high level of false positive predictions (predicting suicide, but being wrong). Compounding the problem is an issue that is more human and interpersonal issue than statistical. An individual who is suffering intensely, seeing no hope for relief, and feeling alienated from others will, in all likelihood, keep suicidal planning to himself or herself. From this standpoint, it would be downright illogical to disclose such thoughts to others.

Postmortem studies consistently support this prediction. In a study of the cases of 76 patients who died by suicide, Busch, Fawcett, and Jacobs (2003) found that 77 percent had denied suicidal ideation at their last communication with a clinician. Of these, more than one-quarter had no-suicide contracts in place at the time of their deaths. This is not to say that all of these patients necessarily were dissimulating. It is likely than many were quite sincere at the time in expressing intentions to stay safe. The fact is that many adverse events that trigger latent schemas (discussed above) are unpredictable, if not downright random—the unexpected death of a friend, being shunned at work after returning from psychiatric hospitalization, or losing money as a stock market bubble bursts. Buffering a vulnerable individual from such challenges and myriad others like them is a challenge for helpers.

Can We Do Better than "Standard of Care"?

As noted above, it is not uncommon to encounter situations in which the community standard of care has been met but the patient nevertheless dies by suicide. "Standard of care" is a legal, not clinical, term used to determine whether providers have delivered services that are consistent with those provided by the typical "reasonably prudent" professional in similar circumstances. Deviations from this standard constitute grounds for a finding of malpractice (Bongar et al., 1998).

The "no fault" finding in Mark's case raises the distinction between standard of care and best practice. Although definitions of best practice vary, in general the term refers to practices that have been shown to be effective and perhaps superior to other approaches in other settings. For our purposes, was meeting standard of care sufficient in Mark's case? More than 2,000 hospital patients in the United States die by suicide each year (Wolfersdorf, 2000). Obviously, there is room for improvement. Without accusing his treaters of malpractice, let us consider some opportunities in his situation that might have made a difference.

Generally speaking, the current standard of care for suicidal patients is characterized by such practices as assessing risk mainly by asking the patient if he or she is suicidal and obtaining a signed no-suicide contract when risk is detected. Although well-standardized instruments, such as the Beck Hopelessness Scale and the Beck Scale for Suicidal Ideation, are available, most clinicians do not use them (Jobes, Eyman, & Yufit, 1995). Similarly, despite the availability of empirically supported treatments developed to address suicidal behavior directly (Ellis & Rutherford, 2008; Linehan, 2006), the field as a whole seems not to have changed much since Shneidman's comment that, following crisis stabilization, "the usual methods of psychotherapy . . . can be usefully employed" (Shneidman, 1981, p. 345).

In Mark's case, we might speculate (and it is *only* speculation) that, given the opportunity (combined with patient education) to address the underlying "drivers" of his suicide attempt, in particular, his overreliance on achievement to sustain his shaky self-esteem, together with his difficulty getting close to people, he might have been better equipped to cope with the adversity he faced after his hospital discharge. It is possible that things might have unfolded differently had he been taught specific coping skills, together with imagined rehearsals of possible future adversities (Wenzel et al., 2009). A written crisis or safety plan also might have proved useful. Unfortunately, as events transpired, Mark was ill-equipped to cope with his stress through means other than drug abuse, and the crisis that followed his being discovered abusing drugs in his workplace was too much for him to bear.

Is there hope for moving standard of care closer to what might be considered best practice? If one considers training programs the best indicator of trends in the field, the evidence suggests cause for concern. Surveys have consistently shown that preparation of students for working with suicidal patients leaves much to be desired (Bongar & Harmatz, 1989; Dexter-Mazza & Freeman, 2003; Ellis, Dickey, & Jones, 1998). Graduate students and psychiatry residents consistently report a high frequency of encounters with suicidal patients (indeed, losing patients to suicide is not uncommon for professionals in training), combined with only superficial training in skills for working with such patients. This is one of the rare areas in which students are found actually to be asking for more training (Dexter-Mazza & Freeman, 2003; Melton & Coverdale, 2009).

In Conclusion: Is the Tragedy of Patient Suicide Inevitable?

It is hoped that this chapter has portrayed the nature of suicidology in the early 21st century. The glass is half empty *and* half full. Unanswered questions abound, including the fundamental questions of how we might do a better job of predicting suicidal behavior in individual cases and whether our interventions are effective in actually saving lives. Shortcomings in professional preparation for working with suicidal patients and research funding relative to the size and scope of the problem are difficult to reconcile with the tragedy of suicide.

At the same time, the progress seen in recent decades is undeniable. Indeed, to call a suicide such as Mark's mysterious is now a sign of an uninformed observer rather than a reflection on the state of the science. We now know enough, not only to understand a tragedy in retrospect, but also to begin looking at suicidal patients and their treatment in a way that permits a collaborative and tailored approach to care that stands to reduce significantly, not only current suicidal thinking and impulses, but also vulnerability to future adversity. We are by no means helpless in the face of this dreaded cause of premature death. Although it is unlikely that we will see a day when suicide is extinguished like an infectious disease by a vaccine, we might hope to see a day when suicides are less often accompanied by a sense that we could have done more to save a life.

NOTE

1. The case described in this chapter is a fictionalized account of an actual patient's hospital course and suicide. By design, it describes characteristics shared by many suicidal individuals, but resemblance to any specific individual, living or dead, is unintended and coincidental.

REFERENCES

Allen, J.G. (2005). *Coping with trauma: Hope through understanding* (2nd ed.). Washington, DC: American Psychiatric Publishing.

Bateman, A., & Fonagy, P. (2009). Eight-year follow-up of patients treated for borderline personality disorder: Mentalization-based treatment versus treatment as usual. *American Journal of Psychiatry, 165,* 631–638.

Beck, A.T. (1998). Beyond belief: A theory of modes, personality, and psychopathology. In P.M. Salkovskis (Ed.), *Frontiers of cognitive therapy.* New York: Guilford.

Bennett, B.E., Bricklin, P.M., Harris, E., Knapp, S., Van de Creek, L., & Younggren, J.N. (2006). *Assessing and managing risk in psychological practice: An individualized approach.* Rockville, MD: The Trust.

Bongar, B., Berman, A.L., Maris, R.W., Silverman, M.M., Harris, E.A., & Packman, W.L. (1998). *Risk management with suicidal patients.* New York: Guilford.

Bongar, B., & Harmatz, M. (1989). Graduate training in clinical psychology and the study of suicide. *Professional Psychology: Research & Practice, 20,* 209–213.

Bostwick, J.M., & Pancratz, V.S. (2000). Affective disorders and suicide risk: A reexamination. *American Journal of Psychiatry, 157,* 1925–1932.

Brown, G.K., Have, T.T., Henriques, G.R., Xie, S.X., Hollander, J.E., & Beck, A.T. (2005). Cognitive therapy for the prevention of suicide attempts: A randomized controlled trial. *Journal of the American Medical Association, 294,* 563–570.

Busch, K.A., Fawcett, J., & Jacobs, D.G. (2003). Clinical correlates of inpatient suicide. *Journal of Clinical Psychiatry, 64,* 14–19.

Dexter-Mazza, E.T., & Freeman, K.A. (2003). Graduate training and the treatment of suicidal clients: The students' perspective. *Suicide & Life-Threatening Behavior, 33,* 211–218.

Ellis, T.E., Dickey, T.O., & Jones, E.C. (1998). Patient suicide in psychiatry residency programs: A national survey of training and postvention practices. *Academic Psychiatry, 22,* 181–189.

Ellis, T.E., & Rutherford, B. (2008). Cognition and suicide: Two decades of progress. *International Journal of Cognitive Therapy, 1,* 47–68.

Elkind, M. (1997). . . . *Or not to be: A collection of suicide notes.* New York: Riverhead.

Fawcett, J., Sheftner, W.A., Fogg, L., Clark, D.C., Young, M.A., Hedeker, D., & Gibbons, R. (1990). Time-related predictors of suicide in major affective disorder. *American Journal of Psychiatry, 147,* 1189–1194.

Hall, R.C.W, Platt, D.E, & Hall, R.C.W. (1999). Suicide risk assessment: A review of risk factors for suicide in 100 patients who made severe suicide attempts. *Psychosomatics, 40,* 18–27.

Hendin, H., Maltsberger, J.T., Haas, A.P., Szanto, K., & Rabinowicz, H. (2004). Desperation and other affective states in suicidal patients. *Suicide & Life-Threatening Behavior, 34,* 386–394.

Inskip, H.M., Harris, E.C., & Barraclough, B. (1998). Lifetime risk of suicide for affective disorder, alcoholism, and schizophrenia. *British Journal of Psychiatry, 172,* 35–37.

Jobes, D.A., Eyman, J.R., & Yufit, R.I. (1995). How clinicians assess suicide risk in adolescents and adults. *Crisis Intervention & Time-Limited Treatment, 2,* 1–12.

Joiner, T. (2007). *Why people die by suicide.* Cambridge, MA: Harvard University Press.

Kan, C. K., Ho, T. P., Dong, J.Y.S., & Dunn, E.L.W. (2007). Risk factors for suicide in the immediate post-discharge period. *Social Psychiatry & Psychiatric Epidemiology, 42,* 208–214.

Linehan, M.M. (2006). Foreword. In T.E. Ellis (Ed.), *Cognition and suicide: Theory, research, and therapy,* pp. xxi–xvi. Washington, DC: American Psychological Association.

Linehan, M.M., Comtois, K.A., Murray, A.M., et al. (2006). Two-year randomized controlled trial and follow-up of Dialectical Behavior Therapy vs. therapy by experts for suicidal behaviors and borderline personality disorder. *Archives of General Psychiatry, 63,* 757–766.

Maris, R. W., Berman, A. L., & Silverman, M. M. (2000). *Comprehensive textbook of suicidology.* New York: Guilford.

Melton, B.B., & Coverdale, J.H. (2009). What do we teach psychiatric residents about suicide? A national survey of chief residents. *Academic Psychiatry, 33,* 47–50.

Mojtabai, R., & Olfson, M. (2010). National trends in psychotropic medication polypharmacy in office-based psychiatry. *Archives of General Psychiatry, 67,* 26–36.

Montgomery, S.A. (1997). Suicide and antidepressants. *Annals of the New York Academy of Sciences, 836,* 329–338.

Page, S.A., & King, M.C. (2008). No-suicide agreements: Current practices and opinions in a Canadian urban health region. *Canadian Journal of Psychiatry, 53,* 169–176.

Pokorny, A. (1983). Prediction of suicide in psychiatric patients: Report of a retrospective study. *Archives of General Psychiatry, 40,* 249–257.

Robins, E. (1981). *The final months.* New York: Oxford University Press.

Rudd, M.D., Mandrusiak, M., & Joiner, T.E. (2006). The case against no-suicide contracts: The commitment to treatment statement as a practice alternative. *Journal of Clinical Psychology, 62,* 243–251.

Shneidman, E.S. (1981). Psychotherapy with suicidal patients. *Suicide & Life-Threatening Behavior, 11,* 341–346.

Shneidman, E.S. (1993). *Suicide as psychache: A clinical approach to self-destructive behavior.* New York: Aronson.

Wenzel, A., Brown, G.K., & Beck, A.T. (2009). *Cognitive therapy for suicidal patients.* Washington, DC: American Psychological Association.

Wolfersdorf, M. (2000). Suicide among psychiatric inpatients. In K. Hawton & K.V. Heeringen (Eds.), *The international handbook of suicide and attempted suicide,* pp. 457–466. West Sussex, UK: Wiley.

Index

About the Editors and Contributors

EDITORS

James R. Rogers earned a PhD in Counseling Psychology from The University of Akron in 1993. He had taught in the Department of Counseling at Youngstown State University, was an adjunct professor of behavioral sciences at The Northeastern Ohio Universities College of Medicine, and a professor in the Collaborative Program in Counseling Psychology at The University of Akron. Dr. Rogers was a licensed psychologist in the state of Ohio and had specialized in the areas of suicide and disaster relief psychology. He was named an American Psychological Association Fellow in the Society of Counseling Psychology and a Fellow of the International Academy of Suicide Research by the IASR Board of Directors.

David Lester has doctoral degrees from Cambridge University (United Kingdom) in social and political science and Brandeis University (United States) in psychology. He is currently Distinguished Professor of Psychology at the Richard Stockton College of New Jersey in Galloway, New Jersey. He is a former president of the International Association for Suicide Prevention. He has published extensively on suicide, murder, and other issues in thanatology. His recent books include *Mass Murder* (2004), *Katie's Diary: Unlocking the Mystery of a Suicide* (2004), *Is there Life after Death?* (2005), *A Multiple-Self Theory of Personality* (2009), *Preventing Suicide: Why We Don't and How We Might* (2010), *Understanding and Preventing College Student Suicide* (2011), and *Suicide in Professional and Amateur Athletes* (2012).

CONTRIBUTORS

Margaret P. Battin, MFA, PhD, is Distinguished Professor of Philosophy and Adjunct Professor of Internal Medicine, Division of Medical Ethics and Humanities, at the University of Utah. She has authored, coauthored, edited, or co-edited some 20 books, including works on philosophical issues in suicide, case-puzzles in aesthetics, ethical issues in organized religion, and various topics in bioethics. She has published two collections of essays on end-of-life issues, *The Least Worst Death* and *Ending Life,* and has been the lead for two multiauthored projects, *Drugs and Justice* and *The Patient as Victim and Vector: Ethics and Infectious Disease.* In 1997, she won the University of Utah's Distinguished Research award, and in 2000, she received the Rosenblatt Prize, the University's most prestigious award. Her current projects include a comprehensive historical sourcebook on ethical issues in suicide and a book on large-scale reproductive problems of the globe, including population growth and decline, teen pregnancy, abortion, male roles in contraception, and more.

Amy M. Brausch has a PhD in Clinical Psychology from Northern Illinois University. She is currently an Assistant Professor of Psychology at Western Kentucky University in Bowling Green, Kentucky. She has been an active member of the American Association of Suicidology for 10 years and has published numerous empirical articles and book chapters on the topics of suicide, nonsuicidal self-injury, risk-taking behaviors, body image, and disordered eating in adolescents and young adults.

Thomas E. Ellis is Director of Psychology at the Menninger Clinic and Professor of Psychiatry in the Menninger Department of Psychiatry and Behavioral Sciences at Baylor College of Medicine in Houston, Texas. He earned his bachelor's degree at the University of Texas at Austin and his doctorate at Baylor University. He is a Fellow of the American Psychological Association, a Diplomate of the American Board of Professional Psychology, and a Founding Fellow of the Academy of Cognitive Therapy. In addition to his clinical, administrative, and teaching activities, he conducts research on the psychology of suicidal individuals and the effectiveness of psychotherapeutic interventions with suicidal patients. His books include *Choosing to Live: How to Defeat Suicide through Cognitive Therapy* (with Cory Newman) and *Cognition and Suicide: Theory, Research, and Therapy.*

Danielle R. Jahn is a doctoral candidate in clinical psychology at Texas Tech University. She completed her undergraduate education at the University of Florida in Gainesville, Florida and received her master's degree in psychology at Texas Tech University in Lubbock, Texas. Her primary research interests are in suicidology, geropsychology, and neuropsychology, and she is especially interested in the integration of these fields. In addition, she has published articles regarding a variety of topics within the field of suicidology, including training and competence in suicide risk assessment and management, the history of the field, survivors of suicide, and older adult suicide.

Bernard S. Jesiolowski is the Executive Director of the Crisis Intervention and Recovery Center in Canton, Ohio, Adjunct Faculty in the Master's and Doctoral Counseling Program at the University of Akron, and a Licensed Professional Clinical Counselor with supervisory endorsement. He received his PhD from Kent State University in Counseling Psychology and his MA in Professional Psychology from Edinboro University. He has been president of the Ohio Council of Behavioral Healthcare and an appointed member of the Ohio Department of Mental Health's Strategic Advisory Committee and Deliver the Promise Committee for the President's New Freedom Commission. He is active in administrative, policy, teaching, and clinical activities, and his interests range from supervision, counselor training, life review, gestalt therapy, crisis intervention, and suicide prevention, to work with the severe and persistently mentally ill and dually disordered individuals.

Jeff Klibert earned his doctoral degree in Counseling Psychology at Oklahoma State University. He is currently the Associate Director of Clinical Training in the PsyD program at Georgia Southern University. He is also a licensed psychologist in the State of Georgia. The majority of his clinical interests are associated with the prevention and treatment of risky behaviors in youth from underserved and/or rural populations. In terms of scholarship, he has published nine articles and book chapters concerning prevention of adolescent health risk behaviors, risk/protective factors for suicide, and suicide interventions.

Dorian A. Lamis is a predoctoral psychology intern at the Emory University School of Medicine, Grady Health System in Atlanta GA. He completed his doctoral work in Clinical Psychology at the University of South Carolina. He received his MA in Clinical Psychology from East Tennessee State University. His research focuses on suicidal behaviors and alcohol use in adolescents and young adults, with a particular emphasis on college students. He has published over 30 peer-reviewed articles on these topics as well as on other risk and protective factors for suicide. He has also edited a book entitled *Understanding and preventing college student suicide* (2011).

Lars Mehlum has a doctoral degree in psychiatry from the University of Oslo (Norway). He is currently Professor of psychiatry and suicidology at the University of Oslo where he is the founding director of the National Centre for Suicide Research and Prevention. He has been a coordinator of the Norwegian National Strategy for suicide prevention, and has established several training programs in suicidology, such as the master's degree in suicide prevention at the University of Oslo. A past president of the International Association for Suicide Prevention, he is also member of the International Academy of Suicide Research, the American Association of Suicidology and the American Foundation for Suicide Prevention. With his research group, he focuses on the clinical course of suicidal behavior with respect to etiological and prognostic factors such as stressors and negative life events, major psychiatric illness, and the effectiveness of interventions, among them Dialectical Behavior Therapy. He has published widely on these subjects and received several national and international awards.

Jennifer J. Muehlenkamp earned her doctoral degree in clinical psychology from Northern Illinois University. She is an associate professor of psychology at the University of Wisconsin-Eau Claire and has held leadership positions within various professional organizations focused on suicide prevention and nonsuicidal self-injury. She has published over 60 empirical articles and book chapters on nonsuicidal self-injury and suicide, as well as assisting with developing and evaluating a school-based self-injury prevention program. Her work is internationally recognized and has earned awards from the American Association of Suicidology.

Maurizio Pompili is currently Professor of Suicidology and part of the Faculty of Medicine and Psychology of Sapienza University of Rome, Italy, where he received his MD degree, trained in Psychiatry (both *summa cum laude*), and has a doctoral degree in Experimental and Clinical Neurosciences. He is the Director of the Suicide Prevention Center at Sant'Andrea Hospital in Rome. He was also part of the Community at McLean Hospital—Harvard Medical School, United States. He is the recipient of the American Association of Suicidology's 2008 Shneidman Award for "Outstanding early career contribution to suicidology." He is part of IASP Task Force for Emergency Medicine and Suicidal Behavior and he has been Italian representative for IASP for several years. He is also member of the International Academy for Suicide Research and the American Association of Suicidology. He has provided validation studies of the Beck Hopelessness Scale, Reason for Living Inventory, and TEMPS-A for the

Italian population researching the interplay of factors that may precipitate suicide both in clinical and in nonclinical samples. He has published about 300 papers on suicide including original research articles, book chapters, and editorials. He co-edited 10 international books on suicide (including the latest *Evidence-based practice in suicidology* with Hogrefe & Huber and *Suicide in the words of suicidologists* with Nova). Maurizio Pompili is particularly active in collaborations with the Italian Ministry of Health and Italian Health Institute for suicide prevention. He is the principal investigator for Italy for the START study directed by Prof. De Leo. He recently launched the Race for Life, a sporting event to support suicide prevention in the community.

Gianluca Serafini is currently Professor of Psychiatry (undergraduate level) at the Faculty of Medicine and Psychology of Sapienza University of Rome, Italy. He obtained his degree in Medicine and Surgery (*summa cum laude*), his training in Psychiatry (*summa cum laude*), and his doctoral degree in Psychiatry (Early Interventions in Psychosis) in the same University. For almost 10 years he has worked as psychiatrist and researcher at Sant'Andrea Hospital in Rome where he is from 2007 an active member of the Service for Suicide Prevention directed by Prof. Pompili. Gianluca Serafini is part of the IASP Task Force for Emergency Medicine and Suicidal Behavior. He is also a member of several scientific societies (International Association for Suicide Prevention, Sociedad Española De Patología Dual, European Psychiatric Association, Associazione Italiana Lotta allo Stigma). He is the author of more than 100 publications in peer-reviewed international journals including original research articles, book chapters, and editorials. From 2007 he was speaker in more than 80 national and international congresses and he is currently Associate Editor of two international journals. Gianluca Serafini is currently reviewer for 30 peer-reviewed international journals, is an Editorial Board member of six international journals, and also an Advisory Board member of one international journal.

Morton M. Silverman, MD, is the Senior Science Advisor to the Suicide Prevention Resource Center (SPRC), Clinical Associate Professor of Psychiatry at the University of Chicago, and Assistant Clinical Professor of Psychiatry at the University of Colorado, Denver. Dr. Silverman served as the Senior Scientific Editor and Writer for the National Strategy for Suicide Prevention: Goals and Objectives for Action (2001). He serves as a Temporary Advisor to the Department of Mental Health and Substance Dependence of the World Health Organization and consults on the development of national suicide prevention programs. From 1996 to 2009 he was the Editor-in-Chief of *Suicide and Life-Threatening Behavior*. Dr. Silverman is a Distinguished Life Fellow of the American Psychiatric Association, and is the coauthor or author of over 45 peer-reviewed journal publications, and over 30 book and monograph chapters on the topics of college student mental health, disease prevention, health promotion, alcohol and other drug abuse, suicide, and standards of care. He is the co-editor or coauthor of six books on topics related to the field of suicidology, including *The Comprehensive Textbook of Suicidology* (2000), and *Adolescent Suicide: Assessment and Intervention* (2006). He is the 2005 recipient of the Louis I. Dublin Award from the American Association of Suicidology. He received his MD degree from Northwestern University in 1974, and in 1978 completed his residency training in Psychiatry at the University of Chicago.

Ian H. Stanley graduated from the University of Rochester in 2012 with a Bachelor of Arts in psychology, with honors. He has worked as a Research Assistant in the Department of Psychiatry at the University of Rochester Medical Center and as a postbaccalaureate Intramural Research Training Award Fellow at the National Institute of Mental Health in Bethesda, Maryland. His research interest focuses on the understanding and prevention of suicidal behaviors across the lifespan.

Kimberly A. Van Orden received her PhD in clinical psychology from Florida State University. She completed a predoctoral internship at Montefiore Medical Center and an NIH-sponsored postdoctoral fellowship in suicide prevention at the University of Rochester Medical Center. She is currently an Assistant Professor in the Department of Psychiatry, University of Rochester Medical Center. Her research interests are in the etiology and prevention of late-life suicide, particularly the role of social connectedness as a protective factor and mechanism of intervention. She has coauthored numerous scientific papers on suicide prevention and is also coauthor of the book *The Interpersonal Theory of Suicide: Guidance for Working with Suicidal Clients*.

Bijou Yang has both master and doctoral degrees from the University of Pennsylvania (United States) in Economics. She is Professor of Economics at the LeBow College of Business, Drexel University in Philadelphia, Pennsylvania, and served as President of the Society for the Advancement of Behavioral Economics. She has published articles on part-time employment, e-commerce and online shopping, the death penalty, and various topics in suicide in the *American Journal of Economics and Sociology, American Economist, Applied Economics, Journal of Socio-Economics, Review of Social Economy, Suicide and Life-Threatening Behavior, Journal of Clinical Psychology, Social Psychiatry & Psychiatric Epidemiology, Medicine & War, International Journal of Contemporary Sociology, International Journal of Social Psychiatry,* and *Journal of Social Psychology.* She has also published two books, *The Economy and Suicide* (1997) and *Suicide and Homicide in the 20th Century* (1998). She is currently working on a book *The Economics of Suicide.*